Closing the Books

An Accountant's Guide

Fourth Edition

Steven M. Bragg

For more information about AccountingTools® products, visit our Web site at www.accountingtools.com.

ISBN-13: 978-1-938910-65-4

Printed in the United States of America

Table of Contents

Preface

One of the most difficult tasks for the practicing accountant is to close the books at the end of each month and produce a quality set of financial statements in a timely manner. From the perspective of the rest of the company, it may be considered the most important accounting function of all. *Closing the Books: An Accountant's Guide* walks you through every aspect of closing the books, including specific closing activities, how to construct the financial statement package, and how to fine-tune the process.

In Chapters 1-3, we address the system within which the closing process is accomplished, including the general ledger and subsidiary ledgers, the trial balance, and different types of journal entries. In Chapters 4 and 5, we delve into the specific steps needed to close the books, as well as how to accelerate the production of financial statements. Next, in Chapters 6-11, we cover the closing activities associated with specific accounting areas, including cash, accounts receivable, inventory, fixed assets, and accounts payable. In Chapter 12-19, we address all aspects of the financial statements that are the end result of closing the books – the income statement, balance sheet, statement of cash flows, disclosures, earnings per share, interim reporting, and more. Finally, we complete the discussion of closing the books in Chapters 20-23 by covering how to close the books of a public company, implement closing controls, set up a record keeping system, and use a soft close or virtual close.

The reader can find the answers to many questions about closing the books in the following chapters, including:

- Can I create financial statements from an extended trial balance?
- When should I use reversing entries?
- Which closing steps can be completed before month-end?
- How can task interdependency analysis improve the closing process?
- Should I use more automation to close the books?
- How do I handle negative cash on the balance sheet?
- How should I record deferred revenue?
- How do I handle delays in the approval of supplier invoices?
- When should I accrue for bonuses?
- What financial statement formats should I use?

Closing the Books is designed for both professional accountants and students. Professionals can use it as a reference tool for improving their existing closing procedures, while it provides students with an overview of the entire process. Given its complete coverage of the closing topic, *Closing the Books* may earn a permanent place on your book shelf.

Centennial, Colorado
November 2015

About the Author

Steven Bragg, CPA, has been the chief financial officer or controller of four companies, as well as a consulting manager at Ernst & Young. He received a master's degree in finance from Bentley College, an MBA from Babson College, and a Bachelor's degree in Economics from the University of Maine. He has been a two-time president of the Colorado Mountain Club, and is an avid alpine skier, mountain biker, and certified master diver. Mr. Bragg resides in Centennial, Colorado. He has written the following books and courses:

Accountants' Guidebook
Accounting Changes and Error Corrections
Accounting Controls Guidebook
Accounting for Derivatives and Hedges
Accounting for Earnings per Share
Accounting for Inventory
Accounting for Investments
Accounting for Managers
Accounting for Stock-Based Compensation
Accounting Procedures Guidebook
Bookkeeping Guidebook
Budgeting
Business Combinations and Consolidations
Business Insurance Fundamentals
Business Ratios
Capital Budgeting
CFO Guidebook
Closing the Books
Constraint Management
Corporate Cash Management
Corporate Finance
Cost Accounting Fundamentals
Cost Management Guidebook
Credit & Collection Guidebook
Developing and Managing Teams
Enterprise Risk Management
Fair Value Accounting

Financial Analysis
Financial Forecasting and Modeling
Fixed Asset Accounting
Foreign Currency Accounting
GAAP Guidebook
Hospitality Accounting
Human Resources Guidebook
IFRS Guidebook
Interpretation of Financial Statements
Inventory Management
Investor Relations Guidebook
Lean Accounting Guidebook
Mergers & Acquisitions
New Controller Guidebook
Nonprofit Accounting
Payables Management
Payroll Management
Project Accounting
Public Company Accounting
Purchasing Guidebook
Real Estate Accounting
Revenue Recognition
The Soft Close
The Statement of Cash Flows
The Year-End Close
Treasurer's Guidebook
Working Capital Management

On-Line Resources by Steven Bragg

Steven maintains the accountingtools.com web site, which contains continuing professional education courses, the Accounting Best Practices podcast, and hundreds of articles on accounting subjects.

Closing the Books is also available as a continuing professional education (CPE) course. You can purchase the course (and many other courses) and take an on-line exam at:

www.accountingtools.com/cpe

Chapter 1
The General Ledger and Other Ledgers

Introduction

Before the books can be closed, it is necessary to understand where the information summarized in the financial statements comes from, since you may have to research and correct errors in that information that are causing problems in the financial statements. The primary source is the general ledger, but information can be fed into the general ledger from subsidiary ledgers too, so you need to understand the flow of information from beginning to end. This chapter addresses how financial information is entered into the accounting system and eventually appears in the general ledger, after which it is aggregated further into the financial statements.

The Ledger Concept

A *ledger* is a book or database in which double-entry accounting transactions are stored or summarized. A *subsidiary ledger* is a ledger designed for the storage of specific types of accounting transactions. The information in a subsidiary ledger is then summarized and posted to an account in the *general ledger*, which in turn is used to construct the financial statements of a company. The account in the general ledger where this summarized information is stored is called a *control account*. Most accounts in the general ledger are not control accounts; instead, transactions are recorded directly into them.

A subsidiary ledger can be set up for virtually any general ledger account. However, they are usually only created for areas in which there are high transaction volumes, which limits their use to a few areas. Examples of subsidiary ledgers are:

- Accounts receivable ledger
- Fixed assets ledger
- Inventory ledger
- Purchases ledger

In order to research accounting information when a subsidiary ledger is used, drill down from the general ledger to the appropriate subsidiary ledger, where the detailed information is stored. Consequently, if you prefer to conduct as much research as possible within the general ledger, use fewer subsidiary ledgers.

As an example of the information in a subsidiary ledger, the inventory ledger may contain transactions pertaining to receipts into stock, movements of stock to the production floor, conversions into finished goods, scrap and rework reporting, and sales of goods to customers.

> **Tip:** Subsidiary ledgers are used when there is a large amount of transaction information that would clutter up the general ledger. This situation typically arises in companies with significant sales volume. Thus, there may be no need for subsidiary ledgers in a small company.

The following chart shows how the various data entry modules within an accounting system are used to create transactions which are recorded in either the general ledger or various subsidiary ledgers, and which are eventually aggregated to create the financial statements.

Transaction Flow in the Accounting System

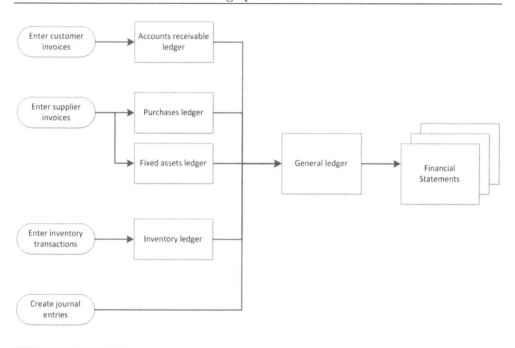

Part of the period-end closing process is to post the information in a subsidiary ledger to the general ledger. This is usually a manual step, so verify that all subsidiary ledgers have been appropriately completed and closed before posting their summarized totals to the general ledger. It can be quite a problem if you forget to post the totals from a subsidiary ledger to the general ledger, since that means the resulting financial statements may be missing a batch of crucial transactions.

> **Tip:** If subsidiary ledgers are used, include a step in the closing procedure to post the balances in all subsidiary ledgers to the general ledger, as well as to verify that the subsidiary ledgers have been closed and shifted forward to the next accounting period.

General Ledger Overview

A general ledger is the master set of accounts in which is summarized all transactions occurring within a business during a specific period of time. The general ledger contains all of the accounts currently being used in a chart of accounts, and is sorted by account number. Either individual transactions or summary-level postings from subsidiary ledgers are listed within each account number, and are sorted by transaction date. Each entry in the general ledger includes a reference number that states the source of the information. The source may be a subsidiary ledger, a journal entry, or a transaction entered directly into the general ledger.

The format of the general ledger varies somewhat, depending on the accounting software being used, but the basic set of information presented for an account within the general ledger is:

- *Transaction number*. The software assigns a unique number to each transaction, so that it can be more easily located in the accounting database if you know the transaction number.
- *Transaction date*. This is the date on which the transaction was entered into the accounting database.
- *Description*. This is a brief description that summarizes the reason for the entry.
- *Source*. Information may be forwarded to the general ledger from a variety of sources, so the report should state the source, in case you need to go back to the source to research the reason for the entry.
- *Debit and credit*. States the amount debited or credited to the account for a specific transaction.

The following sample of a general ledger report shows a possible format that could be used to present information for several transactions that are aggregated under a specific account number.

Sample General Ledger Presentation

Trans. No.	Trans. Date	Description	Source	Debit	Credit
Acct. 10400		**Acct: Accounts Receivable**	**Beginning balance**		**$127,500.00**
10473	3/22/xx	Customer invoice	ARL	93.99	
10474	3/23/xx	Customer invoice	ARL	47.80	
10475	3/24/xx	Credit memo	ARL		43.17
10476	3/25/xx	Customer invoice	ARL	65.25	
18903	3/26/xx	Cash receipt	CRJ		1,105.20
			Ending balance		**$126,558.67**

It is extremely easy to locate information pertinent to an accounting inquiry in the general ledger, which makes it the primary source of accounting information. For example:

- A manager reviews the balance sheet and notices that the amount of debt appears too high. The accounting staff looks up the debt account in the general ledger and sees that a loan was added at the end of the month.
- A manager reviews the income statement and sees that the bad debt expense for his division is very high. The accounting staff looks up the expense in the general ledger, drills down to the source journal entry, and sees that a new bad debt projection was the cause of the increase in bad debt expense.

As the examples show, the source of an inquiry is frequently the financial statements; when conducting an investigation, the accounting staff begins with the general ledger, and may drill down to source documents from there to ascertain the reason(s) for an issue.

We will now proceed to brief discussions of the accounts receivable ledger and purchase ledger, which are representative of the types of subsidiary ledgers that can be used to compile information within the accounting system.

The Accounts Receivable Ledger

The accounts receivable ledger is a subsidiary ledger in which is recorded all credit sales made by a business. It is useful for segregating into one location a record of all amounts invoiced to customers, as well as all credit memos issued to them, and all payments made against invoices by them. The ending balance of the accounts receivable ledger equals the aggregate amount of unpaid accounts receivable.

A typical transaction entered into the accounts receivable ledger will record an account receivable, followed at a later date by a payment transaction from a customer that eliminates the account receivable.

If a manual record of the accounts receivable ledger were to be maintained, it could contain substantially more information than is allowed by an accounting software package. The data fields in a manually-prepared ledger might include the following information for each transaction:

- Invoice date
- Invoice number
- Customer name
- Identifying code for item sold
- Sales tax invoiced
- Total amount billed
- Payment flag (states whether paid or not)

The primary document recorded in the accounts receivable ledger is the customer invoice. Also, if a credit is granted to a customer for such items as returned goods or items damaged in transit, a credit memo is also recorded in the ledger.

The information in the accounts receivable ledger is aggregated periodically and posted to a control account in the general ledger. This account is used to keep from cluttering up the general ledger with the massive amount of information that is typically stored in the accounts receivable ledger. Immediately after posting, the balance in the control account should match the balance in the accounts receivable ledger. Since no detailed transactions are stored in the control account, anyone wanting to research customer invoice and credit memo transactions will have to drill down from the control account to the accounts receivable ledger to find them.

Before closing the books and generating financial statements at the end of an accounting period, all entries must be completed in the accounts receivable ledger, after which the ledger is closed for that period, and totals posted from the accounts receivable ledger to the general ledger.

The Purchase Ledger

The purchase ledger is a subsidiary ledger in which is recorded all purchases made by a business. It is useful for segregating into one location a record of the amounts the company is spending with its suppliers. The purchase ledger shows which purchases have been paid for and which ones remain outstanding. A typical transaction entered into the purchase ledger will record an account payable, followed at a later date by a payment transaction that eliminates the payable. Thus, there is likely to be an outstanding account payable balance in the ledger at any time.

If a manual record of the purchase ledger were to be maintained, it could contain substantially more information than is allowed by an accounting software package. The data fields in a manually-prepared purchase ledger might include the following information for each transaction:
- Purchase date
- Supplier code (or name)
- Supplier invoice number
- Purchase order number (if used)
- Identifying code for item purchased
- Amount paid
- Sales tax paid
- Payment flag (states whether paid or not)

The primary document recorded in the purchase ledger is the supplier invoice. Also, if suppliers grant a credit back to the business for such items as returned goods or items damaged in transit, credit memos issued by suppliers would be recorded in the purchase ledger.

The information in the purchase ledger is aggregated periodically and posted to a control account in the general ledger. The purchase ledger control account is used to keep from cluttering up the general ledger with the massive amount of information that is typically stored in the purchase ledger. Immediately after posting, the balance in the control account should match the balance in the purchase ledger. Since no detailed transactions are stored in the control account, anyone wanting to research purchase transactions will have to drill down from the control account to the purchase ledger to find them.

Before closing the books and generating financial statements at the end of an accounting period, all entries must be completed in the purchase ledger, after which the ledger is closed for that period, and totals posted from the purchase ledger to the general ledger.

Summary

If you are responsible for closing the books, you will likely spend a great deal of time dealing with the general ledger. It is not overly efficient to switch back and forth between the subsidiary ledgers and the general ledger when engaged in research related to the close. Consequently, we recommend that the number of subsidiary ledgers be kept to a minimum, so that as many transactions as possible are available within the general ledger. This also reduces the risk that you will not post the balance in a subsidiary ledger forward into the general ledger, and thereby produce inaccurate financial statements.

We now turn in the next chapter to a discussion of the trial balance. It may be considered the source document for the financial statements, but is in fact a report generated from the information in the general ledger. Consequently, anyone using accounting software to create financial statements will be only slightly aware of the existence of the trial balance. However, it plays a larger role for those people who prepare financial statements by hand, and so is worth discussing.

Chapter 2
The Trial Balance

Introduction

The trial balance is frequently mentioned as a report needed for the production of financial statements. This is not really the case. It used to be the basis from which financial statements were generated when the reports were created by hand, but it is irrelevant when the statements are automatically created with accounting software. In this chapter, we will explore the different trial balance formats, whether or not it can be used to locate errors, and how it can be used to close the books.

Overview of the Trial Balance

The trial balance is a report run at the end of an accounting period. It is primarily used to ensure that the total of all debits equals the total of all credits, which means that there are no unbalanced journal entries in the accounting system that would make it impossible to generate accurate financial statements. Printing the trial balance to match debit and credit totals has fallen into disuse, since accounting software rejects the entry of unbalanced journal entries.

The trial balance can also be used to manually compile financial statements, though with the predominant use of computerized accounting systems that create the statements automatically, the report is rarely used for this purpose.

When the trial balance is first printed, it is called the *unadjusted trial balance*. Then, when the accounting team corrects any errors found and makes adjustments to bring the financial statements into compliance with an accounting framework (such as GAAP or IFRS), the report is called the *adjusted trial balance*. Finally, after the period has been closed, the report is called the *post-closing trial balance*.

The Trial Balance Format

The initial trial balance report contains the following columns of information:
1. Account number
2. Account name
3. Ending debit balance (if any)
4. Ending credit balance (if any)

Each line item only contains the ending balance in an account, which comes from the general ledger. All accounts having an ending balance are listed in the trial balance; usually, the accounting software automatically blocks all accounts having a zero balance from appearing in the report, which reduces its length. A sample trial balance follows:

Sample Trial Balance

Account Number	Account Description	Unadjusted Trial Balance	
		Debit	Credit
1000	Cash	$60,000	
1500	Accounts receivable	180,000	
2000	Inventory	300,000	
3000	Fixed assets	210,000	
4000	Accounts payable		90,000
4500	Accrued liabilities		50,000
4700	Notes payable		420,000
5000	Equity		350,000
6000	Revenue		400,000
7200	Cost of goods sold	290,000	
7300	Salaries expense	200,000	
7400	Payroll tax expense	20,000	
7500	Rent expense	35,000	
7600	Other expenses	15,000	
	Totals	$1,310,000	$1,310,000

The adjusted version of a trial balance may combine the debit and credit columns into a single combined column, and add columns to show adjusting entries and a revised ending balance. An adjusting entry is a journal entry that is used at the end of an accounting period to adjust the balances in various general ledger accounts to meet the requirements of accounting standards. This format is useful for revealing the derivation of the line items in financial statements.

The following sample shows adjusting entries. It also combines the debit and credit totals into the second column, so that the summary balance for the total is (and should be) zero. Adjusting entries are added in the next column, yielding an adjusted trial balance in the far right column.

Sample Adjusted Trial Balance

Account Description	Unadjusted Trial Balance	Adjusting Entries	Adjusted Trial Balance
Cash	$60,000		$60,000
Accounts receivable	180,000	50,000	230,000
Inventory	300,000		300,000
Fixed assets (net)	210,000		210,000
Accounts payable	-90,000		-90,000
Accrued liabilities	-50,000	-25,000	-75,000
Notes payable	-420,000		-420,000
Equity	-350,000		-350,000

Account Description	Unadjusted Trial Balance	Adjusting Entries	Adjusted Trial Balance
Revenue	-400,000	-50,000	-450,000
Cost of goods sold	290,000		290,000
Salaries expense	200,000	25,000	225,000
Payroll tax expense	20,000		20,000
Rent expense	35,000		35,000
Other expenses	15,000		15,000
Totals	$0	$0	$0

The Extended Trial Balance

An extended trial balance is a standard trial balance to which are added categories extending to the right, and in which are listed the account totals for the balance sheet and the income statement. Thus, all asset, liability, and equity accounts are stated in a balance sheet column, and all revenue, expense, gain, and loss accounts are stated in an income statement column.

The extended trial balance is useful for creating a visual representation of where each of the accounts in the standard trial balance goes in the financial statements, and may be useful for detecting anomalies in the trial balance that should be corrected (as discussed further in the next section). A sample of an extended trial balance is shown below. It uses the same trial balance information used to describe the adjusted trial balance format.

Sample Extended Trial Balance

	Unadjusted Trial Balance	Adjusting Entries	Adjusted Trial Balance	Balance Sheet	Income Statement
Cash	$60,000		$60,000	$60,000	
Accounts receivable	180,000	50,000	230,000	230,000	
Inventory	300,000		300,000	300,000	
Fixed assets (net)	210,000		210,000	210,000	
Accounts payable	-90,000		-90,000	-90,000	
Accrued liabilities	-50,000	-25,000	-75,000	-75,000	
Notes payable	-420,000		-420,000	-420,000	
Equity	-350,000		-350,000	-350,000	
Retained earnings				-135,000	
Revenue	-400,000	-50,000	-450,000		-450,000
Cost of goods sold	290,000		290,000		290,000
Salaries expense	200,000	25,000	225,000		225,000
Payroll tax expense	20,000		20,000		20,000
Rent expense	35,000		35,000		35,000
Other expenses	15,000		15,000		15,000
Totals	$0	$0	$0	$0	-$135,000

Any computerized accounting system automatically generates financial statements from the trial balance, so the extended trial balance is not a commonly generated report in computerized systems.

> **Note:** The information in the balance sheet and income statement columns in an extended trial balance do not necessarily match the final presentation of these reports, because some of the line items may be aggregated for presentation purposes.

Trial Balance Error Correction

There may be a number of errors in the trial balance, only a few of which are easy to identify. Here are some suggestions for how to find these problems:

- *Entries made twice.* If a journal entry or other transaction is made twice, the trial balance will still be in balance, so this is not a good report for finding duplicate entries. Instead, you may have to wait for the issue to resolve itself. For example, a duplicate invoice to a customer will be rejected by the customer, while a duplicate invoice from a supplier will (hopefully) be spotted during the invoice approval process.
- *Entries not made at all.* This issue is impossible to find on the trial balance, since it is not there. The best alternative is to maintain a checklist of standard entries, and verify that all of them have been made.
- *Entries to the wrong account.* This may be apparent with a quick glance at the trial balance, since an account that previously had no balance at all now has one. Otherwise, the best form of correction is preventive – use standard journal entry templates for all recurring entries.
- *Reversed entries.* An entry for a debit may be mistakenly recorded as a credit, and vice versa. This issue may be visible on the trial balance, especially if the entry is large enough to change the sign of an ending balance to the reverse of its usual sign.
- *Unbalanced entries.* This issue is listed last, since it is impossible in a computerized environment where entries must be balanced or the system will not accept them. If a manual system is being used, the issue will be apparent in the column totals of the trial balance. However, locating the exact entry causing the problem is vastly more difficult, and will call for a detailed review of every entry, or at least the totals in every subsidiary journal that rolls into the general ledger.

Whenever an error is corrected, be sure to use a clearly labeled journal entry with supporting documentation, so that someone else can verify the work at a later date.

After reviewing the error correction issues in this section, you may have noticed how poor a role the trial balance plays in the detection of errors. In fact, it is nearly impossible to detect an error solely through this report. Instead, it is necessary to use other, more detailed reports to determine the real cause of an error.

The Post-Closing Trial Balance

A post-closing trial balance is a listing of all balance sheet accounts containing balances at the end of a reporting period. The post-closing trial balance contains no revenue, expense, or summary account balances, since these temporary accounts have all been closed and their balances moved into the retained earnings account in the balance sheet. A temporary account is an account used to hold balances during an accounting period for revenue, expense, gain, and loss transactions. These accounts are flushed into the retained earnings account at the end of an accounting period.

The post-closing trial balance contains columns for the account number, account description, debit balance, and credit balance. In most accounting systems, this report does not have a different report title than the usual trial balance.

The post-closing trial balance is used to verify that the total of all debit balances equals the total of all credit balances, which should net to zero. Once you have ensured that this is the case, begin recording accounting transactions for the next accounting period.

A sample post-closing trial balance is shown in the following sample. Notice that there is no column for adjusting entries, and that there are no temporary accounts, such as revenue and expense accounts.

Sample Post-Closing Trial Balance

Account Number	Account Description	Debit	Credit
1000	Cash	$105,000	
1500	Accounts receivable	320,000	
2000	Inventory	500,000	
3000	Fixed assets	2,000,000	
3100	Accumulated depreciation	-480,000	
4000	Accounts payable		$195,000
4500	Accrued liabilities		108,000
5000	Retained earnings		642,000
5500	Common stock		1,500,000
	Totals	$2,445,000	$2,445,000

Evaluation of the Trial Balance

We have described the layout of the trial balance and how it can be used – but is it really needed? The answer depends upon whether a business is using a computerized accounting system or a manual one. In a computerized environment, the system automatically generates financial statements, literally at the touch of a button. In this situation, there is no particular need for a trial balance. The user of a computerized accounting system is more likely to go directly to the general ledger to review the details for each account than to first print out a trial balance to see where a problem *might* lie, and *then* go to the general ledger to spot the problem. In short, a computerized system renders the trial balance unnecessary.

The situation is quite a bit different for the user of a manual accounting system. In this case, you would shift the account balances in the general ledger to the trial balance, and then manually create the financial statements from that information. In essence, the extended trial balance noted in an earlier section becomes the primary tool for constructing financial statements.

The only case in which the user of a computerized accounting system might find it necessary to print a trial balance is when the outside auditors request a copy of it. They copy the trial balance into their auditing software, and use it as the basis for subsequent auditing procedures.

Summary

The trial balance is essentially a summary of the account balances for a business as of a point in time. It was heavily used in an era when financial statements were generated by hand, but has since fallen out of use as computerized systems have taken over the production of financial statements. Nonetheless, we include it in this book both to provide a historical perspective on closing the books, and also because it is still used for the manual creation of financial statements. At a minimum, it is likely to remain on the list of standard computerized accounting reports, so the accountant should be familiar with the information on it, and how it is used.

Chapter 3
Journal Entries

Introduction

An important part of the closing process is the use of journal entries to refine the reported financial results. In this chapter, we discuss various aspects of journal entries – the accruals concept, adjusting entries, reversing entries, and closing entries – and then address a variety of ways to improve the efficiency of journal entry handling. As a result, you should know which journal entries to use, and the most efficient way to incorporate them into the closing process.

Related Podcast Episode: Episodes 172 and 196 of the Accounting Best Practices Podcast discuss accruals and deferrals, and how to prevent over-accruals. They are available at: **accountingtools.com/podcasts** or **iTunes**

The Accruals Concept

An *accrual* allows you to record expenses and revenues for which there is an expectation of expending cash or receiving cash, respectively, in a future reporting period. In double-entry bookkeeping, the offset to an accrued expense is an accrued liability account, which appears in the balance sheet. The offset to accrued revenue is an accrued asset account (such as unbilled consulting fees), which also appears in the balance sheet. Examples of accruals are:

- *Revenue accrual.* A consulting company works billable hours on a project that it will eventually invoice to a client for $5,000. It can record an accrual in the current period so that its current income statement shows $5,000 of revenue, even though it has not yet billed the client.
- *Expense accrual – interest.* A company has a loan with the local bank for $1 million, and pays interest on the loan at a variable rate of interest. The invoice from the bank for $3,000 in interest expense does not arrive until the following month, so the company accrues the expense in order to show the amount on its income statement in the proper month.
- *Expense accrual – wages.* A company pays its employees at the end of each month for their hours worked through the 25th day of the month. To fully record the wage expense for the entire month, it also accrues $32,000 in additional wages, which represents the cost of wages for the remaining days of the month.

Most accruals are initially created as reversing entries, so that the accounting software automatically cancels them in the following month. This happens when you are expecting revenue to actually be billed, or supplier invoices to actually arrive, in the next month. The concept is addressed later in the Reversing Entries section.

Adjusting Entries

Adjusting entries are journal entries that are used at the end of an accounting period to adjust the balances in various general ledger accounts to more closely align the reported results and financial position of a business to meet the requirements of an accounting framework, such as Generally Accepted Accounting Principles (GAAP) or International Financial Reporting Standards (IFRS).

An adjusting entry can be used for any type of accounting transaction; here are some of the more common ones:
- To record depreciation and amortization for the period
- To record an allowance for doubtful accounts
- To record a reserve for obsolete inventory
- To record a reserve for sales returns
- To record a warranty reserve
- To record accrued revenue
- To record accrued expenses
- To record previously paid but unused expenditures as prepaid expenses
- To adjust cash balances for any reconciling items noted in the bank reconciliation

Adjusting entries are most commonly of three types, which are:
- *Accruals*. To record a revenue or expense that has not yet been recorded through a standard accounting transaction.
- *Deferrals*. To defer a revenue or expense that has occurred, but which has not yet been earned or used.
- *Estimates*. To estimate the amount of a reserve, such as the allowance for doubtful accounts or the inventory obsolescence reserve.

When a journal entry is recorded for an accrual, deferral, or estimate, it usually impacts an asset or liability account. For example, if an expense is accrued, this also increases a liability account. Or, if revenue recognition is deferred to a later period, this also increases a liability account. Thus, adjusting entries impact the balance sheet, not just the income statement.

Reversing Entries

When a journal entry is created, it may be to record revenue or an expense other than through a more traditional method, such as issuing an invoice to a customer or recording an invoice from a supplier. In these situations, the journal entry is only meant to be a stopgap measure, with the traditional recordation method still being used at a later date. This means that you have to eventually create a journal entry

14

that is the *opposite* of the original entry, thereby cancelling out the original entry. The concept is best explained with an example.

EXAMPLE

The controller of Lowry Locomotion has not yet received an invoice from a key supplier of materials by the time he closes the books for the month of May. He expects that the invoice will be for $20,000, so he records the following accrual entry for the invoice:

	Debit	Credit
Cost of goods sold (expense)	20,000	
Accrued expenses (liability)		20,000

This entry creates an additional expense of $20,000 for the month of May.

The controller knows that the invoice will arrive in June and will be recorded upon receipt. Therefore, he creates a reversing entry for the original accrual in early June that cancels out the original entry. The entry is:

	Debit	Credit
Accrued expenses (liability)	20,000	
Cost of goods sold (expense)		20,000

The invoice then arrives, and is recorded in the normal manner through the accounts payable module in Lowry's accounting software. This creates an expense during the month of June of $20,000. Thus, the net effect in June is:

June reversing entry	-$20,000
Supplier invoice	+20,000
Net effect in June	$0

Thus, the accrual entry shifts recognition of the expense from June to May.

Any accounting software package contains an option for automatically creating a reversing journal entry when a journal entry is initially set up. Always use this feature when a reversing entry will be needed. By doing so, you can avoid the risk of forgetting to manually create the reversing entry, and also avoid the risk of creating an incorrect entry.

Tip: There will be situations where there is no need to reverse a journal entry for a few months. If so, consider using an automated reversing entry in the *next* month, and creating a replacement journal entry in each successive month. While this approach may appear time-consuming, it ensures that you *always* flush the original entry from the books, thereby avoiding the risk of carrying a journal entry past the date when it should have been eliminated.

Common Adjusting Entries

This section contains a discussion of the journal entries that are most likely to be needed to close the books, along with an example of the accounts most likely to be used in the entries.

Depreciation

This entry is used to gradually charge the investment in fixed assets to expense over the useful lives of those assets. The amount of depreciation is calculated from a spreadsheet or fixed asset software, and is based on a systematic method for spreading recognition of the expense over multiple periods. If you choose to charge the entire depreciation expense in a lump sum to a single account, the entry is:

	Debit	Credit
Depreciation expense	xxx	
Accumulated depreciation		xxx

In this entry, the accumulated depreciation account is a contra asset account, which means that it carries a negative balance that offsets a related asset account (in this case, the fixed assets account on the balance sheet).

A more common approach is to charge the depreciation expense to individual departments, based on their usage of fixed assets. This entry increases the number of depreciation line items, though there is no need to make a similar allocation of accumulated amortization among different accounts. An example of this format is:

	Debit	Credit
Depreciation – Administration	xxx	
Depreciation – Engineering	xxx	
Depreciation – Logistics	xxx	
Depreciation – Production	xxx	
Depreciation – Sales	xxx	
Accumulated depreciation		xxx

If there are intangible assets recorded in the accounting records, charge them to expense over their useful lives. The entry is identical to the depreciation entry, except that we substitute the word "amortization" for "depreciation." A sample entry is:

	Debit	Credit
Amortization expense	xxx	
Accumulated amortization		xxx

It is less necessary to charge amortization expense to individual departments, since it is not always easy to trace the usage of a specific intangible asset to a department. Instead, it is more commonly charged to the general corporate function.

Allowance for Doubtful Accounts

If a business sells goods or services on credit, there is a strong likelihood that a portion of the resulting accounts receivable will eventually become bad debts. If so, update the allowance for doubtful accounts each month. This account is a contra asset account that offsets the balance in the accounts receivable account. Set the balance in this allowance to match the best estimate of how much of the month-end accounts receivable will eventually be written off as bad debts. A sample entry is:

	Debit	Credit
Bad debts expense	xxx	
Allowance for doubtful accounts		xxx

The bad debts expense can be charged to the business as a whole, or it can be charged to a specific department. You could charge it to the accounting department, since that group is responsible for collections. It could also be charged to the treasury department, on the grounds that the treasury staff is responsible for granting credit to customers, and so is responsible for failures to collect on granted credit. Alternatively, it could be charged to the sales department, since the sales staff originally obtained the sale.

Accrued Revenue

If a business has engaged in work for a customer but has not yet billed the customer, it may be possible to recognize some or all of the revenue associated with the work performed to date. This concept usually applies to services rather than to product sales, since the accounting requirements for product-related revenue recognition are quite strict, and generally do not allow accrued revenue to be recorded.

If it is possible to record accrued revenue, the offset to the revenue is a debit to an accrued accounts receivable account. Do not record this accrual in the standard trade accounts receivable account, since that account should be reserved for actual billings to customers. A sample of the accrued revenue entry is:

	Debit	Credit
Accounts receivable – accrued	xxx	
Sales		xxx

It is also possible for the reverse situation to arise, where a customer is billed in advance of completing work on the billed items. In this case, *reduce* recorded sales by the amount of unearned revenue by crediting an unearned sales (liability) account. A sample entry is:

	Debit	Credit
Sales	xxx	
Unearned sales (liability)		xxx

Accrued Expenses

If there are supplier invoices that you are aware of but have not yet received, estimate the amount of the expense and accrue it with a journal entry. There are any number of expense accounts to which such transactions might be charged; in the following sample entry, we assume that the expense relates to a supplier invoice for utilities that has not yet arrived.

	Debit	Credit
Utilities expense	xxx	
Accrued expenses (liability)		xxx

This is likely to be the most frequent of the adjusting entries, as there may be a number of supplier invoices that do not arrive by the time the books are closed.

Prepaid Assets

Occasionally, a significant payment is made in advance to a third party. This advance may be for something that will be charged to expense in a later period, or it may be a deposit that will be returned to the company at a later date. These payments should initially be recorded as assets, usually in the prepaid assets account. Situations where a prepaid asset could be recorded include:

- Rent paid before the month to which it applies
- Medical insurance paid before the month to which it applies
- Rent deposit, to be returned at the conclusion of the lease
- Utilities deposit, to be retained until the company cancels service
- Advance payment to a supplier for custom work

Most of these transactions have the same journal entry, which is:

	Debit	Credit
Prepaid expenses	xxx	
Cash		xxx

The name of the debited account can vary. We use "Prepaid expenses" in the sample entry, but "Prepaid assets" is also used.

Closing Entries

Closing entries are journal entries used to flush out all temporary accounts at the end of an accounting period and transfer their balances into permanent accounts. Doing so resets the temporary accounts to begin accumulating new transactions in the next accounting period. A temporary account is an account used to hold balances during an accounting period for revenue, expense, gain, and loss transactions. These accounts are flushed into the retained earnings account at the end of an accounting period.

The basic sequence of entries is:

1. Debit all revenue accounts and credit the income summary account, thereby clearing out the revenue accounts.
2. Credit all expense accounts and debit the income summary account, thereby clearing out all expense accounts.
3. Close the income summary account to the retained earnings account. If there were a profit in the period, this entry is a debit to the income summary account and a credit to the retained earnings account. If there were a loss in the period, this entry is a credit to the income summary account and a debit to the retained earnings account.

The net result of these activities is to move the net profit or loss for the period into the retained earnings account, which appears in the stockholders' equity section of the balance sheet.

Since the income summary account is only a transitional account, it is also acceptable to close directly to the retained earnings account and bypass the income summary account entirely.

EXAMPLE

Lowry Locomotion is closing its books for the most recent accounting period. Lowry had $50,000 of revenues and $45,000 of expenses during the period. For simplicity, we assume that all of the expenses were recorded in a single account; in a normal environment, there might be dozens of expense accounts to clear out. The sequence of entries is:

1. Empty the revenue account by debiting it for $50,000, and transfer the balance to the income summary account with a credit. The entry is:

	Debit	Credit
Revenue	50,000	
Income summary		50,000

2. Empty the expense account by crediting it for $45,000, and transfer the balance to the income summary account with a debit. The entry is:

	Debit	Credit
Income summary	45,000	
Expenses		45,000

3. Empty the income summary account by debiting it for $5,000, and transfer the balance to the retained earnings account with a credit. The entry is:

	Debit	Credit
Income summary	5,000	
Retained earnings		5,000

These entries have emptied the revenue, expense, and income summary accounts, and shifted the net profit for the period to the retained earnings account.

We should point out that a practicing accountant rarely uses any of these closing entries, since they are handled automatically by any accounting software package. Instead, the basic closing step is to access an option in the software to close the accounting period. Doing so automatically populates the retained earnings account, and prevents any further transactions from being recorded in the system for the period that has been closed.

Correcting Entries

A correcting entry is a journal entry that is made in order to fix an erroneous transaction that had previously been recorded in the general ledger. For example, the monthly depreciation entry might have been mistakenly made to the amortization expense account. If so, the correcting entry is to move the entry to the depreciation expense account by crediting the amortization expense account and debiting the depreciation expense account. Alternatively, the original entry could be reversed and replaced by a new entry that correctly charges the expense to the depreciation account.

Correcting entries are usually only made by the more experienced accounting staff, since these people have a better understanding of the accounting system and the impact of making special journal entries on the financial statements. It can make sense to have the controller approve all proposed correcting entries before they are made, to ensure that a second person verifies that an entry will have the intended effect.

It is especially important to fully document a correcting entry, since these items are particularly difficult to understand after some time has passed. This means attaching documentation of the original error to each correcting entry, as well as notes regarding how the correcting entry is intended to fix the original error. Documentation is especially valuable if it seems likely that the company's auditors will later review a correcting entry.

This type of entry should be made as soon as an error is discovered and evaluated. Otherwise, it is quite likely that the original entry will never be corrected; this is because error correction falls outside of the normal flow of transaction processing, so there is no work calendar or procedure that monitors whether these transactions are pursued.

Journal Entry Efficiencies

This section describes several ways to significantly improve the efficiency and effectiveness of your use of journal entries when closing the books. Knowledge of these refinements is quite useful for creating a streamlined accounting system.

Immaterial Journal Entries

The accounting profession appears to attract an unusually high proportion of people who might be described as picky or excessively detail-oriented. This predilection certainly applies to the use (or misuse) of journal entries, since these people have a strong tendency to create adjusting entries for very small amounts. They seem to believe that making these entries will measurably improve the results of the financial statements. For example, they may accrue $100 supplier invoices that have not yet arrived, even though such amounts are a tiny fraction of total company expenditures. In these situations, consider three issues:

- *Materiality.* Do not create an adjusting entry when the amount of the adjustment is so small that it will not impact the actions of someone who relies on the financial statements. Thus, spending the time to accrue a $10,000 supplier invoice may or may not be worthwhile – it depends on the size of the company. The detail-oriented controller might argue that the sum total of many such invoices *is* material, and therefore they should all be accrued. That argument is fine, as long as there is indeed a grand total for these items that is material. Usually, there is not.

- *Time delay.* Entering a multitude of immaterial adjusting journal entries chews up time at the end of the month, which delays the issuance of financial statements. Good practice is to issue the financial statements as soon as possible, and creating too many journal entries interferes with that goal.

- *Errors.* Every time another adjusting entry is created, there is an increased risk of creating an incorrect entry – either through charging the wrong account, entering the wrong amounts, doing so in the wrong time period, or forgetting to set up a reversing entry in the next period to flush out the original entry. Consequently, it makes considerable sense to adopt a lean attitude when creating journal entries – only create the ones you really need.

> **Tip:** Keep a running total of the transactions that you have elected not to record with adjusting entries. If the total becomes material, then record the transactions. If not, there is at least evidence supporting why you did not choose to record the entries.

Reversing Entries

As noted earlier in the section about reversing entries, take full advantage of the feature in accounting software that automatically reverses a journal entry. By doing so, you avoid the significant risk of retaining an unreversed journal entry through many reporting periods, and of possibly having the auditors find it at the end of the year. Upon discovery, this can result in an embarrassing reversal that can have a significant impact on the financial results that management is expecting.

Journal Entry Templates

The vast majority of journal entries created as part of the closing process are used on an ongoing basis. Given the large number of recurring journal entries, there is a significant opportunity to improve the efficiency of creating journal entries with templates. A journal entry template is a standard form in an accounting software package, into which is entered the following information:

- *Accounts*. Standardize the accounts for which entries will be made. Thus, a depreciation template will contain all depreciation expense and accumulated depreciation accounts involved in the entry.
- *Amounts*. You have the option of entering the exact dollar amount to be recorded with each journal entry. This is generally not recommended, unless you do not expect the amounts to change for a considerable period of time.

Once the templates are set up, access them in the software at the end of each accounting period, enter information as necessary, and post them to the general ledger.

Clearly, journal entry templates can introduce a great deal of efficiency into the closing process. In addition, they reduce the number of journal entry errors related to mistakenly entering incorrect account numbers.

Recurring Journal Entries

A standard feature in many accounting software packages is a feature that allows you to repeat a journal entry in future periods. For example, rather than creating six consecutive journal entries to gradually charge prepaid insurance to expense over six months, just set up the initial journal entry to repeat itself six times. This approach not only saves time, but also eliminates the risk of making an incorrect entry in one of the later journal entries.

Tip: The risk in using recurring journal entries is that you may make an incorrect *initial* journal entry. If so, it will now repeat through all of the specified periods. To mitigate this risk, have a second person review recurring journal entries when they are created, and question the assumptions, calculations, accounts used, and debits and credits.

It is also possible to use a recurring journal entry for large entries that have some variability from month to month. If only a few line items need to be changed, this may still be the most efficient method for creating the entry.

Tip: When a recurring entry is in its final month, verify that the amount in the entry is the correct one. In many cases, the last of a series of journal entries may need to be adjusted slightly to match the underlying transaction. For example, if a prepaid asset is being charged to expense over three months and the amount is $300.01, the first two recurring entries should be for $100.00 each, and the last entry will have to be adjusted to $100.01.

Standard Journal Entry Checklist

A central part of the closing process is the use of a variety of journal entries. Nearly all of these entries are likely to be ones that are used every month, with only a few unique entries. If there are more than a few, it is easy to lose track of which entries have been made (or not), resulting in inconsistent financial statements. For example, if you forget to record a depreciation journal entry in one month, it will be necessary to record an entry in the next month for double the usual amount of depreciation, in order to make up for the missing expense.

It is possible to avoid the issues just noted by creating a journal entry checklist that is specific to your business. The following sample shows the basic structure of the checklist, which should include these columns:

1. *Check off.* There must be a checkbox or space for initials at the beginning or end of each line, so that each journal entry can be checked off as it is completed. Without this feature, you will not know which journal entries have been completed. An add-on to this checkbox is to enter the unique journal entry number assigned by the accounting software to each entry made (if this feature is available). Entering this information into the checklist provides proof that each entry was made and recognized by the system.
2. *Entry description.* List a brief description of the journal entry that uniquely identifies it.
3. *Template ID.* If there is a standard template in the accounting software for the journal entry, enter the identification number of the template. This can be an important issue when the software assigns an otherwise incomprehensible numeric or alphanumeric identification number.
4. *Timing.* State whether the journal entry can be completed in advance. This column is not critical, since you can simply sort the checklist so that the journal entries that can be completed first are located at the top of the list.

Sample Journal Entry Checklist

Check	Journal Entry Description	Template ID	Timing
√	Reserve for obsolete inventory	INV01	-2 days
√	Write down for lower of cost or market	INV02	-2 days
√	Allowance for doubtful accounts	ARE01	-1 days
√	Interest expense	GEN01	-1 days
√	Accrual for unpaid wages	PAY01	-1 days
√	Accrual for unused vacations	PAY02	-1 days
	Bank reconciliation adjustments	GEN02	Closing day
	Accrual for supplier invoices not received	APA01	Closing day
	Allocate overhead	INV03	Closing day
	Accrual for depreciation	FIX01	+1 days
	Accrual for earned, unbilled revenue	REV01	+1 days
	Accrual for commission expense	PAY03	+1 days
	Accrual for income tax liability	GEN03	+2 days

Under the "Timing" column in the sample checklist, some items are noted as being completed several days before closing day; this indicates the date on which sufficient information should be available to complete the journal entry.

Also, the template identification numbers in the sample checklist are keyed to the type of underlying entry. Thus, the template for commission expense accrual is designated as "PAY03," because it is a payroll-related activity, and it is the third of the templates related to payroll. In some accounting systems, this may be a randomly assigned identification with no underlying meaning at all – in such cases, be especially careful to record the correct identification in this column, to ensure that the correct template is used.

As the business changes over time, it may be possible to drop some journal entries that are no longer relevant. These may be entries that apply to parts of the business that have been sold or otherwise eliminated, or which relate to amounts that have gradually become immaterial. For example, a company may have gradually shifted most of its employees to salaried positions from hourly positions, thereby making the month-end wage accrual such a small number that it is no longer worth entering. Situations like this make it worthwhile to occasionally review the standard journal entry checklist for deletions.

Similarly, changing business circumstances may call for the addition of a new set of journal entries to the standard checklist. For example, the acquisition of a patent may call for an ongoing amortization entry to charge the cost of the patent to expense over time. These types of entries will become apparent; they will be the entries that are needed more and more frequently over time.

Journal Entry Responsibility

Though it may seem simple enough to input a journal entry into the accounting software, this is actually an activity that is highly subject to error. It is quite possible to enter the wrong account number, switch debits and credits, enter the wrong amounts, or enter the entire journal entry for the wrong entity. In addition, if there are multiple people entering journal entries into the system, there is a risk that some entries will be made twice, while other entries will not be made at all (because each person thinks that the other person created the entry). Thus, there are a great many ways to incorrectly create a journal entry.

The solution to this problem is to assign responsibility for certain types of journal entries to specific individuals in the accounting department – and they are the *only* people allowed to make those entries. In addition, provide training to these employees regarding how to make entries, and have them sign off on each entry after they have completed it. Finally, password-protect the journal entry screen from unauthorized access in the accounting software. All of these actions are intended to create a system where journal entries are funneled to specific people who are skilled in journal entry data entry, and should reduce the risk of journal entry errors.

Avoid Journal Entries Entirely

This chapter has been all about the use of adjusting journal entries to create financial statements that comply with the applicable accounting framework. The assumption has been that doing so creates better, more precise information. However, what if the information is strictly for internal management use? It is possible that management would prefer to receive approximately correct results immediately, rather than waiting a week for adjusting entries to be made that yield more accurate financial statements. For example, does the management team care if there is a depreciation expense every month, or can it wait until the end of the year for one large depreciation charge?

Usually, this concept should not be taken to the extreme of banning all journal entries. However, it may be possible to adopt a streamlined set of entries for only the largest adjustments, and ignore all other entries until such time as the financial statements must be audited for outside consumption. Thus, you may be able to avoid many journal entries for 11 months of the year, and then spend additional time fine-tuning the financial statements at the end of the fiscal year with additional entries.

Standardize Accounts

When a company has multiple subsidiaries and each one maintains its own records, several problems can arise related to the accounts in which they store information. These issues are:

- *Definitions.* One subsidiary may ascribe a particular meaning to an account that is different from the meaning that another subsidiary gives to the same account. The result is that two subsidiaries record the same type of transaction in different accounts. For example, one subsidiary might record repairs to its telephone system in the repairs and maintenance account, while another subsidiary might record those repairs in the telephone expense account.
- *Unique accounts.* When subsidiaries have different business models, they may use quite different accounts. For example, a consulting business may require more accounts related to the compensation of its workforce, while a manufacturing business may need a number of cost of goods sold accounts. Thus, their account structures are different.

The problem at the core of both issues is that the parent company has not centralized its chart of accounts (which lists all of the accounts used in the general ledger). This presents problems for the corporate accounting staff that must consolidate the results of the individual subsidiaries. This is usually achieved through a process called "mapping," where the consolidation software used by the corporate parent combines the subsidiary-level financial results into a master set of financial statements. When there are inconsistencies in the accounts used at the subsidiary level, the corporate staff may have to manually intervene in the consolidation process to determine which subsidiary-level accounts are to be placed in corporate-level accounts. This can be a time-consuming and inefficient process.

The solution to the uncontrolled use and definition of accounts is to adopt a rigidly-controlled and very standardized set of accounts that are to be used by the entire company. There should be a definition attached to each account, so that accounting people in the subsidiaries know where to record transactions. Also, subsidiaries can only add to the official chart of accounts by applying to the corporate staff for permission to do so. Though this may appear to involve a significant amount of corporate bureaucracy, it ultimately results in more efficiency in the closing process.

Summary

Journal entries are a crucial part of closing the books, so you must know how to create them, when to reverse them, and how to do both as efficiently and correctly as possible. If this is handled in an uncoordinated manner, it is entirely likely that missing or incorrect journal entries will badly skew the results reported in the financial statements. Further, it takes a great deal of time by an experienced accountant to track down and fix incorrect journal entries, so paying attention to the process is essential to reducing the time needed to issue financial statements.

Chapter 4
The Closing Process

Introduction

A great many steps are required to close the books and issue financial statements. In this chapter, we give an overview of the most prevalent closing activities that you are likely to need. In many cases, we refer you to chapters later in the book for more information, such as for the closing of accounts receivable, accounts payable, and inventory. In other cases, the closing steps are sufficiently minor that we can deal with them entirely within this chapter.

The closing process does not begin after a reporting period has been completed. Instead, be prepared for it well in advance. By doing so, you can complete a number of activities in a leisurely manner before the end of the month, leaving fewer items for the busier period immediately following the end of the period. Accordingly, we have grouped closing steps into the following categories:

1. *Prior steps.* These are steps needed to complete the processing of the financial statements, and which can usually be completed before the end of the reporting period.
2. *Core steps.* These are the steps that are required for the creation of financial statements, and which cannot be completed prior to the end of the reporting period.
3. *Delayed steps.* These are the activities that can be safely delayed until after the issuance of the financial statements, but which are still part of the closing process.

The chapter concludes with a lengthy checklist of activities found in most closing processes, along with a case study, both of which can be used as a reference.

The sections in this chapter do not necessarily represent the exact sequence of activities to follow when closing the books; you may want to alter the sequence based on the processes of your company, and the availability of employees to work on them.

Prior Steps: Update Reserves

Under the accrual basis of accounting, create a reserve in the expectation that expenses will be incurred in the future that are related to revenues generated now. This concept is called the matching principle. Under the matching principle, the cause and effect of a business transaction are recorded at the same time. Thus, when revenue is recorded, also record within the same accounting period any expenses directly related to that revenue. Examples of these expenses are the cost of goods sold, the allowance for doubtful accounts, and a sales returns allowance.

The most common of all reserves is the allowance for doubtful accounts, which is described in the Closing Accounts Receivable chapter. It is used to charge to expense the amount of bad debts expected from a certain amount of sales, before you know precisely which invoices will not be paid. There are a number of other reserves to consider, such as:

- *Inventory obsolescence reserve.* If there is an expectation that there are some higher-cost items in inventory that will be rendered obsolete and disposed of, even if you are not sure which items they are, create an obsolescence reserve, and charge losses against the reserve as these items are located and disposed of.
- *Reserve for product returns.* If there is a history of significant product returns from customers, estimate the percentage of these returns based on prior history, and create a reserve using that percentage whenever related sales are recorded.
- *Reserve for warranty claims.* If the company has experienced a material amount of warranty claims in the past, and it can reasonably estimate the amount of these claims in the future, create a reserve in that amount whenever related sales are recorded.

The reserves just noted are among the more common ones. You may find a need for more unique types of reserves that are specific to your company's industry or business model. If so, it is quite acceptable to maintain other reserves.

There is no need to create a reserve if the balance in the account is going to be immaterial. Instead, many businesses can generate perfectly adequate financial statements that only have a few reserves, while charging all other expenditures to expense as incurred.

Core Steps: Issue Customer Invoices

Part of the closing process nearly always includes the issuance of month-end invoices to customers, especially in situations (such as consulting) where billable hours are compiled throughout the month and then billed at one time, or where a company has a practice of shipping most of its products near the end of the month. In other cases, invoices may have been issued throughout the month, leaving only a residual number to be issued as part of the closing process.

Irrespective of the number of invoices to be issued, invoices are always an important part of the closing process, because they are the primary method for recognizing revenue. Consequently, you normally spend a significant part of the closing process verifying that all possible invoices have, in fact, been created. This verification process may include a comparison of the shipping log to the invoice register, or a comparison of the shipping log to the timekeeping system where billable hours are stored or to a listing of open contracts.

If some revenues are considered to not yet be billable, but to have been fully earned by the company, you can accrue the revenue with a journal entry. This process is described in the Closing Accounts Receivable chapter.

Core Steps: Value Inventory

Potentially the most time-consuming activity in the closing process is valuing ending inventory. This involves the following steps:

1. *Physical count.* Either conduct an ending inventory count or have an adequate perpetual inventory system in place that yields a verifiable ending inventory.
2. *Determine the cost of the ending inventory.* There are several methods available for assigning a cost to the ending inventory, such as the first-in first-out method, the last-in first-out method, and standard costing.
3. *Allocate overhead.* Aggregate overhead costs into cost pools and then allocate the amounts in these pools to ending inventory and the cost of goods sold.
4. *Adjust the valuation.* It may be necessary to reduce the amount of ending inventory due to the lower of cost or market rule, or for the presence of obsolete inventory.

All of these steps are described in detail in the Closing Inventory chapter. There are many steps because of the complexity of inventory valuation, but also because the investment in inventory may be so large that you simply cannot afford to arrive at an incorrect valuation – an error here could require a considerable adjustment to the financial statements in a later period.

If there is a relatively small investment in inventory, it may not be so necessary to invest a large amount of time in closing inventory, since the size of potential errors is substantially reduced.

Core Steps: Calculate Depreciation

Once all fixed assets have been recorded in the accounting records for the month, calculate the amount of depreciation (for tangible assets) and amortization (for intangible assets). This is a significant issue for companies with a large investment in fixed assets, but may be so insignificant in other situations that it is sufficient to only record depreciation at the end of the year.

If you are constructing fixed assets (as would be the case for a factory or company headquarters) and have incurred debt to do so, it may be necessary to capitalize some interest expense into the cost of the fixed assets.

Both the depreciation and interest expense capitalization activities are considered to be part of the closing process, and so are described in detail in the Closing Fixed Assets chapter. It is also possible that you may have to record the impairment of a fixed asset, where the recorded amount of the asset is reduced. This is a less-common event, but may be included in the closing process; for that reason, it is also described in the Closing Fixed Assets chapter.

Core Steps: Accrue Expenses

It will probably be necessary to accrue expenses for some items as part of the closing process, usually because the company had not yet received supplier invoices as of the date when the financial statements were released, or because it had not recorded a payroll that spanned the ending days of the month. The concept of accruals and examples of accrual entries are addressed in the Journal Entries chapter.

Core Steps: Consolidate Division Results

If there are company divisions that forward their financial results to the parent company, the largest issue from the perspective of the close is simply obtaining the information in a timely manner. This information may be provided in the format of a trial balance (see the Trial Balance chapter). Then input the summary totals for all accounts provided into the general ledger of the parent company. This process is repeated for all of the divisions.

If the company uses the same accounting software throughout the business, it may be quite simple to consolidate the division results, but only if the software is networked together. Otherwise, it will be necessary to create a separate journal entry to record the results of each division.

> **Tip:** If division results are recorded with a journal entry, the transaction likely involves a large number of line items. To reduce the risk of recording this information incorrectly, create a journal entry template in the accounting software that includes only the relevant accounts. If the entries for the various divisions are substantially different, consider creating a separate template for each one.

Core Steps: Eliminate Intercompany Transactions

If there are several divisions within a company for which accounting transactions are recorded separately, it is possible that they do business with each other. For example, if a company is vertically integrated, some subsidiaries may sell their output to other subsidiaries, which in turn sell their output to other subsidiaries. If this is the case, they are generating intercompany transactions to record the sales. Intercompany transactions must be eliminated from the consolidated financial statements of the business, since not doing so would artificially inflate the revenue of the company as a whole. This elimination requires you to reverse the sale and offsetting account receivable for each such transaction.

Intercompany transactions can be difficult to spot, especially in businesses where such transactions are rare, and therefore not closely monitored. In a larger business, it is relatively easy to flag these transactions as being intercompany when they are created, so that the system automatically reverses them when the financial statements are consolidated. However, this feature is usually only available in the more expensive accounting software packages.

Core Steps: Review Journal Entries

It is entirely possible that some journal entries were made incorrectly, in duplicate, or not at all. These issues can be mitigated, as described in the Journal Entry Efficiencies section of the Journal Entries chapter. Nonetheless, print the list of standard journal entries and compare it to the actual entries made in the general ledger, just to ensure that they were entered in the general ledger correctly. Another test is to have someone review the detailed calculations supporting each journal entry, and trace them through to the actual entries in the general ledger. This second approach takes more time, but is quite useful for ensuring that all necessary journal entries have been made correctly.

If there is an interest in closing the books quickly, the latter approach could interfere with the speed of the close; if so, consider authorizing this detailed review at a later date, when someone can conduct the review under less time pressure. However, any errors found can only be corrected in the *following* accounting period, since the financial statements will already have been issued.

Core Steps: Reconcile Accounts

It is very important to examine the contents of the balance sheet accounts to verify that the recorded assets and liabilities are supposed to be there. It is quite possible that some items are still listed in an account that should have been flushed out of the balance sheet a long time ago, which can be quite embarrassing if they are still on record when the auditors review the company's books at the end of the year. Here are several situations that a proper account reconciliation would have caught:

- *Prepaid assets.* A company issues a $10,000 bid bond to a local government. The company loses the bid, but is not repaid. The asset lingers on the books until year-end, when the auditors inquire about it, and the company then recovers the funds from the local government.
- *Accrued revenue.* A company accrues revenue of $50,000 for a services contract, but forgets to reverse the entry in the following month, when it invoices the full $50,000 to the customer. This results in the double recordation of revenue, which is not spotted until year-end. The controller then reverses the accrual, thereby unexpectedly reducing revenues for the full year by $50,000.
- *Depreciation.* A company calculates the depreciation on several hundred assets with an electronic spreadsheet, which unfortunately does not track when to stop depreciating assets. A year-end review finds that the company charged $40,000 of excess depreciation to expense.
- *Accumulated depreciation.* A company has been disposing of its assets for years, but has never bothered to eliminate the associated accumulated depreciation from its balance sheet. Doing so reduces both the fixed asset and accumulated depreciation accounts by 50%.
- *Accounts payable.* A company does not compare its accounts payable detail report to the general ledger account balance, which is $8,000 lower than the

detail. The auditors spot the error and require a correcting entry at year-end, so that the account balance matches the detail report.

These issues and many more are common problems encountered at year-end. To prevent the extensive embarrassment and error corrections caused by these problems, conduct account reconciliations every month for the larger accounts, and occasionally review the detail for the smaller accounts, too. The following are some of the account reconciliations to conduct, as well as the specific issues to look for:

Sample Account Reconciliation List

Account	Reconciliation Discussion
Cash	There can be a number of unrecorded checks, deposits, and bank fees that are only spotted with a bank reconciliation. It is permissible to do a partial bank reconciliation a day or two before the close, but completely ignoring it is not a good idea.
Accounts receivable, trade	The accounts receivable detail report should match the account balance. If not, you probably created a journal entry that should be eliminated from this account.
Accounts receivable, other	This account usually includes a large proportion of accounts receivable from employees, which are probably being deducted from their paychecks over time. This is a prime source of errors, since payroll deductions may not have been properly reflected in this account.
Accrued revenue	It is good practice to reverse all accrued revenue out of this account at the beginning of every period, so that you are forced to create new accruals every month. Thus, if there is a residual balance in the account, it probably should not be there.
Prepaid assets	This account may contain a variety of assets that will be charged to expense in the short term, so it may require frequent reviews to ensure that items have been flushed out in a timely manner.
Inventory	If a periodic inventory system is being used, match the inventory account to the ending inventory balance, which calls for a monthly reconciliation. However, if a perpetual inventory system is in use, inadequate cycle counting can lead to incorrect inventory balances. Thus, the level of reconciliation work depends upon the quality of the supporting inventory tracking system.
Fixed assets	It is quite likely that fixed assets will initially be recorded in the wrong fixed asset account, or that they are disposed of incorrectly. Reconcile the account to the fixed asset detail report at least once a quarter to spot and correct these issues.
Accumulated depreciation	The balance in this account may not match the fixed asset detail if the accumulated depreciation has not been removed from the account upon the sale or disposal of an asset. This is not a critical issue, but still warrants occasional review.

Account	Reconciliation Discussion
Accounts payable, trade	The accounts payable detail report should match the account balance. If not, you probably included the account in a journal entry, and should reverse that entry.
Accrued expenses	This account can include a large number of accruals for such expenses as wages, vacations, and benefits. It is good practice to reverse all of these expenses in the month following recordation. Thus, if there is a residual balance, there may be an excess accrual still on the books.
Sales taxes payable	If state and local governments mandate the forwarding of collected sales taxes every month, this means that beginning account balances should have been paid out during the subsequent month. Consequently, there should not be any residual balances from the preceding month, unless payment intervals are longer than one month.
Income taxes payable	The amount of income taxes paid on a quarterly basis does not have to match the accrued liability, so there can be a residual balance in the account. However, you should still examine the account, if only to verify that scheduled payments have been made.
Notes payable	The balance in this account should exactly match the account balance of the lender, barring any exceptions for in-transit payments to the lender.
Equity	In an active equity environment where there are frequent stock issuances or treasury stock purchases, these accounts may require considerable review to ensure that the account balances can be verified. However, if there is only sporadic account activity, it may be acceptable to reconcile at much longer intervals.

The number of accounts that can be reconciled makes it clear that this is one of the larger steps involved in closing the books. Selected reconciliations can be skipped from time to time, but doing so presents the risk of an error creeping into the financial statements and not being spotted for quite a few months. Consequently, there is a significant risk of issuing inaccurate financial statements if you continually avoid some reconciliations.

> **Related Podcast Episode:** Episode 168 of the Accounting Best Practices Podcast discusses account reconciliations. It is available at: **accountingtools.com/podcasts** or **iTunes**

Core Steps: Close Subsidiary Ledgers

Depending on the type of accounting software being used, it may be necessary to resolve any open issues in subsidiary ledgers, create a transaction to shift the totals in these balances to the general ledger (called *posting*), and then close the accounting periods within the subsidiary ledgers and open the next accounting period. This may involve ledgers for inventory, accounts receivable, and accounts payable. See the General Ledger and Other Ledgers chapter for more information.

Other accounting software systems (typically those developed more recently) do not have subsidiary ledgers, or at least use ones that do not require posting, and so are essentially invisible from the perspective of closing the books. Posting is the process of copying either summary-level or detailed entries in an accounting journal into the general ledger. Posting is needed in order to have a complete record of all accounting transactions in the general ledger. Posting may be done at any time, in batches, or at the end of an accounting period.

Core Steps: Create Financial Statements

When all of the preceding steps have been completed, print the financial statements, which include the following items:

- Income statement (see the Income Statement chapter)
- Balance sheet (see the Balance Sheet chapter)
- Statement of cash flows (see the Statement of Cash Flows chapter)
- Statement of retained earnings (see the Statement of Retained Earnings chapter)
- Disclosures (see the Financial Statement Disclosures chapter)

It may also be necessary to include segment reporting and earnings per share information. If so, see the Segment Reporting chapter and the Earnings per Share chapter, respectively, for more information.

If the financial statements are only to be distributed internally, it may be acceptable to only issue the income statement and balance sheet, and dispense with the other items just noted. Reporting to people outside of the company generally calls for issuance of the complete set of financial statements.

Core Steps: Review Financial Statements

Once all of the preceding steps have been completed, review the financial statements for errors. There are several ways to do so, including:

- *Horizontal analysis.* Print reports that show the income statement, balance sheet, and statement of cash flows for the past twelve months on a rolling basis. Track across each line item to see if there are any unusual declines or spikes in comparison to the results of prior periods, and investigate those items. This is the best review technique.
- *Budget versus actual.* Print an income statement that shows budgeted versus actual results, and investigate any larger variances. This is a less effective review technique, because it assumes that the budget is realistic, and also because a budget is not usually available for the balance sheet or statement of cash flows.

There will almost always be problems with the first iteration of the financial statements. Expect to investigate and correct several items before issuing a satisfactory set of financials. To reduce the amount of time needed to review financial statement errors during the core closing period, consider doing so a few days prior to month-end; this may uncover a few errors, leaving a smaller number to investigate later on.

Core Steps: Accrue Tax Liabilities

Once the financial statements have been created and finalized, there may be a need to accrue an income tax liability based on the amount of net profit or loss. There are several issues to consider when creating this accrual:

- *Income tax rate*. In most countries that impose an income tax, the tax rate begins at a low level and then gradually moves up to a higher tax rate that corresponds to higher levels of income. When accruing income taxes, use the average income tax rate that you expect to experience for the full year. Otherwise, the first quarter of the year will have a lower tax rate than later months, which is caused by the tax rate schedule, rather than any changes in company operational results.
- *Losses*. If the company has earned a profit in a prior period of the year and has now generated a loss, accrue for a tax rebate, which will offset the tax expense recorded earlier. Doing so creates the correct amount of aggregate tax liability for the year-to-date. If there was no prior profit and no reasonable prospect of one, do not accrue for a tax rebate, since it is more likely than not that the company will not receive the rebate.
- *Net operating loss carryforwards*. If the company has a net operating loss carryforward on its books, you may be able to use it to offset any income taxes in the current period. If so, there is no need to accrue for an income tax expense. A net operating loss (NOL) carryforward is a loss experienced in an earlier period that could not be completely offset against prior-period profits. This residual loss can be carried forward for up to 20 years, during which time it can be offset against any reported taxable income. If there is still an NOL remaining after 20 years have expired, it can no longer be used to offset profits.

Once the income tax liability has been accrued, print the complete set of financial statements.

Core Steps: Close the Month

Once all accounting transactions have been entered in the accounting system, close the month in the accounting software. This means prohibiting any further transactions in the general ledger in the old accounting period, as well as allowing the next accounting period to accept transactions. These steps are important, so that you do not inadvertently enter transactions into the wrong accounting periods.

> **Tip:** There is a risk that an accounting person might access the accounting software to re-open an accounting period to fraudulently adjust the results from a prior period. To avoid this, password-protect the relevant data entry screens in the software.

Core Steps: Calculate Earnings per Share

If the company is publicly-held and the financial statements are being issued to readers other than the management team, add earnings per share information to the bottom of the income statement. This is required when issuing quarterly and annual financial statements. The calculation of earnings per share information, along with examples, is provided in the Earnings per Share chapter.

There are two types of earnings per share information, which are basic earnings per share and diluted earnings per share. If the company has a complex capital structure, it can be time-consuming to calculate the diluted earnings per share. If this is the case, avoid using the earnings per share information in the other eight months of the year when quarterly and annual financial reports are not being issued. This will likely be acceptable to the management team that receives financial statements, since the primary user of earnings per share information is the investment community.

Core Steps: Add Disclosures

If financial statements are being issued to readers other than the management team, consider adding disclosures to the basic set of financial statements. There are many disclosures required under GAAP and IFRS, which are discussed in the Financial Statement Disclosures chapter. It is especially important to include a complete set of disclosures if the financial statements are being audited. If so, the auditors will offer advice regarding which disclosures to include. Allocate a large amount of time to the proper construction and error-checking of disclosures, for they contain a number of references to the financial statements and subsets of financial information extracted from the statements, and this information could be wrong. Thus, every time a new iteration of the financial statements is created, also update the disclosures.

If financial statements are being issued solely for the management team, do not include any disclosures. By avoiding them, you can cut a significant amount of time from the closing process. Further, the management team is already well aware of how the business is run, and so presumably does not need the disclosures. If there are disclosure items that are unusual (such as violating the covenants on a loan), then attach just those items to the financial statements, or note them in the cover letter that accompanies the financials (see the next section).

Core Steps: Write Cover Letter

When financial statements are issued, readers receive several pieces of information that they may not have the time, interest, or knowledge to properly interpret. Accordingly, create a cover letter that itemizes the key aspects of the financial results and position of the business during the reporting period. This should not be an exhaustive analysis. Instead, point out the *key* changes in the business that might be of interest to the readers. Conversely, if changes were expected but did not occur, then point that out. Further, discuss events that will occur in the near future, and their financial impact. Finally, use a standard format for the cover letter that lists all major topic areas, just so that you can refer to each topic as you write the contents of the letter. Doing so ensures that no areas will be missed. A sample cover letter follows:

Sample Cover Letter

To: Lowry Management Team Fr: Controller Re: April Financial Statements **Income statement:** The profit for the past month was $100,000 below budget, because we did not ship the ABC widget order on time. This was caused by a quality problem that was not spotted until the final quality review at the shipping dock. The order could have shipped on time if the quality review had been positioned after the widget trimming machine. We also paid $20,000 more than expected for rent, because we leased 12 storage trailers to accommodate a work-in-process overflow that did not fit into the warehouse. This was caused by the failure of the widget stamping machine. A replacement machine will arrive next week, and we expect it to require two months to eliminate the backlog of stored items. Thus, we will incur most of these leasing costs again through the next two months. **Balance Sheet:** Accounts receivable were lower than expected by $180,000, primarily because of the ABC widget order just noted. This means that incoming cash flows will be reduced by that amount in one month. In anticipation of this cash shortfall, we have finalized an increase in the company's line of credit of $200,000. **Future Events:** We expect to hear from the Marine Corps regarding the Super Widget order in late May. That order could increase the backlog by $1,000,000. Also, the office rent agreement expires on June 1. Market rates have increased, so we expect the replacement lease to cost at least $8,000 more per month.

Note that the sample cover letter addressed three key areas: the income statement, the balance sheet, and future events. These general categories are used as a reminder to review each area for discussion topics. If there are areas of particular ongoing concern, such as cash or debt, it is acceptable to list these items as separate categories.

Tip: When writing the cover letter, always round up the numbers in the report to the nearest thousand (if not higher). Managers will not change their decision if a variance is reported as $82,000 or as $81,729.32, and the report will be much easier to read.

Whenever possible, state the causes of issues in the cover letter, so that recipients do not have to spend time conducting their own investigations. In essence, the ideal cover letter highlights key points, discusses why they happened, and perhaps even points out how to correct them in the future.

Core Steps: Issue Financial Statements

The final core step in closing the books is to issue the financial statements. There are several ways to do this. If there is an interest in reducing the total time required for someone to receive the financial statements, convert the entire package to PDF documents and e-mail the package to recipients. Doing so eliminates the mail float that would otherwise be required. If a number of reports are being incorporated into the financial statement package, this may require the purchase of a document scanner.

When financial statements are issued, always print a copy for yourself and store it in a binder. This gives ready access to the report during the next few days, when managers from around the company are most likely to contact you with questions about it.

Delayed Steps: Issue Customer Invoices

From the perspective of closing the books, it is more important to formulate all customer invoices than it is to issue those invoices to customers.

Taking this delaying step can delay a company's cash flow. The problem is that a customer is supposed to pay an invoice based on pre-arranged terms that may also be stated on the invoice, so a delayed receipt of the invoice delays the corresponding payment. However, this is not necessarily the case. The terms the company sets with customers should state that they must pay the company following a certain number of days from the invoice date, not the date when they receive the invoices. Thus, if invoices are printed that are dated as of the last day of the month being closed, and are then mailed a few days later, the company should still be paid on the usual date.

From a practical perspective, this can still be a problem, because the accounting staff of the customer typically uses the current date as the default date when it enters supplier invoices into its accounting system. If they do so, the company will likely be paid late. You can follow up with any customers that appear to be paying late for this reason, but this will likely be a continuing problem.

Delayed Steps: Closing Metrics

If there is an interest in closing the books more quickly, consider tracking a small set of metrics related to the close. The objective of having these metrics is not necessarily to attain a world-class closing speed, but rather to spot the bottleneck areas of the close that are preventing a more rapid issuance of the financial statements. Thus, it is useful to have a set of metrics that delve sufficiently far into the workings of the closing process to spot the bottlenecks. An example of such metrics follows. Note that the total time required to close the books and issue financial statements is six days, but that the closing time for most of the steps needed to close the books is substantially shorter. Only the valuation of inventory and the bank reconciliation metrics reveal long closing intervals. This type of metric measurement and presentation allows you to spot where there are opportunities to compress the closing process.

Sample Metrics Report for Closing the Books

	Day 1	Day 2	Day 3	Day 4	Day 5	Day 6
Issue financials	xxx	xxx	xxx	xxx	xxx	**Done**
Supplier invoices	xxx	**Done**				
Customer invoices	xxx	xxx	**Done**			
Accrued expenses	xxx	xxx	**Done**			
Inventory valuation	xxx	xxx	xxx	xxx	**Done**	
Bank reconciliation	xxx	xxx	xxx	**Done**		
Fixed assets	xxx	**Done**				
Payroll	**Done**					

Delayed Steps: Document Future Closing Changes

After reviewing the closing metrics in the preceding step, you will likely want to make some improvements to the closing process. If so, incorporate these changes into a schedule of activities for the next close, and review any resulting changes in responsibility with the accounting staff. Do this as soon after the close as possible, since this is the time when any problems with the close will be fresh in your mind, and you will be most interested in fixing them during the next close.

Even if the timing of closing activities appears to be adequate, it is possible that one or more employees in the accounting department will be on vacation during the next close, so it will be necessary to incorporate their absence into the plan. Further, if there are inexperienced people in the department, consider including them in peripheral closing activities, and then gradually shifting them into positions of greater responsibility within the process. Thus, from the perspective of improvements, employee absences, and training, it is important to document any changes to the next closing process.

Delayed Steps: Update Closing Procedures

When a rigorous set of closing procedures is first implemented, you will find that they do not yield the expected results. Some steps may be concluded too late to feed into another step, or some activities may be assigned to the wrong employee. As you gradually sort through these issues, update the closing procedures and schedule of events. This process will require a number of iterations, after which the closing procedures will yield more satisfactory results. Further, every time the company changes its operations, it will be necessary to update the procedures again. Examples of situations that may require a change in the closing procedures are:

Situation	Impact on Closing Procedure
New accounting software	Every accounting package has a different built-in methodology for closing the books, which must be incorporated into the closing procedures.
New business transaction procedures	If other parts of the business alter their approaches to processing purchasing, inventory counts, shipping, and so forth, adjust the closing procedures to accommodate the changes.
Acquisition or sale of a subsidiary	Add procedures to encompass new lines of business, while shutting down closing activities for those segments that have been disposed of.
Change in bank accounts	Different banks have different systems for providing on-line access to bank account information, which may alter the bank reconciliation procedure.
Change in credit policy	This may require a different method for compiling the allowance for doubtful accounts.
Change in inventory management system	If a business changes to just-in-time inventory management, it may flush out many older LIFO inventory layers, or uncover more obsolete inventory. These changes may also require different inventory costing methods, new overhead allocation methodologies, or altered obsolescence reserves.

The preceding list is by no means all-encompassing. It merely illustrates the fact that you should consider the impact of almost *any* change in the business on the closing procedures. It is quite likely that at least minor tweaking will be needed every few months for even the most finely-tuned closing procedures. In particular, be wary of closing steps that are no longer needed, or whose impact on the financial statements have become so minor that their impact is immaterial; such steps clutter up the closing process and can significantly delay the issuance of financial statements.

Case Study

This section contains a case study that shows how a business uses many of the concepts noted earlier in this chapter to close the books and create financial statements.

The Billabong Machining Company manufactures a variety of widgets and also provides widget installation services to its customers. Jason Jones is the controller of Billabong, and he is closing the April books for the company.

To give us a beginning reference point for Jason's closing process, we start with his trial balance before he initiates any closing activities. The trial balance is:

Unadjusted Trial Balance before Closing Activities

Account Number	Account Description	Debit	Credit
1000	Cash	$60,000	
1100	Petty cash	1,000	
1200	Accounts receivable	180,000	
1300	Accounts receivable - accrued		
1350	Allowance for doubtful accounts		$4,800
1400	Rebillable expenses	8,000	
1500	Prepaid assets	30,000	
2000	Inventory	300,000	
3000	Fixed assets	710,000	
3100	Accumulated depreciation		320,000
3200	Accumulated amortization		21,000
4000	Accounts payable		98,000
4500	Accrued liabilities		50,000
4700	Notes payable		420,000
5000	Equity		374,300
6000	Revenue		720,000
7100	Cost of goods sold – Materials	180,000	
7120	Cost of goods sold – Labor	25,000	
7130	Cost of goods sold – Overhead	130,000	
7200	Wage expense	200,000	
7210	Bonus expense	15,000	
7220	Commission expense	6,000	
7230	Payroll tax expense	20,000	
7300	Benefits expense	36,000	
7400	Depreciation expense	35,000	
7450	Amortization expense	3,000	
7500	Rent expense	30,000	
7600	Office supplies expense	900	
7700	Meals expense	600	

Account Number	Account Description	Debit	Credit
7800	Bad debt expense	2,500	
7850	Bank fees	300	
7900	Interest expense	21,000	
7950	Interest income		1,200
8000	Other expenses	15,000	
	Totals	$2,009,300	$2,009,300

Next, Jason has the field service staff enter its billable hours into the Billabong timekeeping system. After issuing some pointed reminders to dilatory employees, these hours are all recorded in the timekeeping system, which he uses to create a batch of customer invoices. The billing module of the Billabong accounting software creates the following entry as a result of these billing activities:

	Debit	Credit
Accounts receivable	32,500	
Revenue		32,500

In addition, several customer contracts allow the field service staff to charge their travel expenses to customers. Jason checks the rebillable expenses account (which is a current asset), and sees that there are $8,000 to be rebilled. Again, he uses the billing module of the accounting software to create a batch of customer invoices, which creates the following entry:

	Debit	Credit
Accounts receivable	8,000	
Rebillable expenses		8,000

There are also a few widget shipments that were mailed at the end of the month, and which Jason invoices to customers. He uses the billing module to accomplish this, though the resulting entry is somewhat different, since it must also relieve the shipped widgets from inventory and charge them to the cost of goods sold. The entry for the $10,000 of widgets and their $4,000 cost is:

	Debit	Credit
Accounts receivable	10,000	
Revenue		10,000
Cost of goods sold	4,000	
Inventory		4,000

Jason finds that he cannot issue a $6,500 invoice to one customer, which only accepts invoices from Billabong on a quarterly basis, so he elects to accrue the revenue instead. This is a reversing journal entry, and he records it as:

	Debit	Credit
Accounts receivable - accrued	6,500	
Revenue		6,500

Jason has now completed customer billings, and moves on to accounts payable. He has entered all supplier invoices into the system, and now compares the receiving log to his list of supplier invoices to see if any invoices have not yet been received. He uncovers one receipt for which there is no corresponding invoice; according to the purchase order, the missing invoice should be for $14,000. He records the following reversing journal entry to replicate the missing invoice:

	Debit	Credit
Inventory	14,000	
Accrued liabilities		14,000

Jason then turns to the fixed assets area. Billabong has just taken out a loan to fund the construction of its new widget factory. The amount of interest applicable to construction of the factory is $21,000, so Jason shifts the money out of the interest expense account and into the fixed assets account with the following entry:

	Debit	Credit
Fixed assets	21,000	
Interest expense		21,000

In addition, Jason reviews the depreciation and amortization spreadsheet that he uses to calculate the monthly amount of depreciation and amortization, and finds that there should be $9,200 of depreciation and $1,000 of amortization expense for the month. He records this with the following entry:

	Debit	Credit
Depreciation expense	9,200	
Amortization expense	1,000	
Accumulated depreciation		9,200
Accumulated amortization		1,000

Jason turns to the closing of inventory. He goes to the warehouse and confirms with the warehouse manager that the staff set aside all incoming deliveries after midnight on the last day of the month, and so did not improperly include them in the preceding month. Thus, he achieved a correct month-end cutoff.

Billabong uses a perpetual inventory system and standard costing. The warehouse manager updated all inventory transaction records as of the close of business on the last day of the month and then printed the extended inventory report, which reveals an ending balance of $280,000. Since the preliminary balance in the account was $300,000, Jason creates the following entry to charge the difference to the cost of goods sold, thereby reducing the inventory asset account to $280,000:

	Debit	Credit
Cost of goods sold – Materials	20,000	
Inventory		20,000

There have historically been few differences between standard and actual costs, so Jason only calculates the purchase price variance on a quarterly basis. Since this is April, he does not bother to run the calculation. If there had been a variance, he would have charged it to the cost of goods sold account.

The manufacturing overhead cost pool for April contains $40,000, which Jason must allocate to the cost of goods sold and ending inventory. The basis of allocation for Billabong is machine hours used. There were 1,000 machine hours in April, so the allocation rate is $40 per machine hour used. Since the average widget uses 0.5 machine hours, this means that $20 of manufacturing overhead is allocated to each widget. Since 500 widgets were added to ending inventory, this means that $10,000 of the overhead cost pool can be allocated to ending inventory. Jason does this with the following entry:

	Debit	Credit
Inventory	10,000	
Cost of goods sold - Overhead		10,000

To complete the inventory analysis, the accounting staff reviews those inventory items with the largest total carrying cost and find that there have been no losses due to the lower of cost or market rule (see the Closing Inventory chapter).

Jason then moves to the standard set of journal entries that should at least be reviewed on a monthly basis, and makes the following adjustments:

- *Allowance for doubtful accounts.* Billabong derives its allowance for doubtful accounts from a straight 2.4% of the entire ending amount of trade accounts receivable, which Jason adjusts periodically to match actual experience. Using this percentage, the balance in the allowance at month-end should be $5,500. The balance is currently $4,800, so Jason records the following entry to increase the balance in the account:

	Debit	Credit
Bad debt expense	700	
Allowance for doubtful accounts		700

- *Accrued vacations.* Few Billabong employees took vacation time during April, preferring to retain it for use during the summer months. Accordingly, the amount of earned but unused vacation time increased by $11,000. In addition, pay raises for several employees effectively increased the amount of their existing accruals of unused vacation time, which increased the accrual by another $3,500. Accordingly, Jason records the following entry to increase the vacation accrual:

	Debit	Credit
Wage expense	14,500	
Accrued liabilities		14,500

- *Accrued wages.* The hourly employees of the company were paid on the last day of the month for hours worked through the 27th day of the month. Thus, there were three business days of earned but unpaid work at month-end, which amounted to $3,800. In addition, there were $300 of payroll taxes associated with the accrued wages. Jason records both expenses with the following reversing entry:

	Debit	Credit
Wage expense	3,800	
Payroll tax expense	300	
Accrued liabilities		4,100

- *Bonus expense.* The management team has a set of performance plans under which they can collectively earn $120,000 in bonuses if the company meets certain performance targets by the end of the calendar year. Based on current and estimated results, it is more likely than not that the management team in aggregate will earn a reduced bonus of $60,000. Accordingly, Jason accrues $1/12^{th}$ of this reduced amount for April, along with a related amount of payroll tax expense. The entry is:

	Debit	Credit
Bonus expense	5,000	
Payroll tax expense	350	
Accrued liabilities		5,350

- *Commission expense.* The accounting staff compiles the commission payments for the sales staff. Following the approval of the sales manager, Jason records the following reversing entry (the commission payment will be made in the following month) for $2,000 of commissions, plus $100 of related payroll taxes:

	Debit	Credit
Commission expense	2,000	
Payroll tax expense	100	
Accrued liabilities		2,100

The bank statement arrives from the bank for Billabong's checking account, and Jason completes the bank reconciliation. He finds that there are unrecorded service charges of $200, a not-sufficient-funds fee of $100, and interest income of $400. He records these changes with the following entry:

	Debit	Credit
Cash	100	
Bank fees	300	
Interest income		400

The manager of the petty cash fund forwards to Jason her itemization of petty cash expenditures during the month, which reduces petty cash by $500, due to $200 for meals and $300 for office supplies. He records this change with the following entry:

	Debit	Credit
Meals expense	200	
Office supplies expense	300	
Petty cash		500

Jason reviews the prepaid assets account and finds that $7,500 of prepaid rent and $12,000 of medical insurance payments should be charged to expense. He does so with the following entry:

	Debit	Credit
Rent expense	7,500	
Benefits expense	12,000	
Prepaid assets		19,500

Jason then examines the accrued liabilities account and finds that the accrued wages expense entry from the preceding month had not been set to reverse automatically in the current month. He rectifies the problem with the following entry:

	Debit	Credit
Accrued liabilities	6,100	
Wage expense		5,700
Payroll tax expense		400

After all of these entries have been made, Jason prints the following adjusted trial balance. Note that the debits and credits from the unadjusted version of the trial balance have been consolidated into a single column, thereby making room for the adjusting entries.

Adjusted Trial Balance after Closing Activities

Account Number	Account Description	Unadjusted Balance	Debit	Credit	Adjusted Balance
1000	Cash	$60,000	100		$60,100
1100	Petty cash	1,000		500	500
1200	Accounts receivable	180,000	50,500		230,500
1300	Accounts receivable - accrued		6,500		6,500
1350	Allowance for doubtful accounts	-4,800		700	-5,500
1400	Rebillable expenses	8,000		8,000	0
1500	Prepaid assets	30,000		19,500	10,500
2000	Inventory	300,000	24,000	24,000	300,000
3000	Fixed assets	710,000	21,000		731,000
3100	Accumulated depreciation	-320,000		9,200	-329,200
3200	Accumulated amortization	-21,000		1,000	-22,000
4000	Accounts payable	-98,000			-98,000
4500	Accrued liabilities	-50,000	6,100	40,050	-83,950
4700	Notes payable	-420,000			-420,000
5000	Equity	-374,300			-374,300
6000	Revenue	-720,000		49,000	-769,000
7100	Cost of goods sold – Materials	180,000	24,000		204,000
7120	Cost of goods sold – Labor	25,000			25,000
7130	Cost of goods sold – Overhead	130,000		10,000	120,000
7200	Wage expense	200,000	18,300	5,700	212,600
7210	Bonus expense	15,000	5,000		20,000
7220	Commission expense	6,000	2,000		8,000
7230	Payroll tax expense	20,000	750	400	20,350
7300	Benefits expense	36,000	12,000		48,000
7400	Depreciation expense	35,000	9,200		44,200
7450	Amortization expense	3,000	1,000		4,000
7500	Rent expense	30,000	7,500		37,500
7600	Office supplies expense	900	300		1,200
7700	Meals expense	600	200		800
7800	Bad debt expense	2,500	700		3,200
7850	Bank fees	300	300		600
7900	Interest expense	21,000		21,000	0
7950	Interest income	-1,200		400	-1,600
8000	Other expenses	15,000			15,000
	Totals	$0	$189,450	$189,450	$0

Jason then prints the income statement and the balance sheet from the accounting software, which are as follows:

Income Statement

Revenue	$769,000
Cost of goods sold – Materials	204,000
Cost of goods sold – Labor	25,000
Cost of goods sold – Overhead	120,000
Gross margin	$420,000
Other expenses	
Wage expense	212,600
Bonus expense	20,000
Commission expense	8,000
Payroll tax expense	20,350
Benefits expense	48,000
Depreciation expense	44,200
Amortization expense	4,000
Rent expense	37,500
Office supplies expense	1,200
Meals expense	800
Bad debt expense	3,200
Bank fees	600
Interest expense	0
Interest income	-1,600
Other expenses	15,000
Net profit	$6,150

Balance Sheet

Assets	
Cash	$60,100
Petty cash	500
Accounts receivable	230,500
Accounts receivable - accrued	6,500
Allowance for doubtful accounts	-5,500
Prepaid assets	10,500
Inventory	300,000
Fixed assets	731,000
Accumulated depreciation	-329,200
Accumulated amortization	-22,000
Total assets	$982,400
Liabilities	
Accounts payable	$98,000
Accrued liabilities	83,950
Notes payable	420,000
Total liabilities	$601,950
Equity	
Equity	$374,300
Current year income	6,150
Total equity	$380,450
Total liabilities and equity	$982,400

Note that the net year-to-date profit shown in the income statement also appears under the equity section of the balance sheet.

Closing Checklist

This section contains a listing of the key steps to follow to close the books. They are not presented in an exact numerical sequence, since it may be necessary to alter the order of certain tasks, depending upon the structure and procedures of the organization.

Customer Billings

- Issue recurring invoices to customers.
- Verify that all billable time has been included in the timekeeping system.
- Issue invoices to customers for all services provided and goods shipped through month-end. If the billings are related to customer contracts, first verify that there is sufficient funding to support the invoices.
- Accumulate rebillable expenses and issue invoices for them to customers.
- Reconcile invoices to shipping log.
- Verify that all subcontractor invoices were received and included in customer billings.
- Accrue revenue as applicable.

Accounts Payable

- Notify all employees to submit their expense reports.
- Enter all supplier invoices in the system by the designated cutoff date.
- Enter all employee expense reports.
- Accrue for any material expenses for which the supplier invoice has not yet been received.

Fixed Assets

- Verify that all fixed asset additions and deletions are correctly reflected in the fixed asset register.
- Capitalize interest on applicable projects.
- Record depreciation and amortization expense.
- Record the impairment of applicable fixed assets.

Inventory

- Verify that there was a proper inventory cutoff.
- Count the inventory or run a perpetual inventory report.
- Determine the cost of the ending inventory.
- Allocate overhead to ending inventory and the cost of goods sold.
- Adjust the ending inventory valuation for the lower of cost or market rule.

Journal Entries

- *Allowance for doubtful accounts.* Do not run this calculation early if a large part of company billings are issued at month-end.
- *Accrued revenue.* Only accrue revenue if the amount accrued meets all revenue recognition rules. When in doubt, do not accrue revenue. **[this is a reversing entry]**
- *Accrued royalties.* Accrue the amount of any royalties owed to third parties who own the intellectual property. **[this is a reversing entry]**

- *Accrued supplier billings.* If supplier invoices do not appear in time for the closing date, accrue the expense if it is material. **[this is a reversing entry]**
- *Accrued vacations.* Accrue for any changes in the amount of earned but unused vacation time. This balance can go up or down, depending upon actual vacation usage.
- *Accrued wages.* Accrue the earned but unpaid amount of wages at month-end. It usually makes sense to also accrue for the related amount of payroll taxes. **[this is a reversing entry]**
- *Bonus expense.* Accrue for the incremental amount of bonuses earned in the period.
- *Commission expense.* Accrue for the commission amount earned but not paid in the period. Consider also accruing the related amount of payroll taxes. **[this is a reversing entry]**
- *Depreciation and amortization.* If depreciation and amortization are being calculated with a spreadsheet, verify that the calculations do not run past the useful life of the asset, and that any salvage values are reasonable.
- *Income tax liability.* Adjust the income tax liability. This amount could increase or decrease, depending upon whether there was a gain or a loss, and whether there is a net operating loss carryforward.
- *Interest expense.* Accrue for any interest expense for which a billing has not yet been received from the lender. **[this is a reversing entry]**
- *Reserve for obsolete inventory.* Estimate the amount of obsolete inventory likely to be in the warehouse and adjust the reserve to match the estimate. This can be run at any time of the month.
- *Reserve for sales returns.* If the historical amount of sales returns is immaterial, this entry can be avoided.
- *Reserve for warranty claims.* If the historical amount of warranties is immaterial, this entry can be avoided.

Balance Sheet Reconciliations

- *Bank reconciliation(s).* Access the bank's online account records and reconcile all bank accounts. It is preferable to do so in advance for the bulk of the month's transactions, and then complete the last few days of the reconciliation during the core closing period.
- *Petty cash.* Reconcile the amount of petty cash on hand. This is usually such a small amount that it can be done outside of the core closing period.
- *Accounts receivable (trade).* Match the total in the ending aged accounts receivable report to the trade accounts receivable account in the general ledger.
- *Accounts receivable (other).* Verify that all items remaining in this general ledger account are still unpaid and are valid receivables. Adjust as necessary.
- *Prepaid expenses.* Review this general ledger account to see if any items should be charged to expense.

- *Inventory*. Match the total in the extended ending inventory report to the balance in the inventory account in the general ledger.
- *Fixed assets*. Match the subtotals for each asset classification in the fixed asset register to the corresponding accounts in the general ledger.
- *Accounts payable*. Match the total in the ending aged accounts payable report to the trade accounts payable account in the general ledger.
- *Sales taxes payable*. Most sales taxes are paid in the following month, so there should not be any residual balances from the preceding month (unless payment intervals are longer than one month).
- *Income taxes payable*. The amount of income taxes paid on a quarterly basis does not have to match the accrued liability, but verify that the quarterly payments were made.
- *Accrued liabilities*. Inspect the contents of each accrued liability account in the general ledger and verify that it matches the supporting detail.
- *Notes payable*. The balance in this general ledger account should exactly match the account balance provided by the lender, barring any exceptions for in-transit payments.
- *Equity*. Inspect the contents of each equity account in the general ledger and verify that it matches the supporting detail.

Consolidate Results

- *Convert currencies*. Convert the results forwarded from subsidiaries to the parent company's reporting currency.
- *Map results*. Map the converted subsidiary results to the chart of accounts of the parent company.
- *Eliminate intercompany transactions*. Aggregate the supporting schedule detailing all intercompany transactions and use it to eliminate these transactions from the consolidated results.

Error Checking

- *Journal entry review*. Review all journal entries for incorrect accounts, transpositions, and the incorrect use of reversing flags.
- *Income statement review*. Print a preliminary version of the income statement and review it for obvious errors. This works best if you can compare it to the results of previous periods using horizontal analysis, or compare it to budgeted results.
- *Negative cash*. If there is negative cash on the balance sheet, set the cash balance to zero with a journal entry and move the difference to a current liability account.

Preparation of the Financial Statements – Private Company

- If the financial statements are being prepared by hand:
  1. Print the ending trial balance report.
  2. Transfer the account totals into an income statement and balance sheet.
  3. Create a closing entry to shift temporary account balances to retained earnings.
- If the financial statements are being prepared with accounting software:
  1. Verify that budget information for the month has been entered.
  2. Print the financial statements.
- Complete the following for both manually and automatically prepared financial statements:
  1. Prepare a cover letter to accompany the financial statements.
  2. Prepare all necessary supporting disclosures.
  3. Complete all supporting schedules that accompany the main set of financial statements.
  4. Convert the complete financial statement package to PDF format.
  5. E-mail the PDF package to the financial statement distribution list.

Preparation of the Financial Statements – Public Company

1. Calculate basic and diluted earnings per share.
2. Add those disclosures required for publicly held companies. This includes segment reporting.
3. Prepare all supporting schedules associated with the SEC-mandated disclosures.
4. Complete the first draft of the Form 10-Q or Form 10-K.
5. Prepare schedules requested by auditors.
6. Support the auditors' review or audit of the financial statements and systems.
7. Obtain officer certifications of the Forms.
8. Obtain audit committee approval of the Form 10-Q (if applicable).
9. Obtain board of directors approval of the Form 10-K (if applicable).
10. EDGARize the applicable Form.
11. Obtain final auditor approval of the EDGARized Form.
12. File the Form with the SEC.

Final Tasks – Month-End

- Mail any customer invoices that have not yet been issued.
- Generate metrics regarding the speed with which the books were closed.
- Update the error tracking database for errors found during the close.
- Update controls based on system flaws found.
- Document any future changes to the closing process.
- Request programming changes from the information technology staff.

- Update the closing procedures, as necessary. This may involve the reallocation of work among the accounting staff if someone is expected to be out of the office during the next closing period.
- Close all activity in the subsidiary ledgers and the general ledger for the closed month and open the next month for the recordation of transactions.
- Update the month-end closing binder with all applicable supporting documentation related to the close. This should include:
  o Master activity list with steps initialed
  o Journal entry support
  o Schedules
  o Account reconciliations
  o Bank reconciliation
- If applicable, also update the month-end closing binder for a public company with the audit committee approval, officer certifications, and auditor-approved copy of the EDGARized Form 10-Q or 10-K filing.

Final Tasks – Year-End

- Update the year-end binder. This should include:
  o Financial statements
  o Trial balance
  o General ledger
  o Subsidiary ledgers
  o Ending inventory report
  o Fixed asset register
  o Fixed asset roll forward
  o Invoice register
  o Ending accounts receivable aging report
  o Ending accounts payable aging report

Summary

This chapter has outlined a large number of steps that are needed to close the books. The level of organization required to close the books in this manner may appear to be overkill. However, consider that the primary work product of the accounting department as a whole, and the controller in particular, is the financial statements. If you can establish a reputation for consistently issuing high-quality financial statements within a reasonable period of time, this will likely be the basis for the company's view of the entire department.

This chapter itemized the closing steps needed for a privately-held company. If you are closing the books for a publicly-held company, then also apply all of the preceding steps, plus the steps described in the Public Company Close chapter.

It is quite possible that additional closing steps are needed beyond the extensive list noted in this chapter. This is particularly common when a business has an unusual operating model, or operates in an industry with unique accounting rules. If so, incorporate the additional closing steps into the list described in this chapter.

Chapter 5
Fine-Tune the Closing Process

Introduction

The discussion of the closing process in this book is concerned solely with the proper closing of the books and production of financial statements – which can be a lengthy process. In this chapter, we focus on how to fine-tune the closing process with a variety of management techniques, with the goal of accelerating the closing process by being more efficient. The core concepts are:

- *Task interdependency analysis.* This involves examining the work flow to determine which tasks are delaying the completion of the close.
- *Early activities.* This involves completing selected closing tasks prior to the core closing period at month-end. Such activities include early reconciliations, accruals, and commission calculations.
- *Standardize and centralize.* This is the imposition of identical accounting procedures in all locations, and possibly the complete centralization of the accounting function.
- *Reduce reporting.* This is the reduction of the information contained within the financial statements.
- *Defer activities.* This is the shifting of non-closing activities out of the core closing period.
- *Use automation.* This is the use of technology to enhance the efficiency of the closing process.

Related Podcast Episodes: Episodes 16 through 21 of the Accounting Best Practices Podcast discuss scheduling, centralization, and journal entries as they relate to closing the books. They are available at: **accountingtools.com/podcasts** or **iTunes**

Task Interdependency Analysis

This chapter contains many suggestions for improving the closing process, but the main issue concerning most controllers is not having a more efficient close – just issuing financial statements more promptly. The simplest tool for achieving that goal is task interdependency analysis. In essence, this analysis seeks out the few processes within the entire system of closing activities that keep you from issuing financial statements more quickly. This concept is best illustrated with an example.

EXAMPLE

The accounting team of Lowry Locomotion finds that it can consistently issue financial statements in about six business days. The controller hires a process analyst, who constructs the following table to break down the start and stop times of some of the more important activities needed to produce the financial statements:

Closing Activity	Day 1	Day 2	Day 3	Day 4	Day 5	Day 6
Payroll	Collect timesheets	Accrue wages	Review billable hours			
Customer invoicing	Invoice shipments		Invoice billable hours	Accrue commissions		
Supplier payables		Accrue expenses	Update fixed assets			
Fixed assets				Record depreciation		
Inventory valuation	Count inventory		Value inventory	Allocate overhead		
General ledger		Reconcile cash account	Reconcile other accounts			
Financial statements					Compile and review financials	Add commentary and issue

The chart of task interdependencies reveals that (obviously) the financial statements cannot be prepared until a variety of other closing tasks have first been completed. In particular, the accounting team needs to eliminate all of the activities appearing in Day 4 in order to accelerate the compilation and review of the financial statements by one day. To do so, it needs to address three issues:

- *Customer invoicing.* The accrual of commissions in Day 4 can be completed earlier if the invoicing of billable hours in Day 3 can be accelerated. That is achievable if the employees tasked with payroll activities can review billable hours in Day 2 instead of Day 3.
- *Fixed assets.* The recordation of depreciation in Day 4 can be shifted to Day 3 if the updating of fixed assets by the employees tasked with supplier payables can be moved from Day 3 to Day 2.
- *Inventory valuation.* The allocation of overhead in Day 4 can be moved to Day 3 by increasing the workload of the employees tasked with inventory valuation on Day 3.

The accounting staff enacts these changes, resulting in the following table that reflects the altered schedule, and which allows the company to issue financial statements one day sooner.

Closing Activity	Day 1	Day 2	Day 3	Day 4	Day 5
Payroll	Collect timesheets	Accrue wages, review billable hours			
Customer invoicing	Invoice shipments	Invoice billable hours	Accrue commissions		
Supplier payables	Accrue expenses	Update fixed assets			
Fixed assets			Record depreciation		
Inventory valuation	Count inventory		Value inventory and allocate overhead		
General ledger		Reconcile cash account	Reconcile other accounts		
Financial statements				Compile and review financials	Add commentary and issue

As the example demonstrated, it may be necessary to shift the timing of a number of activities in order to issue financial statements more quickly. As the closing process is gradually refined, this will mean that a large number of activities will be compressed into a very small time period, which requires extremely tight scheduling of activities. As a result, the controller may find it necessary to adopt the role of master scheduler and shift a number of hands-on closing tasks to other people.

Correct Errors Early

Transactional errors can arise throughout the month, which means it is possible to run the financial statements a few days prior to month-end and spot most of them. This is a vast improvement over waiting until you are in the midst of the closing process and *then* finding problems. By spotting errors a few days early, the accounting staff can research and correct items at their leisure, rather than doing so in a hurry at month-end. Also, a rushed error correction at month-end may not yield a proper fix, which means that someone has to research and correct the issue a second time – which may delay closing the books.

If early error correction is used, there will still be a few days near the end of the month when errors may arise, since the accounting staff will not have reviewed financial statements that include those days. Still, there should be far fewer errors to deal with.

Reconcile Accounts Early

One of the lengthier tasks at month-end is to reconcile all of the accounts in the balance sheet that have significant ending balances, to ensure that their contents are correct. The accounting staff could start these reconciliations a few days before month-end, and then update them for any transactions that occurred during the last couple of days of the month. This is not a cure-all by any means, since many accruals are generated at month-end, and so will not appear in early versions of account reconciliations. Nonetheless, it can remove a fair amount of reconciliation labor from the core closing period.

The concept of reconciling early is especially important for the bank reconciliation. The cash account may have many adjustments each month that are caused by unrecorded bank fees, transactional errors, not-sufficient-funds check rejections, and so forth. These accounts can be reconciled a few days early based on the on-line account information that most banks make available to their customers over the Internet. This leaves just a day or two of final reconciliation work during the core closing period.

Tip: Many banks automatically generate PDF versions of monthly bank statements and post them to their web sites, where they can be downloaded. These statements should be available within 24 hours of the end of each month; the monthly bank reconciliation can be completed with this report.

Adjust Reserves Early

It may be possible to adjust reserves early, rather than waiting until month-end. For example, if the company maintains a reserve for obsolete inventory, schedule a review of inventory at any time of the month and adjust the reserve at that time, rather than waiting to do so at month-end. This approach is less useful for the allowance for doubtful accounts, since proportionately more accounts receivable are generated at month-end than at any other time of the month; this makes it difficult to adjust that reserve early.

Tip: Use the simplest possible estimation method to adjust the allowance for doubtful accounts, such as a simple percentage of the total amount of receivables outstanding. The simplest method may not be as accurate as a more complex method, such as conducting a review of individual receivables. However, the calculation of this allowance is difficult to move out of the core closing period, so it may make sense to trade time for accuracy.

Alter Overhead Allocations Early

If a company engages in production activities, it should allocate manufacturing overhead to its ending inventory and cost of goods sold. The usual method for doing so is to add up all manufacturing overhead costs during the period and allocate them based on an activity, such as direct labor hours or machine time used. The trouble with this approach is that you have to wait until the month has been completed to determine (for example) how many direct labor hours or machine hours were used during the period, which then forms the basis for the allocation. It can take time to compile this allocation information, so consider using the allocation information from the immediately preceding month, or perhaps an average for the preceding three months. By doing so, there is no need to wait for the compilation of any operational information for the month that was just completed, thereby shifting work out of the core closing period.

Review the Shipping Log Early

Some organizations have procedural difficulties in issuing invoices to all of the customers to whom they have shipped goods, resulting in some missed billings. This issue can be rectified by comparing all issued invoices to the shipping log that is maintained by the shipping department. In companies where missed invoices is a recurring problem, matching invoices to the shipping log is a key part of the closing process. It can be tedious to crosscheck invoices against the shipping log, and so can interfere with the closing process. To mitigate this issue, consider conducting the comparison shortly before the end of the month; doing so will spot any missed billing opportunities for the bulk of the month. It will still be necessary to conduct the review during the core closing period, but only for the last few days of the month.

Review Billable Hours Early

When a business earns revenue by billing its staff time to customers, an important part of the closing process is to ensure that those billable hours are correct. Thus, there should be closing activities to verify that:
- Hours have been billed to the correct customers
- Hours billed are for the correct activities
- The rates per hour are correct
- There is sufficient funding remaining on customer contracts to be billed

When billable time is the core revenue-generating part of a business, these verification steps are likely to be the most important of all closing activities. To keep this verification work from inundating the closing team, consider conducting a preliminary review of billable hours a day or two prior to month-end. Doing so will not spot all errors and adjustments, because many employees wait until month-end to enter their time in the timekeeping system. Nonetheless, catching even a few errors in advance will shift work out of the core closing period.

Accrue Early

There are likely to be a standard number of expenses that should be accrued as part of every month-end close, so that expenses are recorded even in the absence of a supplier invoice or other documentation. While these accruals are usually completed in the core closing period, it is possible to calculate and record some of them in advance. For example:
- *Interest expense.* If a company has outstanding debt, accrue interest expense for it, or else wait for the lender to send an invoice for the interest expense. It may be possible to estimate the amount of interest expense prior to month-

end. Even if there are sudden changes in the debt level in the last day or two of the month, the amount of interest expense associated with this change is likely to be small, and will be immaterial to the reported results of the business.

- *Vacation expense.* If there is a large amount of accrued but unused vacation time, there should be an expense adjustment each month (or at least every quarter) to update the expense. This can be a significant issue in companies that have a large number of employees, liberal vacation policies, and/or do *not* have "use it or lose it" vacation policies. Any one of these three circumstances can result in large amounts of accrued vacation expense. You can typically make this accrual immediately after the last pay period of the month, when employees have recorded their vacation time taken through that date.
- *Wage expense.* If there are any employees paid on an hourly basis, there are likely to be a few days at month-end when those employees have earned wages but have not yet been paid for them. You can estimate the amount of these hours worked but not paid prior to month-end and accrue the expense. The estimate may be slightly different from actual results, but the difference should not be material. The accrual may be somewhat more difficult if the hourly staff is also incurring a significant amount of overtime that is not easily predicted in advance; if so, this accrual may have to wait until all time recording has been completed for the month.

Tip: Have the company follow a policy of having employees record their time every day in the timekeeping system. This means that the wage information available for accrual purposes is very nearly current, which makes it easier to calculate a reasonably accurate wage accrual just prior to month-end.

Accelerate Depreciation Calculations

It is not necessary to wait until the core closing period to calculate the depreciation and amortization expense for the month. Instead, it can be done a day or two in advance for all fixed assets that have been recorded through that point. If any fixed assets are recorded subsequent to that date, consider the impact on the financial statements of *not* recording the associated monthly amount of depreciation:

- Missing $1/36^{th}$ of the expense for an asset depreciated over three years.
- Missing $1/60^{th}$ of the expense for an asset depreciated over five years.
- Missing $1/120^{th}$ of the expense for an asset depreciated over ten years.

In short, the impact on a single accounting period is extremely small. Further, you can record double the amount of depreciation in the next month for any fixed assets that missed the prior month depreciation, so there is no impact on the financial statements at all over even a short period of time.

The only time of the year when depreciation calculations cannot be accelerated is at the end of the fiscal year, since the auditors will certainly want to see depreciation calculations that link back to the ending fixed asset balance.

Examine Commissions Early

It can be difficult to prepare the commissions payable documentation prior to month-end, especially when a large part of the monthly invoices are not issued until month-end, and commissions are based on the invoices. Still, there are some tasks or system changes to consider that might ease the commission calculation work. They are:

- *Switch to commissions paid from cash receipts.* If commissions are paid based on cash received from customers, you can reliably calculate commissions throughout the month, as cash comes in. This may work better from a closing perspective than paying based on invoices issued, since many businesses issue a disproportionate number of invoices at month-end, which delays commission calculations until month-end.
- *Ask about plan changes.* Commission plans are notorious for incorporating a vast array of arcane payment features, such as retroactive rate increases if quarterly or annual targets are met, altered commissions for certain products, bonuses, and splits between multiple salespeople. If the sales manager has made yet another change to these plans, it is useful to document the changes in advance.
- *Itemize trigger points.* If some salespeople are about to receive different commission percentages or bonuses because they have achieved certain performance targets, ascertain these trigger points in advance and incorporate them into the commission calculations for the month.

Tip: The sales manager nearly always reviews and approves the commission calculations generated by the accounting department. This review process may be so lengthy that it interferes with closing the books. If so, it may be acceptable to close the books *without* the approval of the sales manager. This situation arises when the most likely alteration that the sales manager will make is to shift a commission payment from one salesperson to another. This does not affect the total commission expense, which is the chief concern from the perspective of closing the books.

Standardize the Accounting System

If a company has a number of subsidiaries that report their information to corporate headquarters for consolidation, it is quite possible that the headquarters accounting staff will spend an inordinate amount of time trying to consolidate the disparate results that it has received. Further, if the corporate staff detects a possible error in the results forwarded from a division, it must make inquiries with that division, which make take quite a long time to respond. Also, some subsidiaries may use different procedures that require more time to forward closing information to headquarters. The result of these issues is a slower close.

The solution is a high degree of standardization throughout the accounting operations of the business. Standardization can be applied in a number of areas, including:

- *Software*. It is very useful to have a single company-wide enterprise resources planning (ERP) system, but that solution is so expensive that it may not be cost-effective. Instead, consider installing the same accounting software in all locations, so that common procedures can be designed around them.
- *Chart of accounts*. Use an identical chart of accounts in all locations. This makes it much easier to map the month-end results of the subsidiaries to the general ledger of the parent company.
- *Procedures*. Use an identical set of procedures for all accounting transactions. This can be difficult if some transactions are based on non-standard systems elsewhere in the company, so there will likely be some variability in procedures.
- *Policies*. Accounting policies should be the same in all locations, so that business transactions are treated in the same way. For example, different capitalization policies would mean that an expenditure would be recorded as a fixed asset in one location and as an expense in another location.
- *Journal entries*. There should be a standard set of journal entries that are used in all locations, and which use the same accounts. Thus, journal entry templates are standardized.
- *Calendars*. The same activity schedules are used everywhere, so that the managers of all accounting operations know when they are supposed to complete assigned deliverables.

Tip: Encourage the selective testing of new ways to streamline accounting processes further. This may involve the use of an in-house team of accountants, internal auditors, or perhaps a group of process consultants. If successful, you can then roll them out throughout the company.

When there is a high level of standardization within the business, it is much easier to compare the closing performance of each accounting area. This is useful for spotting promotion-worthy employees. In addition, develop closing metrics for all subsidiaries, and use this information to improve the operations of those accounting units that persistently perform at sub-par levels.

Tip: Allocate a large amount of time to the standardization task. This involves the construction of operational manuals, training classes, and follow-up system testing by the internal audit staff to ensure that standardized approaches are being followed. In a large company, this could be a multi-year task.

Centralize the Accounting System

When there are multiple accounting locations that forward their results to the corporate staff for consolidation, the overall closing process will be less efficient. The trouble is that some locations will be less efficient than others, due to different policies, procedures, training, staff availability, management skills, and so on. The result is that a few locations will always be late in forwarding their results to the headquarters staff, which delays the close.

These issues can be avoided by shutting down the local accounting operations and instead centralizing all accounting activities in one place. Doing so yields the following advantages:

- *Coordination.* The closing team is located in a single place, so there is tight coordination within the team. There is also no need for a workflow management system, since everyone involved in the close is likely sitting next to each other.
- *Intercompany eliminations.* When the entire accounting system is in one place, it is much easier to flag intercompany transactions and eliminate them as part of the consolidation process. This is a much more difficult issue when there are different accounting systems in every location, and no one tracks intercompany transactions at the local level.
- *Research.* If someone uncovers a problem during the closing process, it is much easier to research the issue in a centralized environment, since the closing team has on-site access to the detailed transaction, and so can research it at once.
- *Software.* The company only needs one accounting software package. This yields considerable benefits over a distributed solution, since everyone is trained on a single system and procedures can be tailored to that system. Though it does not relate to the closing process, a company will also likely realize cost reductions from having to pay maintenance on only one software package, as well as from only creating custom interfaces between other systems and that single accounting package.
- *Standardization.* It is much easier to standardize all accounting policies and procedures when there is only one accounting location. This means that you can more easily fine-tune the accounting systems to close quickly.
- *Transaction factory.* It is much more efficient to deal with all of a company's credit, collection, customer billing, and accounts payable transactions in one place – essentially creating a "transaction factory" to reduce transaction costs. This approach carries the added benefit of being so efficient that those aspects of the closing process related to transactions can be completed extremely quickly.

It is a considerable chore to centralize all accounting activities. The best approach is to do so gradually and by functional area. Thus, you could centralize all supplier invoice processing activities, and perhaps then move on to the centralization of customer invoices, payroll processing, and so forth.

> **Tip:** Local managers may be concerned about losing all local accounting employees, so it may be necessary to retain a few people at the subsidiary level to handle a few issues that are closely related to local business transactions. If it is necessary to do so, at least keep them away from any activities that could increase the time required for the closing process.

If the company routinely acquires other businesses, it is quite possible that any one of these acquisitions will delay the closing process for a long time to come. The reason is that the accounting staff of the acquired company may set a low priority on the closing process, and so routinely completes closing activities many days late. If this is the case, the easiest alternative is to standardize their closing processes by providing them with the company's standard closing procedures and as much training as is needed to comply with it. However, it is also possible that they never attain the standards at which the rest of the company operates; if, so you may be forced to shift their accounting operations to the centralized company facility. The key point to remember is that any acquisition can severely delay the overall closing process if the acquiree's accounting operations are substandard.

> **Tip:** If there is a plan to shift the accounting operations of all acquired companies to the corporate accounting center, have a standardized plan in place that is enacted as part of the initial integration process for every acquired company. Though these transitions are painful, there is less impact on the closing process if the acquiree's accounting operations can be shifted to the central location as soon as possible.

Standardize Exception Handling

Errors and a variety of other issues are bound to arise as part of any closing process. If so, there can be a serious delay if the resolutions to these issues must first be reviewed and approved by a senior-level accounting person. To avoid the delay, create an exception handling policy. The policy describes the materiality thresholds that must be exceeded before senior management needs to approve a correction. The thresholds should be set high, so that most changes are corrected at the clerical level.

When creating this policy, be aware that some line items in the financial statements are more sensitive than others, so the materiality threshold may vary. For example, the gross margin percentage is closely watched, so the controller may be more interested in issues relating to the cost of goods sold than to depreciation.

Also, do not allow the clerical staff to correct errors and other issues with no supervisory review until the staff has been properly trained. Doing so may require not just an initial training session, but also the use of a procedure with explanatory examples, and an occasional audit to see if guidelines are still being followed.

Centralize Travel Bookings

In some companies, the expense reports submitted by employees are substantial, and therefore can have a major impact on the financial results of the month.

Unfortunately, they also tend to be submitted late, so that expenses do not appear in the month in which they were incurred. While this issue can be mitigated through the use of employee reminders in advance of month-end, another option is to remove travel costs from employee expense reports. This can be done by requiring all employees to use an approved travel agency for all airfare bookings, if not for hotels, as well. By doing so, these charges appear on a company credit card, which the accounting staff can easily access and record in the accounting system well before any employee expense reports arrive. The end result is that employee expense reports contain far fewer expenses, and so it is less important to have them submitted in a timely manner.

Process Centering

A significant problem with the closing process is the participation of too many people, because there are too many hand-offs of closing tasks between employees. Every time there is a hand-off, there is a risk not only of a task being inadvertently dropped, but also of it waiting in the work queue of the person to whom it was given. Thus, if a task is passed through multiple hands, there is a strong likelihood that it will not be completed in time, and will delay the closing process.

The solution is to reduce the number of people who are involved in the closing process, and then have as many of the remaining employees as possible handle closing processes from end-to-end. This approach is called *process centering*. The intent is to reduce the number of participants in the closing process to the point where queue times have been largely eliminated, but without shrinking the headcount so much that they cannot complete the closing tasks within a reasonable period of time. Thus, there will be an optimum number of people on the closing team that minimizes the amount of time needed to close the books. If too many people are eliminated from the closing process, there may be no queue times left, but the burden of the close will be on so few people that the time required to close the books will *increase*.

Tip: When the entire accounting department assists in the closing process, this means that it does not have enough time for other ongoing activities during the close – such as issuing customer invoices. Process centering keeps a few accounting people away from closing activities, which means that they can return to their normal day-to-day tasks, thereby eliminating work stoppages elsewhere in the department.

The best way to determine the optimum team size for process centering is to review the entire closing process, ascertain where queue times are actively interfering with the production of financial statements, and take one of the following actions:
- If the queue time is caused by waiting for an approval, find a workaround to the approval
- Route the transaction to someone else who does not have a work queue

- Have the person currently working on the activity complete the additional task(s) for which it was to be transferred to another person

Once the point is reached where queue times are no longer interfering with the close, there is no need to continue with process centering; doing so would only impact other activities that are not crucial to the closing process.

Mitigate Information Dependencies

It is possible that the entire closing process is being delayed because another department is supposed to forward information to the accounting department and has not done so. Examples of this situation are the completion of a physical inventory count and the forwarding of shipping information for customer billing purposes. In these cases, the controller will have a difficult time improving the closing process, because the generation of the required information is simply out of his control. The situation can be improved with one or more of the following options:

- *Eliminate the information requirement.* It may be possible to exclude the information from the financial statements entirely. For example, if you are waiting for performance metrics from the production department, shift this information to a metrics report that is issued separately from the financial statements.
- *Upgrade information systems.* If you are waiting for the manual collection and forwarding of information, install systems that automate these steps. For example, if you are waiting for the shipping log from the shipping department, have the shipping staff enter shipment information directly into a computer system that is accessible by the accounting staff. Similarly, switch to a perpetual inventory system (see the Closing Inventory chapter) in order to avoid a physical inventory count.
- *Assign data collection to accounting.* There may be a few cases where data collection activities can be assigned to the accounting staff. This gives the controller direct control over data collection.
- *Assign coordinators to source departments.* It can be helpful to assign an employee to the departments from which information is sourced, in order to gain insights into why the information flow is delayed. Having this interface can increase the cooperation between the departments in finding a better way to handle the situation.

Standardize the Report Layout

Some managers who receive the financial statements prefer them in a certain layout, with perhaps more detail in one area and less in another. If so, the controller must prepare a variety of different reporting packages for distribution to the management team, which can require a significant amount of additional time. This is a particularly pernicious problem if some managers want special calculations included in their financial statement packages (such as different forms of net profit, or operational metrics). The solution is to persuade senior management to adopt a single reporting package that is used throughout the company.

Having a standardized report layout can be difficult to achieve, because of pressure from report recipients. If so, a possible solution is to issue additional information to the most importunate managers after the basic financial statement package has been released.

Tip: It is very important to standardize the calculation of any measurements included within the financial statement package. Otherwise, some managers may apply pressure for the accounting department to use calculations that favor the reported performance of those managers. To avoid this, prepare a report stating how all measurements are to be calculated, and have the chief executive officer approve it.

Reduce the Financial Statements

The financial statements can be considered just the income statement and balance sheet, but tend to grow over time, eventually encompassing a cover letter, statement of cash flows, statement of retained earnings, departmental results, and a variety of operational and financial metrics. While a large and comprehensive financial statement package makes for plenty of in-depth reading by the management team, it also plays havoc with the closing schedule. The primary issue is that any report not automatically generated by the accounting software can require a considerable amount of time to prepare by hand. Further, it may be necessary to use separate information collection systems to obtain the data needed for these additional reports, and that additional information may not be ready at month-end.

The solution is quite simple. The contents of the primary financial statement package should only contain those reports that qualify under both of the following criteria:

- The reports are automatically generated by the accounting system; and
- The information from which the reports are compiled have been recorded in the accounting system no later than the scheduled issuance date of the financial statements.

These criteria exclude any manually-prepared reports. These additional reports do not have to be eliminated entirely, but their issuance should be delayed until after the financial statements have been issued. By doing so, the accounting team does not waste time on anything other than the primary product of the closing process – the financial statements. In particular, consider shifting to a separate reporting package any information about the cost or profit of specific products, services, or contracts, since these items are usually compiled manually.

> **Tip:** The one exception to the report issuance rules just described is the cover letter to the financial statements. As described in the Closing Process chapter, the cover letter can provide valuable insights into the financial results achieved by a business. As such, it is worthwhile to spend extra time preparing it, rather than issuing financial statements without any accompanying explanations.

Also, if there are a number of metrics related to the company's financial or operational results, consider shifting them to a separate report; they can take time to prepare, and so may delay the issuance of the financial statements.

> **Tip:** Many reporting packages allow you to include metrics within financial reports that are automatically compiled from the financial information in the reports. If so, these metrics are not interfering with the issuance of financial statements, and so can be included in the basic reporting package.

If there is uncertainty about which parts of the financial statements and related metrics are being read by the recipients, interview them to find out. Based on this information, it may be possible to eliminate large blocks of information from the financial statement package.

Collect Report Information Early

It may not be possible to reduce the content of the financial statements. If so, there may be some line items in those reports that you can complete or at least start work on prior to the closing period. For example:

- *Commentary.* If there is a cover letter or disclosures that accompany the financial statements, review them in advance and update any information that you can. If there are areas that cannot be completed before printing the final version of the financial statements, highlight them in the word processing software to indicate that further updates are needed.
- *Variance analysis.* If there was a significant variance earlier in the month and you are aware of what happened, document it in the financial statement package as soon as there is complete information about it.
- *Metrics.* In a few instances, you may receive or calculate financial or operational metrics prior to month-end. If so, include it in the reports as soon as it is available.

Electronic Delivery

The time required to produce financial statements can be considered to include the time it takes to deliver the financial statements into the hands of their intended recipients. If so, the least efficient method of delivery is to print out the financial statements and mail them to the distribution list. Instead, consider converting the entire financial statement package into PDF format and e-mailing the package. Many accounting systems create PDF-format financial statements, or you can simply run the entire set of printed documents through a scanner, which will convert it into PDF format automatically.

Defer Activities

The closing process can be seriously delayed if the accounting staff is forced to engage in all of its normal day-to-day activities at the same time. Instead, block out a certain amount of time in which the staff does nothing but close the books. For example:

- *Meetings*. If the staff is normally required to attend various meetings during the closing period, defer the meetings to a later date, or do not attend.
- *Accounts payable*. The payment terms with most suppliers are reasonably lengthy, so you do not have to enter them into the accounting system the moment they arrive in the mail. Instead, let them pile up until the financial statements have been issued. This comment refers to invoices relating to the *next* reporting period; invoices for the *last* reporting period must be entered at once, in order to recognize the related expense in the correct period.
- *Reports*. If there are standard daily or weekly reports that the accounting staff issues to other departments, make it clear that these reports will not be issued until the close has been completed.
- *Tax returns*. Government entities usually allow a reasonable number of days for you to prepare tax returns (20 days for sales tax returns is common), so defer the preparation of these returns until after the close.

There will inevitably be a few issues that need to be handled at once, irrespective of closing activities. Examples of these issues are depositing cash at the bank and handling rush requests for supplier payments. A good way to address these occasional issues is to keep a few of the accounting staff completely away from the closing process, and task them with all day-to-day activities. Doing so minimizes any interruptions of closing activities.

The deferral of some activities will likely mean that the intense pressure to close the books will be followed by the intense pressure to catch up on all items that had been deferred. Nonetheless, you should have closed the books and be caught up on all deferred activities within roughly one week of month-end.

Tip: Make it clear to the rest of the company that the accounting department is not available for *anything* during the closing period. While a few crises will still leak through to the department, it is likely that the request to be left alone for a few days each month will be honored by other employees.

Automation Solutions

There are many ways to create an efficient and cost-effective closing process, and few of them involve the use of automation. This is partially because the core improvements to the closing process involve scheduling and procedural changes (which are largely free), and partially because automated solutions involve the installation of comprehensive company-wide accounting systems (which are fabulously expensive and difficult to install). Consequently, do not place the solutions set forth in this section at the top of the closing agenda. Instead, implement the other solutions recommended in this chapter, and *then* scan through this section to see if there are any topics of interest. That is also why this section was placed at the end of the chapter.

Intercompany Transactions

An area that can seriously impede the closing process is the reconciliation of intercompany transactions. If a company routinely buys and sells between its divisions, these transactions must be removed from the consolidated results of the parent company, in order to avoid the recordation of sales that do not really exist. Given the difficulty of identifying and eliminating these transactions, it can make a great deal of sense to purchase software that tracks this information for you. This is usually a separate module within an enterprise resources planning (ERP) system. All transactions between subsidiaries are flagged when they are initially generated, and this module backs them out of the consolidated financial results of the company. The main issue with this solution is cost – the underlying ERP system is quite expensive, and must be used by all subsidiaries that engage in intercompany transactions.

If subsidiaries use different accounting software, then an alternative is to upload the payables and receivables records of all subsidiaries into a centralized matching program. This program matches receivable and payable transactions between the entities, and generates a report showing which transaction records are mismatched. The accounting staffs of the subsidiaries use this report as the basis for a manual reconciliation of their transaction records.

Consolidation Software

If it is necessary to consolidate the financial results of multiple entities into consolidated financial statements, consolidation software could be useful. This is accounting software that takes the financial information from multiple sources, converts it into a single currency, maps the incoming information to the corporate chart of accounts, and produces consolidated financial statements. This is expensive software that can also be costly to install, depending upon the number and complexity of custom interfaces needed to link it the company's various accounting software packages.

Consolidation software is not of much use if you have a simple consolidation environment, with few subsidiaries that all use the same chart of accounts and the same currency.

Enterprise Resources Planning Systems

An enterprise resources planning system is a comprehensive company-wide system that ties together all of the operations of a business, possibly for all locations. Having such a system is a clear benefit for the closing process, since all

71

intercompany transactions can be flagged when they are produced, and eliminated for the purposes of creating consolidated financial statements. An ERP system also makes it much easier to produce consolidated financial statements.

ERP systems are enormously expensive and very time-consuming to install. When installed incorrectly, they can even put a company's operations at risk of failure. Given these issues, it is certainly not cost-effective to acquire an ERP system solely to improve the closing process. Instead, there should be many other reasons for acquiring an ERP system; its impact on the closing process should only be considered a useful side benefit of the installation.

The main providers of ERP systems are SAP and Oracle. You can learn more about their software at www.sap.com and www.oracle.com.

Workflow Management Systems

A workflow management system is a software application that routes work to specific people, and monitors their progress in completing assigned tasks. It can also re-route work items to a different person if the person who was initially assigned those tasks is not responsive. It tracks the amount of time required for a person to complete a task, which is useful not only for calculating the duration of a process, but also for measuring the efficiency of the person assigned to the task. In essence, it is designed to improve the flow of complex processes through a business.

Will a workflow management system improve your ability to close the books? In most situations, it probably will not play a direct role in the process flow. The trouble is that workflow management systems were designed to aid in the completion of complex tasks that involve many people, whereas the closing process typically involves very few people. When you have a small closing team (see the earlier section about process centering), there is little need for anything that monitors work flow, since everyone already knows their assigned tasks. Furthermore, they are likely located together within a small area, so that any issue can be addressed simply by walking over to someone and discussing it.

A workflow management system can be of considerably greater use when the closing process is distributed across multiple locations. Under this scenario, it is difficult to personally keep track of the work of people who may be on different continents, so the system could introduce a good oversight capability to the process.

In short, workflow management software is most useful for closing the books in a highly dispersed environment. If there is a small closing team that operates from one location, the system is probably not necessary.

Incremental Automation

The closing team may spot possible enhancements to the closing process that require extremely minor adjustments to the existing accounting systems. If so, prioritize them and make programming requests to the information technology staff in an orderly manner; the intent is not to overwhelm the programmers with requests. Instead, implement the improvements at a measured pace over a period of time, ensuring that each one is properly tested and integrated into the closing process before proceeding to the next request.

Automation Summary

Some of the automation choices noted in this section are quite expensive. However, they can also be a godsend for larger companies that have multiple subsidiaries and the cash to pay for fully-integrated accounting solutions. For these companies, it may be highly cost-effective to acquire computerized solutions to improve their closing processes. Nonetheless, that is not the case for smaller companies that are unable or unwilling to spend large sums on automation. This latter group should concern itself with the other solutions outlined in this chapter, and will still be able to achieve excellent results with their closing processes.

Tip: Before purchasing an automated solution, consider its cost in comparison to the benefit to be gained from the closing process. In most cases, few automation solutions are worth the corresponding improvement in the closing process. Instead, there must be benefits in other parts of the business to make them worthwhile.

A final consideration is to first improve a process to the greatest extent possible, and wring out all possible efficiencies from it. At that point, consider some additional level of automation. By taking this approach, you are avoiding the automation of a process that is fundamentally inefficient and quite possibly flawed. In short, do not automate a process too soon, thereby locking in a process that is still too inefficient.

Ongoing Process Improvements

A basic rule of any system is that it is either being improved or it is in a state of decline – there is no steady state. This is because even the most perfect system will be continually assailed by changes in other systems within the business, resulting in alterations that make the "perfect" system less perfect over time. Thus, if you stop the ongoing review and improvement of the closing process, the amount of time and effort needed to close the books will soon begin to increase.

This degradation in the system can be avoided by adopting an issue tracking and review system. In essence, write down every issue that arises during the closing process over multiple periods, and periodically examine these issues to determine how they can be resolved. In particular, aggregate these issues by type, so that it becomes apparent over time if there are recurring problems that require more immediate attention. Issues that do not recur can be considered outlier problems, and which can therefore be assigned a lower priority for resolution.

The error tracking system may be a simple spreadsheet on which is recorded the date of the issue, a description, and a code that designates the type of issue. Then sort the spreadsheet by issue code to more easily determine which issues appear to be a problem. It may also be useful to record on the spreadsheet how issues were resolved. A sample format for such a spreadsheet is shown below:

Sample Error Tracking Spreadsheet

Date	Code	Description
03/20x1	Accrue	Did not set wage accrual to automatically reverse
03/20x1	Accrue	Missing rent expense accrual
03/20x1	Cutoff	Incorrect month-end cutoff at receiving dock
04/20x1	Accrue	No termination set for royalty accrual
04/20x1	Cutoff	Incorrect month-end cutoff at receiving dock
04/20x1	Calculate	Over-depreciated fixed assets
05/20x1	Posting	Missed posting of final customer invoice batch
06/20x1	Cutoff	Incorrect month-end cutoff at receiving dock
06/20x1	Accrual	Double accrual of rent expense
06/20x1	Accrual	Did not set wage accrual to automatically reverse

In the sample error tracking spreadsheet, we can see that there has been a month-end inventory cutoff problem at the receiving dock that has occurred so many times that it is probably most worthy of attention. There is also an issue with wage accrual reversals that has arisen with less frequency, so it can probably be assigned second priority for examination.

It is particularly important to encourage the accounting staff to contribute to the issue tracking system as soon as possible, since these issues tend to be forgotten in the midst of the closing process. Accordingly, the controller may want to take charge of issue collection and walk through the closing team each day, asking for issues to include in the system.

Once a problem with the closing process has been tracked down and corrected, be sure to document it. By doing so, you can develop a history of which actions were taken in the past. This is a useful training tool for new accounting managers, and also may provide clues to how to resolve similar problems in the future. For example, if you were able to resolve inventory cutoff issues with a training class for the receiving department, it may be worthwhile to require another class at some point in the future if a cutoff problem were to appear again.

Another ongoing process improvement is to schedule an annual review of the closing process with the entire closing team. This review examines all steps in the closing process, opportunities for automation, and the presence of any non-value added activities. Consider having an outside expert on the topic attend the meeting, if they can provide usable insights. These types of reviews should be scheduled at sufficiently long intervals to make them of some interest to the closing team.

Tip: Schedule an update of the closing procedures at least once a year, if not more frequently. This is less of a concern if the closing process is well-refined and has changed little, but may require more frequent revisions if there have been many changes, or if the closing team is inexperienced and therefore relies upon the procedures to complete the close.

Summary

This chapter has described a variety of techniques that can help accelerate the closing process. When deciding which ones to install, consider that there should not be too many changes to the closing process in any one month. If there is already a functional closing process, then there is already a closely-knit set of functional procedures in place, which are now going to be disrupted. Consequently, it is better to implement one or two changes per month, so that you can measure their impact on the total closing process and figure out how to integrate them seamlessly into the process. If it takes several months complete the implementation of a specific modification, then so be it; do not try to rush these modifications. Over a period of time, an accelerated close will be achieved. The trick is doing so without disrupting the process along the way.

Since it may take years to implement all of the improvements suggested in this chapter, concentrate on those ideas that will have the most immediate impact on the closing process. Accordingly, it is most useful to determine which suggestions will immediately improve the speed of your closing process, and implement them first. For example, if switching from a physical inventory count to a perpetual inventory system will immediately reduce the time needed to close the books and issue financial statements by several days, that may be the best immediate improvement to pursue.

Chapter 6
Closing Cash

Introduction

Closing cash is all about the bank reconciliation, because it matches the amount of cash recorded by the company to what its bank has recorded. Once a valid bank reconciliation has been completed, you can have considerable confidence that the amount of cash appearing on the balance sheet is correct.

This chapter shows how to create a bank reconciliation format, as well as how to complete it as expeditiously as possible. There are also discussions of how to close petty cash, and how to deal with a negative cash balance on the balance sheet.

Overview of the Bank Reconciliation

A bank reconciliation is the process of matching the balances in an entity's accounting records for a cash account to the corresponding information on a bank statement, with the goal of ascertaining the differences between the two and booking changes to the accounting records as appropriate. The information on the bank statement is the bank's record of all transactions impacting the entity's bank account during the past month.

At a minimum, conduct a bank reconciliation shortly after the end of each month, when the bank sends the company a bank statement containing the bank's beginning cash balance, transactions during the month, and its ending cash balance. It is even better to conduct a bank reconciliation every day based on the bank's month-to-date information, which should be accessible on the bank's web site. By completing a daily bank reconciliation, problems can be spotted and corrected immediately.

It is extremely unlikely that a company's ending cash balance and the bank's ending cash balance will be identical, since there are probably multiple payments and deposits in transit at all times, as well as bank service fees, penalties, and not sufficient funds (NSF) deposits (which is a check not cleared, because the payer's bank account does not contain sufficient funds) that the company has not yet recorded.

The essential process flow for a bank reconciliation is to start with the bank's ending cash balance, add to it any deposits in transit from the company to the bank, subtract any outstanding (uncleared) checks, and either add or deduct any other items. Then, go to the company's ending cash balance and deduct from it any bank service fees, NSF checks and penalties, and add to it any interest earned. At the end of this process, the adjusted bank balance should equal the company's ending adjusted cash balance.

The Bank Reconciliation Procedure

The following bank reconciliation procedure assumes that the bank reconciliation is being created in an accounting software package, which makes the reconciliation process easier. The steps are:

1. Enter the bank reconciliation software module. A listing of uncleared checks and uncleared deposits will appear.
2. Check off in the bank reconciliation module all checks that are listed on the bank statement as having cleared the bank.
3. Check off in the bank reconciliation module all deposits that are listed on the bank statement as having cleared the bank.
4. Enter as expenses all bank charges appearing on the bank statement, and which have not already been recorded in the company's records.
5. Enter the ending balance on the bank statement. If the book and bank balances match, post all changes recorded in the bank reconciliation, and close the module. If the balances do not match, continue reviewing the bank reconciliation for additional reconciling items. Look for the following issues:

   - Checks recorded in the bank records at a different amount from what is recorded in the company's records.
   - Deposits recorded in the bank records at a different amount from what is recorded in the company's records.
   - Checks recorded in the bank records that are not recorded at all in the company's records.
   - Deposits recorded in the bank records that are not recorded at all in the company's records.
   - Inbound wire transfers from which a lifting fee has been extracted. A lifting fee is the transaction fee charged to the recipient of a wire transfer, which the recipient's bank imposes for handling the transaction. The term also applies to foreign bank processing fees, which may be applied to a variety of other financial transactions besides a wire transfer.

EXAMPLE

Lowry Locomotion is closing its books for the month ended April 30. Lowry's controller must prepare a bank reconciliation based on the following issues:

1. The bank statement contains an ending bank balance of $320,000.
2. The bank statement contains a $200 check printing charge for new checks that the company ordered.
3. The bank statement contains a $150 service charge for operating the bank account.
4. The bank rejects a deposit of $500, due to not sufficient funds, and charges the company a $10 fee associated with the rejection.
5. The bank statement contains interest income of $30.
6. Lowry issued $80,000 of checks that have not yet cleared the bank.

7. Lowry deposited $25,000 of checks at month-end that were not deposited in time to appear on the bank statement.

Based on this information, the controller creates the following reconciliation:

	$	Item No.	Adjustment to Books
Bank balance	$320,000	1	
- Check printing charge	-200	2	Debit expense, credit cash
- Service charge	-150	3	Debit expense, credit cash
- NSF fee	-10	4	Debit expense, credit cash
- NSF deposit rejected	-500	4	Debit receivable, credit cash
+ Interest income	+30	5	Debit cash, credit interest income
- Uncleared checks	-80,000	6	None
+ Deposits in transit	+25,000	7	None
Book balance	$264,170		

Bank Reconciliation Problems

There are several problems that continually arise as part of the bank reconciliation, and which you should be aware of. They are:

- *Uncleared checks that continue to not be presented.* There will be a residual number of checks that either are not presented to the bank for payment for a long time, or which are never presented for payment. In the short term, treat them in the same manner as any other uncleared checks – just keep them in the uncleared checks listing in the accounting software, so they will be an ongoing reconciling item. In the long term, contact the payee to see if they ever received the check; you will likely need to void the old check and issue them a new one.
- *Checks clear the bank after having been voided.* As just noted, if a check remains uncleared for a long time, you will probably void the old check and issue a replacement check. But what if the payee then cashes the original check? If the check was voided with the bank, the bank should reject the check when it is presented. If you did not void it with the bank, then record the check with a credit to the cash account and a debit to indicate the reason for the payment. If the payee has not yet cashed the replacement check, void it with the bank at once to avoid a double payment. Otherwise, you will need to pursue repayment of the second check with the payee.
- *Deposited checks are returned.* There are cases where the bank will refuse to deposit a check, usually because it is drawn on a bank account located in another country. In this case, reverse the original entry related to that deposit, which will be a credit to the cash account to reduce the cash balance, with a corresponding debit (increase) in the accounts receivable account.

The three items noted here are relatively common, and you will likely have to deal with each one at least once a year.

The Bank Reconciliation Statement

When the bank reconciliation process is complete, print a report through the accounting software that shows the bank and book balances, the identified differences between the two (mostly uncleared checks), and any remaining unreconciled difference. Retain a copy of this report for each month. The auditors will want to see it as part of their year-end audit. The format of the report will vary by software package; a simplistic layout is:

Sample Bank Reconciliation Statement

For the month ended March 31, 20X3:	$	Notes
Bank balance	$850,000	
Less: Checks outstanding	-225,000	See detail
Add: deposits in transit	+100,000	See detail
+/- Other adjustments	0	
Book balance	$725,000	

The Timing of the Bank Reconciliation

It is possible to wait for a bank reconciliation to be generated by the bank within a day or two of month-end, and then download the document as a PDF file and use it as the basis for a bank reconciliation. Including the time required to complete the bank reconciliation, this introduces a two-to-three day delay to the closing process. Since the adjustments normally found in a typical bank reconciliation are not substantial, this means that you are spending time on a closing activity whose results are likely to be immaterial to the financial statements as a whole.

Rather than incorporating this delay into the closing process, consider running a periodic bank reconciliation throughout the month. This involves accessing the bank's website to view the most recent information about deposits and recently cleared checks, and updating this information in the bank reconciliation module of the accounting software. By doing so, you are gradually making adjustments to the company's accounting records throughout the month, so that completing the final month-end bank reconciliation should be a simple matter – after all, it should only involve any activity in the bank account for the last day of the month.

By engaging in daily bank reconciliations, it may be possible to avoid the final month-end bank reconciliation until after you have closed the books. With only a one-day reconciliation to complete, the risk of not recording a material adjustment in the accounting records is quite small. Instead, you can complete the reconciliation immediately after issuing the financial statements, and record any remaining adjustments in the accounting records of the following month.

The situation is somewhat different for the year-end financial statements, since the auditors will likely want to see a bank reconciliation that exactly matches the company's cash balance as of the end of the year. The same situation applies on a quarterly basis for publicly-held companies, since auditors will conduct a review of their financial statements as of the end of the first, second and third quarters, and will also want to see a complete bank reconciliation. Thus, if the year-end financial statements are audited or the quarterly financial statements are reviewed, it makes sense to wait for the official period-end bank statement to arrive before closing the books.

Negative Cash on the Balance Sheet

It is possible for a negative cash balance to appear on the balance sheet if checks were issued for more funds than exist in the cash account. If so, it is customary to use a journal entry to move the amount of the overdrawn checks into a liability account, and set up the entry to automatically reverse at the beginning of the next reporting period. Doing so eliminates the negative cash balance.

There are two options for which liability account to use to store the overdrawn amount, which are:

1. *Separate account.* The more theoretically correct approach is to segregate the overdrawn amount in its own account, such as "Overdrawn Checks" or "Checks Paid Exceeding Cash." However, since this is likely to be a small account balance, it clutters the balance sheet with an extra line. Or, if you are aggregating smaller accounts together on the balance sheet, it will not appear by itself on the balance sheet, and so conveys no real information to the user. If so, try the next option.

2. *Accounts payable account.* Enter the amount into the "Accounts Payable" account. If you do, the accounts payable detail report will no longer exactly match the total account balance. However, as long as the entry automatically reverses, the overdrawn amount should not clutter up the account for long. This approach is especially appealing if overdrawn checks are a rarity.

Based on this discussion, it is reasonable to assume that any time you see a company's balance sheet with a zero cash balance, it probably has an overdrawn bank account; this brings up questions about its liquidity, and therefore its ability to continue as a going concern. To allay such concerns for anyone reading your financial statements, try to avoid being in a situation where there is a zero cash balance.

Closing Petty Cash

The amount of petty cash on hand should be so small that it is completely immaterial to the reported results of a business, and so can be safely ignored from the perspective of closing the books. Petty cash is a small amount of cash kept on hand in a business to pay for incidental expenses.

If you insist on closing petty cash as part of closing the books, doing so centers on the petty cash book. This is, in most cases, an actual ledger book or spreadsheet, rather than a computer record, in which are recorded petty cash expenditures.

There are two primary types of entries in the petty cash book, which are a debit to record cash received by the petty cash clerk (usually in a single block of cash at infrequent intervals), and a large number of credits to reflect cash withdrawals from the petty cash fund. These credits can be for such transactions as payments for meals, flowers, office supplies, stamps, and so forth. A somewhat more useful format is to record all debits and credits in a single column, with a running cash balance in the column furthest to the right, as shown in the following example. This format is an excellent way to monitor the current amount of petty cash remaining on hand.

Sample Petty Cash Book (Running Balance)

Date	Purchase/Receipt	Amount	Balance
4/01/xx	Opening balance	$250.00	$250.00
4/05/xx	Kitchen supplies	-52.80	197.20
4/08/xx	Birthday cake	-24.15	173.05
4/11/xx	Pizza lunch	-81.62	91.43
4/14/xx	Taxi fare	-25.00	66.43
4/23/xx	Kitchen supplies	-42.00	24.43

Yet another variation on the petty cash book is to maintain it as a spreadsheet, where each item is recorded in a specific column that is designated for a particular type of receipt or expense. This format makes it easier to record petty cash activity in the general ledger. An example of this format, using the same information as the preceding example, follows:

Sample Petty Cash Book (Columnar)

Date	Description	Meals	Supplies	Travel
4/05/xx	Kitchen supplies		$52.80	
4/08/xx	Birthday cake	$24.15		
4/11/xx	Pizza lunch	81.62		
4/14/xx	Taxi fare			$25.00
4/23/xx	Kitchen supplies		42.00	
	Totals	$105.77	$94.80	$25.00

When the amount of petty cash on hand declines to near zero, as is caused by withdrawals for various expenditures, the petty cash clerk obtains additional cash from the cashier and records this cash influx as a new debit. The petty cash clerk also turns in a copy of the petty cash book to the general ledger accountant or cashier, who creates a journal entry to record how the petty cash was used.

From the perspective of closing the books, three levels of increasing detail can be used to ensure that all petty cash that has been used during the reporting period is recorded by the end of the month. The options are:

1. *Easiest.* Rely on the occasional recordation of expenses by the general ledger accountant that is based on the petty cash book. This may be at long intervals, and so tends to under-report the expenses for which cash may have been expended.

2. *Intermediate.* Have the petty cash clerk update the petty cash book through month-end and submit it to the general ledger accountant for recording in the general ledger. This accurately records all uses of petty cash through month-end.

3. *Hardest.* Count the amount of petty cash on hand, reconcile it to the petty cash book, and record any adjustments through the end of the month. This approach ensures that all expenses have been accurately recorded through the end of the month, and records any missing cash.

We do not recommend *any* form of petty cash closing activities at the end of the month, since any results will be immaterial. If you insist on closing petty cash, then we recommend the easiest of the three alternatives just described. The other two options require valuable staff time during the closing period, when accounting personnel are needed for more important tasks.

Summary

The key issue to consider when closing cash is whether you can continually generate a bank reconciliation throughout the month. Doing so leaves so little reconciliation work at the end of the month that you can either spend a short period of time to complete it, or even delay the final reconciliation until after having closed the books. In either case, remember that closing cash is one of the *least* significant activities in the list of closing activities, so do not spend much time on it during the period when you are closing the books.

Chapter 7
Closing Accounts Receivable

Introduction

To close accounts receivable, ensure that all billings to customers have been completed properly. In some situations, it can also mean that you need to record accrued revenue, and possibly also contra revenue. In this chapter, we address a variety of closing issues related to issuing invoices to customers, as well as revenue recognition, reconciling accounts receivable, and the calculation of several allowance accounts.

Related Podcast Episode: Episode 25 of the Accounting Best Practices Podcast discusses billing in relation to closing the books. It is available at: **accounting-tools.com/podcasts** or **iTunes**

The Shipping Log Interface

When the accounting department creates customer invoices, it uses shipping documentation as the basis for those invoices. In a traditionally-organized company, that means the accounting staff must wait for the shipping information to be forwarded to it from the shipping department. This is not normally a problem during the month, but can cause a delay at month-end, when the accounting department is typically operating under a tight closing deadline. Ideally, the shipping information from the preceding day should be in the accounting department as of the start of business on the next day. If not, the simplest approach is to have someone in the accounting department go to the shipping department to collect the missing documentation. This may be acceptable, but can be an issue if doing so will delay closing the books, and is not possible if the shipping department is located elsewhere.

A good alternative is to have the shipping department enter all shipments into shipping software that is accessible by the accounting department. This has the following advantages:

- *Information accessibility*. The accounting department can access the information as soon as it is entered into the system, which may even allow for some limited invoicing on the day of shipment.
- *Errors*. The accounting staff can match the information in the on-line shipping log to its records of invoices issued, to see if any shipments were not invoiced.

> **Tip:** Match the shipping log to the invoice register just before the end of the month to verify if all shipped items have been properly invoiced. Doing so may retrieve some revenue that would otherwise have been lost, while not interfering with the month-end closing process.

Revenue Accruals

There may be situations where the company has completed all contractual requirements for recognizing revenue, but is not allowed to issue an invoice until a later date. In this case, you can accrue revenue, using a credit to an accrued revenue account and a debit to an accrued accounts receivable asset account. If you use this approach, be sure to address the following issues:

- *Auditor documentation.* Auditors do not like accrued revenue, since there are a number of restrictions placed on its use under GAAP. Consequently, this means fully documenting the reasons for accruing revenue, with complete backup of the revenue calculations. The auditors will review this information. However, if revenue is only being accrued for partway through a year, it may not be necessary to document the transactions in detail, since they should no longer be present on the balance sheet by the end of the fiscal year.
- *Reversing entry.* When revenue is accrued, the assumption is that you are likely to issue an invoice soon thereafter, probably in the next month. Consequently, set up every revenue accrual journal entry to automatically reverse in the next month. This clears the revenue accrual from the books, leaving room to record the revenue on the invoice. The following example illustrates the technique.

EXAMPLE

Lowry Locomotion has fulfilled all of the terms of a contract with a customer to deliver a diesel locomotive, but is unable to issue an invoice until July, which is the following month. Accordingly, the controller of Lowry creates a revenue accrual with the following entry in June:

	Debit	Credit
Accrued revenue receivable (asset)	6,500,000	
Accrued revenue (revenue)		6,500,000

The controller sets the journal entry to automatically reverse in the next month, so the accounting software creates the following entry at the beginning of July:

	Debit	Credit
Accrued revenue (revenue)	6,500,000	
Accrued revenue receivable (asset)		6,500,000

In July, Lowry is now able to issue the invoice to the customer. When the invoice is created, the billing module of the accounting software creates the following entry in July:

	Debit	Credit
Accounts receivable	6,500,000	
Revenue		6,500,000

Thus, the net impact of these transactions is:

June:	Accrued revenue =	$6,500,000
July:	Accrued revenue reversal =	-$6,500,000
	Invoice generated =	+6,500,000
	Net effect in July =	$0

There are a large number of revenue recognition rules. The key ones are noted in the following section.

Revenue Recognition Rules

Consider the following two factors when determining the proper date and amount of revenue to recognize:

- *Is the sale realized or realizable?* A sale is realized when goods or services are exchanged for cash or claims to cash. You generally cannot recognize revenue until a sale is realized or realizable.
- *Has the sale been earned?* A sale has been earned when an entity has substantially accomplished whatever is needed in order to be entitled to the benefits represented by the revenue.

More specifically, an entity can record revenue when it meets *all* of the following criteria:

- The price is substantially fixed at the sale date.
- The buyer has either paid the seller or is obligated to make such payment. The payment is not contingent upon the buyer reselling the product.
- The buyer's obligation to pay does not change if the product is destroyed or damaged.
- The buyer has economic substance apart from the seller.
- The seller does not have any significant additional performance obligations related to the sale.
- The seller can reasonably estimate the amount of future returns.

Treatment of Deferred Revenue

There are times when the company may have invoiced a customer, but should defer recognition of the related revenue. This is called *deferred revenue*. You generally account for deferred revenue situations as part of the closing process.

Record deferred revenue as a liability, which means that the initial entry to record it is a debit to the cash or accounts receivable account and a credit to the deferred revenue liability account. As the company earns this revenue over time, it reduces the balance in the deferred revenue liability account (with a debit) and increases the balance in the revenue account (with a credit). The deferred revenue liability account is normally classified as a current liability on the balance sheet.

EXAMPLE

Lowry Locomotion hires Bozeman Plowing to plow its parking area, and pays $2,500 in advance, so that Bozeman will give the company top plowing priority throughout the winter. Upon payment, Bozeman has not earned any of the revenue, so it records the entire $2,500 in a deferred revenue liability account with the following entry:

	Debit	Credit
Cash	2,500	
Deferred revenue (liability)		2,500

Bozeman expects to be plowing for Lowry for five months, so it elects to recognize $500 of the deferred revenue per month in each of the five months. Thus, in each of these months, Bozeman records the following entry:

	Debit	Credit
Deferred revenue (liability)	500	
Revenue		500

Issues with Subcontractors

There may be situations where a company is the prime contractor to a customer, and has one or more subcontractors working for it. In these situations, the normal flow of paperwork is for the subcontractors to compile their billings and forward them to the company, which then includes the information on these invoices in its billing to the final customer. The problem with this flow of paper is that you have to wait, sometimes more than a week, before the subcontractors forward their billings; this seriously impacts the issuance of the company's month-end billings, which in turn delays closing the books. There are several ways to deal with this problem:

- *Set due date*. State in the contract with each subcontractor that they must provide a monthly invoice to the company by a certain date, or else risk termination of the contract. This clause usually allows contractors several days to create invoices, so there is still a built-in delay in the closing process.

- *Electronic transmission.* Require subcontractors to forward their invoices to the company by an e-mailed PDF document. Doing so eliminates the mail float.
- *Require use of company systems.* Require the billable staff of subcontractors to use the company's online timekeeping system. By doing so, you can create invoices as soon as the subcontractor employees have entered their information into the system. This is the fastest approach for creating invoices, but it requires subcontractor employees to enter their billable time twice – once in the company's timekeeping system, and once in their employer's timekeeping system.

The third option results in the fastest closing process, but requires the presence of an online timekeeping system that everyone can access, as well as the cooperation of subcontractors.

Recurring Invoices

There may be situations where a business issues invoices for exactly the same amounts to its customers, month after month. Such invoices usually relate to ongoing subscription, lease, or service contracts. For example, a landlord may issue a rent invoice to its lessees every month, while a maintenance company may charge a fixed monthly fee to its customers to review and update their air conditioning systems.

If there is a recurring invoice situation, a business probably includes these billings in its month-end invoicing activities. If so, it represents a work load in the midst of the closing activities that can be avoided simply by issuing them in advance. If you already know the amount of each invoice, it is quite possible to process and mail the invoices several days in advance. If customers are accustomed to having these invoices dated as of the last day of the month, you can simply set the date on these invoices to the last day of the month.

A side benefit of this approach is that the recipients of the invoices may process them for payment sooner, since they receive the invoices sooner.

The only downside of this technique is to make sure that prices have not changed before issuing the early invoices. This can happen when there is a contractually-authorized change in price, so be sure to review all related contracts before issuing the invoices.

Tip: Contracts may state that recurring invoices be dated as of the first day of the *next* month. If so, you can still print them in advance, as long as you set the accounting period in the accounting software to the next month. In particular, be sure to return to the original accounting month once the printing is complete; otherwise, you will then record subsequent accounting transactions in the wrong month.

Rebillable Expenses

There are situations where a company may incur expenses on behalf of a customer, and then bill the customer for these expenses. This situation arises most frequently under a longer-term services contract. For example, an investment banker may be hired by a company to assist it in locating other companies to acquire, and the investment banker is allowed to rebill its travel expenses on behalf of the company. When there are rebillable expenses, a company normally accumulates these expenses in a current asset account, waits until the end of the month for these expenses to accumulate, and then invoices them to the customer as part of its normal month-end invoice.

> **Tip:** Initially record rebillable expenses in an asset account, not an expense account. If you were to record them in an expense account, you would have to rebill them in the same month as you initially recorded them, or risk having the expense appear in the financial statements in the month of recordation, followed by a reversal in the financial statements for the next month, when the expenses are billed to the customer. By recording rebillable expenses in an asset account, there is not impact on the income statement.

There are several issues with rebillable expenses that make them a troublesome component of the closing process. These issues are:
- *Supplier invoices.* You may have to wait for supplier invoices to arrive, since customers may only accept billings for actual expenses, not accrued ones.
- *Receipts.* Some customers want to see the receipts related to a rebilled expense. This is particularly common when you are billing a government agency.
- *Approvals.* A manager may want to review all rebillable expenses before they are invoiced to a customer, to see if they should be rebilled or charged to expense. This can be a time-consuming process, especially if the manager wants to review the supporting detail for each expense.

These issues can require a significant amount of time in the midst of the closing process, even though the amount billed may be relatively small. There are several ways to deal with rebillable expenses, which are:
1. *Adopt longer billing cycle.* If the contract with a customer is a long one, it may be acceptable to let rebillable expenses accumulate over a longer period of time, with perhaps a separate quarterly billing for these items. This may be a particularly attractive option if the amounts involved are small.
2. *Adopt an offset billing cycle.* Since rebilled expenses should initially be recorded as assets in the seller's general ledger, there is no impact on the income statement if you adopt a billing cycle for rebilled expenses that varies from the normal monthly billing cycle. For example, you could issue invoices for rebillable expenses for the period from the 16th day of the pre-

ceding month to the 15th day of the current month. Doing so keeps this type of invoicing away from the closing process, though it means that some re-billable items will remain on the balance sheet at month-end. The ideal time for this type of invoicing is whenever the accounting staff has sufficient time available to deal with it.

3. *Separate invoices.* If you are issuing a services billing to a customer at month-end, it may make sense to issue the services invoice first, and then delay the invoice for rebilled expenses until after you have closed the books for the month. Doing so shifts this extra billing activity out of the busiest part of the closing process. This approach does not work if customers only want to receive one invoice per month, or they are closing out the contract and do not want to wait for an additional invoice.

4. *Retroactively adjust invoices.* You could ignore rebillable expenses when creating customer invoices during the closing process, but then re-open the month after the financial statements have been issued, and shift rebillable expenses onto the invoices and then issue the invoices. Doing so does not impact the reported results on the income statement, though it will shift assets on the balance sheet from the rebillable expenses line item to the accounts receivable line item. This approach may appear too complicated, or give financial statement readers the impression that a company is altering its results after a reporting period has been closed.

Many customers only want to be billed once a month, which eliminates most of the options just described. If so, the final option may prove to be the best one. It is somewhat complicated, but allows you to close the books quickly, while still issuing a single invoice per month.

Reconciling Accounts Receivable

The accounting software should have an accounts receivable module that you use to enter customer invoices. This module automatically populates the accounts receivable account in the general ledger when you create invoices. Thus, at month-end, you should be able to print the open accounts receivable report and have the grand total on it match the ending balance in the accounts receivable general ledger account. This means that there are no reconciling items between the open accounts receivable report and the general ledger account.

If there is a difference between the two numbers, it is almost certainly caused by the use of a journal entry that debited or credited the accounts receivable account. *Never* create such a journal entry, because there is so much detail in the accounts receivable account that it is very time-consuming to wade through it to ascertain the source of the variance.

The primary transaction that you will be tempted to record in the accounts receivable account is accrued revenue. Instead, create a current asset account called "Accrued Revenue Receivable" and enter the accruals in that account. By doing so, you are segregating normal accounts receivable transactions from special month-end accrual transactions. Accrual transactions require special monitoring, since they may linger for several months, so keeping them in a separate account makes it easier to reconcile accounts receivable.

Non-Trade Receivables

Non-trade receivables are amounts due for payment that are not related to the normal customer invoices for merchandise shipped or services performed. Examples of non-trade receivables are amounts owed to a business by its employees for loans or wage advances, tax refunds owed to it by taxing authorities, and insurance claims owed to it by an insurance company.

Non-trade receivables are usually classified as current assets on the balance sheet, since there is typically an expectation that they will be paid within one year. If you anticipate that payment will be over a longer period of time, classify it as a non-current asset.

Non-trade receivables are typically not billed using a company's invoicing software. Instead, they are recorded as journal entries. This is a key distinction, since there should be few (if any) journal entries impacting the accounts receivable account. Indeed, the use of a journal entry to record a transaction can be considered a key indicator that a receivable should be treated as a non-trade receivable.

Periodically evaluate the individual items recorded in the non-trade receivables account to see if the company is still likely to receive full payment. If not, reduce the amount in the account to the level you expect to receive, and charge the difference to expense in the period in which you make the determination. There is no need to conduct this evaluation during the month-end close. Instead, schedule it for somewhat earlier in the month, so that the accounting staff does not waste time on it in the midst of the close.

The Allowance for Doubtful Accounts

The allowance for doubtful accounts is a reduction of the total amount of accounts receivable appearing on a company's balance sheet, and is listed as a deduction immediately below the accounts receivable line item. The allowance represents management's best estimate of the amount of accounts receivable that will not be paid by customers. This allowance should be updated as part of the closing process.

There are several possible ways to estimate the allowance, which are:

- *Risk classification.* Assign a risk score to each customer, and assume a higher risk of default for those having a higher risk score.
- *Historical percentage.* If a certain percentage of accounts receivable became bad debts in the past, then use the same percentage in the future. This method works best for large numbers of small account balances.
- *Pareto analysis.* Review the largest accounts receivable that make up 80% of the total receivable balance, and estimate which specific customers are most likely to default. Then use the preceding historical percentage method

for the remaining smaller accounts. This method works best if there are a small number of large account balances.

You can also evaluate the reasonableness of an allowance for doubtful accounts by comparing it to the total amount of seriously overdue accounts receivable, which are presumably not going to be collected. If the allowance is less than the amount of these overdue receivables, the allowance is probably insufficient.

You should review the balance in the allowance for doubtful accounts as part of the month-end closing process, to ensure that the balance is reasonable in comparison to the latest bad debt forecast. For companies having minimal bad debt activity, a quarterly update may be sufficient. The following example demonstrates how the allowance is handled.

EXAMPLE

Lowry Locomotion records $10,000,000 of sales to several hundred customers, and projects (based on historical experience) that it will incur 1% of this amount as bad debts, though it does not know exactly which customers will default. It records the 1% of projected bad debts as a $100,000 debit to the bad debt expense account and a credit to the allowance for doubtful accounts. The bad debt expense is charged to expense right away, and the allowance for doubtful accounts becomes a reserve account that offsets the accounts receivable of $10,000,000 (for a net receivable on the balance sheet of $9,900,000). The entry is:

	Debit	Credit
Bad debt expense	100,000	
Allowance for doubtful accounts		100,000

Later, several customers default on payments totaling $40,000. Accordingly, the company credits the accounts receivable account by $40,000 to reduce the amount of outstanding accounts receivable, and debits the allowance for doubtful accounts by $40,000. This entry reduces the balance in the allowance account to $60,000. The entry does not impact earnings in the current period. The entry is:

	Debit	Credit
Allowance for doubtful accounts	40,000	
Accounts receivable		40,000

A few months later, a collection agency succeeds in collecting $15,000 of the funds that Lowry had already written off. The company can now reverse part of the previous entry, thereby increasing the balances of both the accounts receivable and the allowance for doubtful accounts. The entry is:

	Debit	Credit
Accounts receivable	15,000	
Allowance for doubtful accounts		15,000

Recording Contra Revenue

There may be isolated instances where you need to accrue for contra revenue as part of the closing process. Contra revenue is a deduction from gross revenue. Examples of contra revenue are sales returns, sales allowances, and sales discounts. These transactions are recorded in one or more contra revenue accounts, which usually contain a debit balance.

A sales return is merchandise sent back by a customer to the seller, presumably due to defects. A sales allowance is a reduction in the price charged by a seller, due to a problem with the sold product or service, such as a quality problem or a short shipment. Finally, a sales discount is a reduction in the price of a product or service that is offered by the seller in exchange for early payment by the buyer. A company may deal with one or more of these situations.

If there are only immaterial amounts of sales returns, sales allowances, and sales discounts, there is no need to set up one or more contra revenue accounts to accrue for them. However, if the amounts are material and the company incurs a predictable amount of them over time, you should accrue an expense for them at the end of each month, and subsequently adjust the balances in these accounts based on actual experience. In most companies, the amounts are so small that there is no need to accrue; instead, simply record these items as incurred.

Summary

Closing accounts receivable is one of the most important parts of the entire closing process. It is more important to do a thorough job of ensuring that revenue and related receivables have been correctly recorded than it is to close the books fast. Thus, if you suspect that there may be a billing problem, it is better to delay issuing financial statements and track down the issue than to produce the financial statements first and defer resolution of the suspected problem until the following month. The reason is that both management and investors are generally quite sensitive to incorrect revenue reporting.

Further, pay particular attention to the balance in the allowance for doubtful accounts at the end of the fiscal year, since auditors will examine it at that time, and will question an account balance that does not match their expectations based on the company's historical experience with bad debts. Thus, you can sometimes get away with giving the allowance only cursory attention during the year, but do not make that mistake at the end of the year.

Chapter 8
Closing Inventory

Introduction

If a company has a large amount of inventory, it is likely that calculating the value of ending inventory is the most time-consuming step required to close the books. An ending inventory valuation is needed to calculate a large part of the cost of goods sold – and since that is typically the largest expense in a business, closing inventory properly is critical.

Unfortunately, as you will see in this chapter, there are a number of complicated steps involved in creating an ending inventory valuation. The key steps are:

1. *Inventory quantities*. Determine the inventory quantities on hand at the end of the reporting period.
2. *Inventory cost*. Calculate the cost at which the inventory was acquired. There are multiple methods of inventory valuation, depending on the type of inventory involved.
3. *Overhead allocation*. Calculate the allocation of indirect costs to inventory.
4. *Inventory valuation*. Note whether the value of the inventory has declined since it was purchased.

In this chapter, we address all four components of the inventory valuation process.

> **Related Podcast Episode:** Episode 23 of the Accounting Best Practices Podcast discusses inventory in relation to closing the books. It is available at: **accounting-tools.com/podcasts** or **iTunes**

Valuation Step 1: The Quantity of Inventory on Hand

The following two sections describe the initial step in the valuation process, which is ensuring that correct inventory quantities are used. There are two alternative counting methods, which are the periodic inventory system and the perpetual system. The periodic inventory system requires you to physically count the inventory from time to time, whereas the perpetual system instead uses continual updating of the inventory records as each inventory transaction occurs.

An interesting method for estimating ending inventory is the gross profit method, which is also described in a separate section.

The Periodic Inventory System

The *periodic inventory system* only updates the ending inventory balance when you conduct a physical inventory count. Since physical inventory counts are time-consuming, few companies do them more than once a quarter or year. In the meantime, the inventory account continues to show the cost of the inventory that was recorded as of the last physical inventory count.

Under the periodic inventory system, all purchases made between physical inventory counts are recorded in a purchases account. When a physical inventory count is done, you then shift the balance in the purchases account into the inventory account, which in turn is adjusted to match the cost of the ending inventory.

The calculation of the cost of goods sold under the periodic inventory system is:

Beginning inventory + Purchases = Cost of goods available for sale

Cost of goods available for sale – Ending inventory = Cost of goods sold

---

EXAMPLE

Lowry Locomotion has beginning inventory of $100,000, has paid $170,000 for purchases, and its physical inventory count reveals an ending inventory cost of $80,000. The calculation of its cost of goods sold is:

$100,000 Beginning inventory + $170,000 Purchases - $80,000 Ending inventory

= $190,000 Cost of goods sold

The periodic inventory system is most useful for smaller businesses that maintain minimal amounts of inventory. For them, a physical inventory count is easy to complete, and they can estimate cost of goods sold figures for interim periods. However, there are also several problems with the system:

- It does not yield any information about the cost of goods sold or ending inventory balances during interim periods when there has been no physical inventory count.
- You must estimate the cost of goods sold during interim periods, which will likely result in a significant adjustment to the actual cost of goods whenever a physical inventory count is eventually completed.
- There is no way to adjust for obsolete inventory or scrap losses during interim periods, so there tends to be a significant (and expensive) adjustment for these issues when a physical inventory count is eventually completed.

A more up-to-date and accurate alternative to the periodic inventory system is the perpetual inventory system, which is described in the next section.

The Perpetual Inventory System

Under the *perpetual inventory system*, an entity continually updates its inventory records to account for additions to and subtractions from inventory for such activities as received inventory items, goods sold from stock, and items picked from inventory for use in the production process. Thus, a perpetual inventory system has the advantages of both providing up-to-date inventory balance information and requiring a reduced level of physical inventory counts. However, the calculated inventory levels derived by a perpetual inventory system may gradually diverge from actual inventory levels, due to unrecorded transactions or theft, so you should periodically compare book balances to actual on-hand quantities with cycle counting. Cycle counting is the process of counting a small proportion of the total inventory on a daily basis, and not only correcting any errors found, but also investigating the underlying reasons why the errors occurred.

EXAMPLE

This example contains several journal entries used to account for transactions in a perpetual inventory system. Lowry Locomotion records a purchase of $1,000 of widgets that are stored in inventory:

	Debit	Credit
Inventory	1,000	
Accounts payable		1,000

Lowry records $250 of inbound freight cost associated with the delivery of the widgets:

	Debit	Credit
Inventory	250	
Accounts payable		250

Lowry records the sale of widgets from inventory for $2,000, for which the associated inventory cost is $1,200:

	Debit	Credit
Accounts receivable	2,000	
Revenue		2,000
Cost of goods sold	1,200	
Inventory		1,200

Lowry records a downward inventory adjustment of $500, caused by inventory theft, and detected during a cycle count:

	Debit	Credit
Inventory shrinkage expense	500	
Inventory		500

The Gross Profit Method

The *gross profit method* can be used to estimate the amount of ending inventory. This is useful for interim periods between physical inventory counts, or when inventory was destroyed and you need to back into the ending inventory balance for the purpose of filing a claim for insurance reimbursement. Follow these steps to estimate ending inventory using the gross profit method:

1. Add together the cost of beginning inventory and the cost of purchases during the period to arrive at the cost of goods available for sale.
2. Multiply (1 - expected gross profit %) by sales during the period to arrive at the estimated cost of goods sold.
3. Subtract the estimated cost of goods sold (step #2) from the cost of goods available for sale (step #1) to arrive at the ending inventory.

The gross profit method is not an acceptable method for determining the year-end inventory balance, since it only estimates what the ending inventory balance may be. It is not sufficiently precise to be reliable for audited financial statements.

EXAMPLE

Lowry Locomotion is calculating its month-end widget inventory for March. Its beginning inventory was $175,000 and its purchases during the month were $225,000. Thus, its cost of goods available for sale is:

$175,000 beginning inventory + $225,000 purchases

= $400,000 cost of goods available for sale

Lowry's gross margin percentage for all of the past 12 months was 35%, which is considered a reliable long-term margin. Its sales during March were $500,000. Thus, its estimated cost of goods sold is:

(1 - 35%) × $500,000 = $325,000 cost of goods sold

By subtracting the estimated cost of goods sold from the cost of goods available for sale, Lowry arrives at an estimated ending inventory balance of $75,000.

There are several issues with the gross profit method that make it unreliable as the sole method for determining the value of inventory, which are:

- *Applicability.* The calculation is most useful in retail situations where a company is simply buying and reselling merchandise. If a company is instead manufacturing goods, the components of inventory must also include labor and overhead, which make the gross profit method too simplistic to yield reliable results.
- *Historical basis.* The gross profit percentage is a key component of the calculation, but the percentage is based on a company's historical experience. If the current situation yields a different percentage (as may be caused by a special sale at reduced prices), the gross profit percentage used in the calculation will be incorrect.

- *Inventory losses.* The calculation assumes that the long-term rate of losses due to theft, obsolescence, and other causes is included in the historical gross profit percentage. If not, or if these losses have not previously been recognized, the calculation will likely result in an inaccurate estimated ending inventory (and probably one that is too high).

Valuation Step 2: Inventory Costing (Typical Inventory)

Five methods for calculating the cost of inventory are shown in the following sections. Of the methods presented, only the first in, first out method and the weighted average method have gained worldwide recognition. The last in, first out method cannot realistically be justified based on the actual flow of inventory, and is only used in the United States under the sanction of the Internal Revenue Service; it is specifically banned under international financial reporting standards. Standard costing is an acceptable alternative to cost layering, as long as any associated variances are properly accounted for. Finally, the retail inventory method should be used only to derive an approximation of the ending inventory cost, and so should be limited to interim reporting periods when a company does not intend to issue any financial results to outside parties.

The First In, First Out Method

The first in, first out (FIFO) method of inventory valuation operates under the assumption that the first goods purchased are also the first goods sold. In most companies, this accounting assumption closely matches the actual flow of goods, and so is considered the most theoretically correct inventory valuation method.

Under the FIFO method, the earliest goods purchased are the first ones removed from the inventory account. This results in the remaining items in inventory being accounted for at the most recently incurred costs, so that the inventory asset recorded on the balance sheet contains costs quite close to the most recent costs that could be obtained in the marketplace. Conversely, this method also results in older historical costs being matched against current revenues and recorded in the cost of goods sold, so the gross margin does not necessarily reflect a proper matching of revenues and costs. The gross margin is revenues less the cost of goods sold. The gross margin reveals the amount that an entity earns from the sale of its products and services, before the deduction of any sales and administrative expenses.

EXAMPLE

Lowry Locomotion decides to use the FIFO method for the month of January. During that month, it records the following transactions:

	Quantity Change	Actual Unit Cost	Actual Total Cost
Beginning inventory (Layer 1)	+100	$210	$21,000
Sale	-75		
Purchase (Layer 2)	+150	280	42,000
Sale	-100		
Purchase (Layer 3)	+50	300	15,000
Ending inventory	=125		

The cost of goods sold in units is calculated as:

100 Beginning inventory + 200 Purchased – 125 Ending inventory = 175 Units

Lowry's accounting staff uses the information in the preceding table to calculate the cost of goods sold for January, as well as the cost of the inventory balance as of the end of January.

	Units	Unit Cost	Total Cost
Cost of goods sold			
FIFO layer 1	100	$210	$21,000
FIFO layer 2	75	280	21,000
Total cost of goods sold	175		$42,000
Ending inventory			
FIFO layer 2	75	280	$21,000
FIFO layer 3	50	300	15,000
Total ending inventory	125		$36,000

Thus, the first FIFO layer, which was the beginning inventory layer, is completely used up during the month, as well as half of Layer 2, leaving half of Layer 2 and all of Layer 3 to be the sole components of the ending inventory.

Note that the $42,000 cost of goods sold and $36,000 ending inventory equals the $78,000 combined total of beginning inventory and purchases during the month.

The Last In, First Out Method

The last in, first out (LIFO) method operates under the assumption that the last item of inventory purchased is the first one sold. Picture a store shelf where a clerk adds items from the front, and customers also take their selections from the front; the remaining items of inventory that are located further from the front of the shelf are rarely picked, and so remain on the shelf – that is a LIFO scenario.

The trouble with the LIFO scenario is that it is rarely encountered in practice. If a company were to use the process flow embodied by LIFO, a significant part of its inventory would be very old, and likely obsolete. Nonetheless, a company does not actually have to experience the LIFO process flow in order to use the method to calculate its inventory valuation.

The reason why companies use LIFO is the assumption that the cost of inventory increases over time, which is a reasonable assumption in times of inflating prices. If you were to use LIFO in such a situation, the cost of the most recently acquired inventory will always be higher than the cost of earlier purchases, so the ending inventory balance will be valued at earlier costs, while the most recent costs appear in the cost of goods sold. By shifting high-cost inventory into the cost of goods sold, a company can reduce its reported level of profitability, and thereby defer its recognition of income taxes. Since income tax deferral is the only justification for LIFO in most situations, it is banned under international financial reporting standards (though it is still allowed in the United States under the approval of the Internal Revenue Service).

EXAMPLE

Lowry Locomotion decides to use the LIFO method for the month of March. The following table shows the various purchasing transactions for the company's purple widgets. The quantity purchased on March 1 actually reflects the inventory beginning balance.

Date Purchased	Quantity Purchased	Cost per Unit	Units Sold	Cost of Layer 1	Cost of Layer 2	Total Cost
March 1	150	$210	95	(55 × $210)		$11,550
March 7	100	235	110	(45 × $210)		9,450
March 11	200	250	180	(45 × $210)	(20 × $250)	14,450
March 17	125	240	125	(45 × $210)	(20 × $250)	14,450
March 25	80	260	120	(25 × $210)		5,250

The following bullet points describe the transactions noted in the preceding table:
- *March 1.* Lowry has a beginning inventory balance of 150 units, and sells 95 of these units between March 1 and March 7. This leaves one inventory layer of 55 units at a cost of $210 each.
- *March 7.* Lowry buys 100 additional units on March 7, and sells 110 units between March 7 and March 11. Under LIFO, we assume that the latest purchase was sold

first, so there is still just one inventory layer, which has now been reduced to 45 units.

- *March 11.* Lowry buys 200 additional units on March 11, and sells 180 units between March 11 and March 17, which creates a new inventory layer that is comprised of 20 units at a cost of $250. This new layer appears in the table in the "Cost of Layer #2" column.
- *March 17.* Lowry buys 125 additional units on March 17, and sells 125 units between March 17 and March 25, so there is no change in the inventory layers.
- *March 25.* Lowry buys 80 additional units on March 25, and sells 120 units between March 25 and the end of the month. Sales exceed purchases during this period, so the second inventory layer is eliminated, as well as part of the first layer. The result is an ending inventory balance of $5,250, which is derived from 25 units of ending inventory, multiplied by the $210 cost in the first layer that existed at the beginning of the month.

Before you implement the LIFO system, consider the following points:

- *Consistent usage.* The Internal Revenue Service states that a company using LIFO for its tax reporting must also use LIFO for its financial reporting. Thus, a company wanting to defer tax recognition through early expense recognition must show those same low profit numbers to the outside users of its financial statements.
- *Layering.* Since the LIFO system is intended to use the most recent layers of inventory, you may never access earlier layers, which can result in an administrative problem if there are many layers to document.
- *Profit fluctuations.* If early layers contain inventory costs that depart substantially from current market prices, a company could experience sharp changes in its profitability if those layers are ever used.

In summary, LIFO is only useful for deferring income tax payments in periods of cost inflation. It does not reflect the actual flow of inventory in most situations, and may even yield unusual financial results that differ markedly from reality.

The Weighted Average Method

When using the weighted average method, divide the cost of goods available for sale by the number of units available for sale, which yields the weighted-average cost per unit. In this calculation, the cost of goods available for sale is the sum of beginning inventory and net purchases. You then use this weighted-average figure to assign a cost to both ending inventory and the cost of goods sold.

The singular advantage of the weighted average method is the complete absence of any inventory layers, which avoids the record keeping problems that would be encountered with either the FIFO or LIFO methods that were described earlier.

EXAMPLE

Lowry Locomotion elects to use the weighted-average method for the month of May. During that month, it records the following transactions:

	Quantity Change	Actual Unit Cost	Actual Total Cost
Beginning inventory	+150	$220	$33,000
Sale	-125		
Purchase	+200	270	54,000
Sale	-150		
Purchase	+100	290	29,000
Ending inventory	=175		

The actual total cost of all purchased or beginning inventory units in the preceding table is $116,000 ($33,000 + $54,000 + $29,000). The total of all purchased or beginning inventory units is 450 (150 beginning inventory + 300 purchased). The weighted average cost per unit is therefore $257.78 ($116,000 ÷ 450 units.)

The ending inventory valuation is $45,112 (175 units × $257.78 weighted average cost), while the cost of goods sold valuation is $70,890 (275 units × $257.78 weighted average cost). The sum of these two amounts (less a rounding error) equals the $116,000 total actual cost of all purchases and beginning inventory.

In the preceding example, if Lowry used a perpetual inventory system to record its inventory transactions, it would have to recomputed the weighted average after every purchase. The following table uses the same information in the preceding example to show the recomputations:

	Units on Hand	Purchases	Cost of Sales	Inventory Total Cost	Inventory Moving Average Unit Cost
Beginning inventory	150	$ --	$ --	$33,000	$220.00
Sale (125 units @ $220.00)	25	--	27,500	5,500	220.00
Purchase (200 units @ $270.00)	225	54,000	--	59,500	264.44
Sale (150 units @ $264.44)	75	--	39,666	19,834	264.44
Purchase (100 units @ $290.00)	175	29,000	--	48,834	279.05
Total			$67,166		

Note that the cost of goods sold of $67,166 and the ending inventory balance of $48,834 equal $116,000, which matches the total of the costs in the original example. Thus, the totals are the same, but the weighted average calculation results in slight differences in the apportionment of costs between the cost of goods sold and ending inventory.

Standard Costing

The preceding methods (FIFO, LIFO, and weighted average) have all operated under the assumption that some sort of cost layering is used, even if that layering results in nothing more than a single weighted-average layer. The standard costing methodology arrives at inventory valuation from an entirely different direction, which is to set a standard cost for each item and to then value those items at the standard cost – not the actual cost at which the items were purchased.

Standard costs are stored separately from all other accounting records, usually in a bill of materials for finished goods, and in the item master file for raw materials. An item master is a record that lists the name, description, unit of measure, weight, dimensions, ordering quantity, and other key information for a component part.

At the end of a reporting period, follow these steps to integrate standard costs into the accounting system:

1. *Cost verification.* Review the standard cost database for errors and correct as necessary. Also, if it is time to do so, update the standard costs to more accurately reflect actual costs.
2. *Inventory valuation.* Multiply the number of units in ending inventory by their standard costs to derive the ending inventory valuation.
3. *Calculate the cost of goods sold.* Add purchases during the month to the beginning inventory and subtract the ending inventory to determine the cost of goods sold.
4. *Enter updated balances.* Create a journal entry that reduces the purchases account to zero and which also adjusts the inventory asset account balance to the ending total standard cost, with the offset to the cost of goods sold account.

EXAMPLE

Lowry Locomotion is using a standard costing system to calculate its inventory balances and cost of goods sold. The company conducts a month-end physical inventory count that results in a reasonably accurate set of unit quantities for all inventory items. The accounting staff multiplies each of these unit quantities by their standard costs to derive the ending inventory valuation. This ending balance is $2,500,000.

The beginning inventory account balance is $2,750,000 and purchases during the month were $1,000,000, so the calculation of the cost of goods sold is:

Beginning inventory	$2,750,000
+ Purchases	1,000,000
- Ending inventory	(2,500,000)
= Cost of goods sold	$1,250,000

To record the correct ending inventory balance and cost of goods sold, Hodgson records the following entry, which clears out the purchases asset account and adjusts the ending inventory balance to $2,500,000:

	Debit	Credit
Cost of goods sold	1,250,000	
Purchases		1,000,000
Inventory		250,000

Standard costing is clearly more efficient than any cost layering system, simply because there are no layers to keep track of. However, its primary failing is that the resulting inventory valuation may not equate to the actual cost. The difference is handled through several types of variance calculations, which may be charged to the cost of goods sold (if minor) or allocated between inventory and the cost of goods sold (if material).

The Retail Inventory Method

The retail inventory method is sometimes used by retailers that resell merchandise to estimate their ending inventory balances. This method is based on the relationship between the cost of merchandise and its retail price. To calculate the cost of ending inventory using the retail inventory method, follow these steps:

1. Calculate the cost-to-retail percentage, for which the formula is (Cost ÷ Retail price).
2. Calculate the cost of goods available for sale, for which the formula is (Cost of beginning inventory + Cost of purchases).
3. Calculate the cost of sales during the period, for which the formula is (Sales × cost-to-retail percentage).
4. Calculate ending inventory, for which the formula is (Cost of goods available for sale - Cost of sales during the period).

EXAMPLE

Lowry Locomotion's retail division sells toy locomotives for an average of $200, and which cost it $140. This is a cost-to-retail percentage of 70%. Lowry's beginning inventory has a cost of $1,000,000, it paid $1,800,000 for purchases during the month, and it had sales of $2,400,000. The calculation of its ending inventory is:

Beginning inventory	$1,000,000	(at cost)
Purchases	+ 1,800,000	(at cost)
Goods available for sale	= 2,800,000	
Sales	-1,680,000	(sales of $2,400,000 × 70%)
Ending inventory	= $1,120,000	

The retail inventory method is an easy way to determine an approximate ending inventory balance. However, there are also several issues with it:

- The retail inventory method is only an estimate. Do not rely upon it too heavily to yield results that will compare with those of a physical inventory count.
- The retail inventory method only works if you have a consistent mark-up across all products sold. If not, the actual ending inventory cost may vary wildly from what was derived using this method.
- The method assumes that the historical basis for the mark-up percentage continues into the current period. If the mark-up was different (as may be caused by an after-holidays sale), then the results of the calculation will be incorrect.

Valuation Step 3: Overhead Allocation

The preceding valuation step was concerned with charging the direct costs of production to inventory, but what about overhead expenses? In many businesses, the cost of overhead is substantially greater than direct costs, so you should expend considerable attention on the proper method of allocating overhead to inventory.

There are two types of overhead, which are administrative overhead and manufacturing overhead. *Administrative overhead* includes those costs not involved in the development or production of goods or services, such as the costs of front office administration and sales; this is essentially all overhead that is not included in manufacturing overhead. *Manufacturing overhead* is all of the costs that a factory incurs, other than direct costs.

It is necessary to allocate the costs of manufacturing overhead to any inventory items that are classified as work-in-process or finished goods. Overhead is not allocated to raw materials inventory, since the operations giving rise to overhead costs only impact work-in-process and finished goods inventory.

The following items are usually included in manufacturing overhead:

Depreciation of factory equipment	Quality control and inspection
Factory administration expenses	Rent, facility and equipment
Indirect labor and production supervisory wages	Repair expenses
Indirect materials and supplies	Rework labor, scrap and spoilage
Maintenance, factory and production equipment	Taxes related to production assets
Officer salaries related to production	Uncapitalized tools and equipment
Production employees' benefits	Utilities

The typical procedure for allocating overhead is to accumulate all manufacturing overhead costs into one or more cost pools, and to then use an activity measure to apportion the overhead costs in the cost pools to inventory. A cost pool is a grouping of individual costs, typically by department or service center. Cost allocations are then made from the cost pool. For example, the cost of a maintenance department is accumulated in a cost pool and then allocated to those departments using its services. Thus, the overhead allocation formula is:

Cost pool ÷ Total activity measure = Overhead allocation per unit

---

EXAMPLE

Lowry Locomotion has a small production line for toy locomotives. During April, it incurs costs for the following items:

Cost Type	Amount
Building rent	$65,000
Building utilities	12,000
Factory equipment depreciation	8,000
Production equipment maintenance	7,000
Total	$92,000

All of these items are classified as manufacturing overhead, so Lowry creates the following journal entry to shift these costs into an overhead cost pool:

	Debit	Credit
Overhead cost pool	92,000	
Depreciation expense		8,000
Maintenance expense		7,000
Rent expense		65,000
Utilities expense		12,000

It is allowable to allocate overhead costs by any reasonable measure, as long as it is consistently applied across reporting periods. Common bases of allocation are direct labor hours charged against a product, or the amount of machine hours used during the production of a product. The amount of allocation charged per unit is known as the *overhead rate*.

The overhead rate can be expressed as a proportion, if both the numerator and denominator are in dollars. For example, ABC Company has total indirect costs of $100,000 and it decides to use the cost of its direct labor as the allocation measure. ABC incurs $50,000 of direct labor costs, so the overhead rate is calculated as:

$$\frac{\$100,000 \text{ Indirect costs}}{\$50,000 \text{ Direct labor}}$$

The result is an overhead rate of 2.0.

Alternatively, if the denominator is not in dollars, the overhead rate is expressed as a cost per allocation unit. For example, ABC Company decides to change its allocation measure to hours of machine time used. ABC has 10,000 hours of machine time usage, so the overhead rate is now calculated as:

$$\frac{\$100,000 \text{ Indirect costs}}{10,000 \text{ Machine hours}}$$

The result is an overhead rate of $10.00 per machine hour.

EXAMPLE

Lowry Locomotion has a toy locomotive production line, which manufactures a titanium version and an aluminum version. Considerable machining is required for both versions, so Lowry concludes that it should allocate overhead to these products based on the total hours of machine time used. In May, production of the titanium model requires 5,400 hours of machine time, while the aluminum version needs 2,600 hours. Thus, 67.5% of the overhead cost pool is allocated to the titanium model and 32.5% to the aluminum model.

In May, Lowry accumulates $100,000 of costs in its overhead cost pool, and allocates it between the two products with the following journal entry:

	Debit	Credit
Finished goods – Titanium model	67,500	
Finished goods – Aluminum model	32,500	
Overhead cost pool		100,000

This entry clears out the balance in the overhead cost pool, readying it to accumulate overhead costs in the next reporting period.

If the basis of allocation does not appear correct for certain types of overhead costs, it may make more sense to split the overhead into two or more overhead cost pools, and allocate each cost pool using a different basis of allocation. For example, if warehouse costs are more appropriately allocated based on the square footage consumed by various products, then store warehouse costs in a warehouse overhead cost pool, and allocate these costs based on square footage used.

Thus far, we have assumed that only actual overhead costs incurred are allocated. However, it is also possible to set up a standard overhead rate that you continue to use for multiple reporting periods, based on long-term expectations regarding how much overhead will be incurred and how many units will be produced. If the difference between actual overhead costs incurred and overhead allocated is small, charge the difference to the cost of goods sold. If the amount is material, allocate the difference to both the cost of goods sold and inventory.

EXAMPLE

Lowry Locomotion incurs overhead of $93,000, which it stores in an overhead cost pool. Lowry uses a standard overhead rate of $20 per unit, which approximates its long-term experience with the relationship between overhead costs and production volumes. In September, it produces 4,500 widgets, to which it allocates $90,000 (allocate rate of $20 × 4,500 units). This leaves a difference between overhead incurred and overhead absorbed of $3,000. Given the small size of the variance, Lowry charges the $3,000 difference to the cost of goods sold, thereby clearing out the overhead cost pool.

Overhead absorbed is manufacturing overhead that has been applied to products or other cost objects. Overhead is *overabsorbed* when the amount allocated to a product or other cost object is higher than the actual amount of overhead, while the amount is *underabsorbed* when the amount allocated is lower than the actual amount of overhead.

A key issue is that overhead allocation is not a precisely-defined science – there is plenty of latitude in how you can go about allocating overhead. The amount of allowable diversity in practice can result in slipshod accounting, so be sure to use a standardized and well-documented method to allocate overhead using the same calculation in every reporting period. This allows for great consistency, which auditors appreciate when they validate the supporting calculations.

Valuation Step 4: Inventory Valuation

Many accountants may complete the preceding steps to create an inventory valuation, and go no further. However, there are two situations worth reviewing on a regular basis, which are to reduce the recorded cost of inventory under either the lower of cost or market rule, or to account for obsolete inventory. The next two sections address these issues. Of the two, the one to be most careful of is obsolete inventory, which nearly always is present in any inventory that has been in existence for more than a few years.

The Lower of Cost or Market Rule

The lower of cost or market rule (LCM) is required by GAAP, and essentially states that you record the cost of inventory at whichever cost is lower – the original cost or its current market price (hence the name of the rule). More specifically, the rule mandates that the recognized cost of an inventory item should be reduced to a level that does not exceed its replacement cost as derived in an open market. This replacement cost is subject to the following two conditions:

- The recognized cost cannot be greater than the likely selling price minus costs of disposal (known as net realizable value).
- The recognized cost cannot be lower than the net realizable value minus a normal profit percentage.

This situation typically arises when inventory has deteriorated, or has become obsolete, or market prices have declined. The following example illustrates the concept.

EXAMPLE

Mulligan Imports resells five major brands of golf clubs, which are noted in the following table. At the end of its reporting year, Mulligan calculates the upper and lower price boundaries of the LCM rule for each of the products, as noted in the table:

Product	Selling Price	-	Completion/ Selling Cost	=	Upper Price Boundary	-	Normal Profit	=	Lower Price Boundary
Free Swing	$250		$25		$225		$75		$150
Golf Elite	190		19		171		57		114
Hi-Flight	150		15		135		45		90
Iridescent	1,000		100		900		300		600
Titanium	700		70		630		210		420

The normal profit associated with these products is a 30% margin on the original selling price.

The information in the preceding table for the upper and lower price boundaries is then included in the following table, which completes the LCM calculation:

Product	Upper Price Boundary	Lower Price Boundary	Existing Recognized Cost	Replacement Cost*	Market Value**	Lower of Cost or Market
Free Swing	$225	$150	$140	$260	$225	$140
Golf Elite	171	114	180	175	171	171
Hi-Flight	135	90	125	110	110	110
Iridescent	900	600	850	550	600	600
Titanium	630	420	450	390	420	420

* The cost at which the item could be acquired on the open market
** The replacement cost, as limited by the upper and lower pricing boundaries

The LCM decisions noted in the last table are explained as follows:
- *Free Swing clubs.* It would cost Mulligan $260 to replace these clubs, which is above the upper price boundary of $225. This means the market value for the purposes of this calculation is $225. Since the market price is higher than the existing recognized cost, the LCM decision is to leave the recognized cost at $140 each.
- *Golf Elite clubs.* The replacement cost of these clubs has declined to a level below the existing recognized cost, so the LCM decision is to revise the recognized cost to $171. This amount is a small reduction from the unadjusted replacement cost of $175 to the upper price boundary of $171.
- *Hi-Flight clubs.* The replacement cost is less than the recognized cost, and is between the price boundaries. Consequently, there is no need to revise the replacement cost. The LCM decision is to revise the recognized cost to $110.

- *Iridescent clubs.* The replacement cost of these clubs is below the existing recognized cost, but is below the lower price boundary. Thus, the LCM decision is to set the market price at the lower price boundary, which will be the revised cost of the clubs.
- *Titanium clubs.* The replacement cost is much less than the existing recognized cost, but also well below the lower price boundary. The LCM decision is therefore to set the market price at the lower price boundary, which is also the new product cost.

If the amount of a write-down caused by the LCM analysis is minor, charge the expense to the cost of goods sold, since there is no reason to separately track the information. If the loss is material, track it in a separate account (especially if such losses are recurring), such as "Loss on LCM adjustment." A sample journal entry for a large adjustment is:

	Debit	Credit
Loss on LCM adjustment	147,000	
Finished goods inventory		147,000

Additional factors to consider when applying the LCM rule are:
- *Analysis by category.* You normally apply the LCM rule to a specific inventory item, but it can be applied to entire inventory categories. In the latter case, an LCM adjustment can be avoided if there is a balance within an inventory category of items having market below cost and in excess of cost.
- *Hedges.* If inventory is being hedged by a fair value hedge, add the effects of the hedge to the cost of the inventory, which frequently eliminates the need for an LCM adjustment. A fair value hedge is a hedge of the exposure to changes in the fair value of an asset or liability that are attributable to a specific risk.
- *Last in, first out layer recovery.* You can avoid a write-down to the lower of cost or market in an interim period if there is substantial evidence that inventory amounts will be restored by year end, thereby avoiding recognition of an earlier inventory layer.
- *Raw materials.* Do not write down the cost of raw materials if the finished goods in which they are used are expected to sell either at or above their costs.
- *Recovery.* You can avoid a write-down to the lower of cost or market if there is substantial evidence that market prices will increase before you sell the inventory.
- *Sales incentives.* If there are unexpired sales incentives that will result in a loss on the sale of a specific item, this is a strong indicator that there may be an LCM problem with that item.

> **Tip:** When there is an LCM adjustment, it must be taken at once – the expense cannot be recognized over multiple reporting periods.

Obsolete Inventory Accounting

What do you do if there is obsolete inventory on hand? Determine the most likely disposition of the obsolete items, subtract the amount of this projected amount from the book value of the obsolete items, and set aside the difference as a reserve. As the company later disposes of the items, or the estimated amounts to be received from disposition change, adjust the reserve account to reflect these events.

EXAMPLE

Lowery Locomotion has $100,000 of excess widgets that it cannot sell. However, it believes there is a market for the widgets through a reseller in China, but only at a sale price of $20,000. Accordingly, the Lowry accounting staff recognizes a reserve of $80,000 with the following journal entry:

	Debit	Credit
Cost of goods sold	80,000	
Reserve for obsolete inventory		80,000

After finalizing the arrangement with the Chinese reseller, the actual sale price is only $19,000, so the accounting staff completes the transaction with the following entry, recognizing an additional $1,000 of expense:

	Debit	Credit
Reserve for obsolete inventory	80,000	
Cost of goods sold	1,000	
Inventory		81,000

The example makes inventory obsolescence accounting look simple enough, but it is not. The issues are:
- *Timing*. You can improperly alter a company's reported financial results by altering the timing of the actual dispositions. As an example, if a supervisor knows that he can receive a higher-than-estimated price on the disposition of obsolete inventory, he can either accelerate or delay the sale in order to shift gains into whichever reporting period needs the extra profit.
- *Optimism*. Those responsible for determining inventory obsolescence may feel that they can find a use for certain inventory items, even though there is not currently any usage planned in the production schedule, and no special deals are being offered to customers. If so, the result can be a gradual buildup in inventory balances that really should have been flagged for disposal at an earlier date, followed by a sudden write-down once they finally realize that full-price dispositions cannot be achieved.

- *Expense recognition.* Management may be reluctant to suddenly drop a large expense reserve into the financial statements, preferring instead to recognize small incremental amounts which make inventory obsolescence appear to be a minor problem. Since GAAP mandates immediate recognition of any obsolescence as soon as it is detected, the controller may have a struggle forcing immediate recognition through the objections of management.

- *Timely reviews.* Inventory obsolescence is likely to be a minor issue as long as management reviews inventory on a regular basis, so that the incremental amount of obsolescence detected is small in any given period. However, if management does not conduct a review for a long time, this allows obsolete inventory to build up to quite impressive proportions, along with an equally impressive amount of expense recognition. To avoid this issue, conduct frequent obsolescence reviews, and maintain a reserve based on historical or expected obsolescence, even if the specific inventory items have not yet been identified. Also, encourage the warehouse manager to make full use of the reserve, which he should treat as an opportunity to eliminate ancient items from stock.

- *Management resistance.* Senior managers may not believe the controller when he presents them with a massive write down, and so will reject any attempt to recognize an obsolescence reserve. If so, hire outside consultants who will independently review the inventory and present their own obsolescence report to management. This second opinion may bring sufficient professional weight to bear that management will grudgingly allow you to create the reserve.

EXAMPLE

Lowry Locomotion sets aside an obsolescence reserve of $25,000 for obsolete widgets. However, in January the purchasing manager knows that the resale price for obsolete widgets has plummeted, so the real reserve should be closer to $35,000, which would call for the immediate recognition of an additional $10,000 of expense. However, since this would result in an overall reported loss in Lowry's financial results in January, he waits until April, when Lowry has a very profitable month, and completes the sale at that time, thereby delaying the additional obsolescence loss until the point of sale.

Summary

This chapter has described the four steps involved in creating an accurate inventory valuation. All four are fraught with problems. There are a multitude of ways in which to incorrectly arrive at the quantity of units in stock, and a similar number of ways in which to arrive at an incorrect product cost. Further, given the large amount of costs in overhead, even a small change in the overhead allocation methodology can result in a startling change in reported profit levels. And finally, many companies do not spend sufficient time reviewing inventory obsolescence issues, so that their inventories should be valued lower than the cost at which they are actually reported. Given this potential morass of concerns, it is no surprise that inventory valuation can cause significant problems during the closing process. Inventory issues may halt the closing process entirely, while the accounting staff tries to determine why ending inventory and/or the cost of goods sold results appear to vary so much from expectations.

Chapter 9
Closing Fixed Assets

Introduction

Closing the books for fixed assets can be quite easy, as long as you shift most of the transactions related to fixed assets away from the closing process. The following table describes the various transactions that relate to fixed assets. Note how only three of them need to be addressed within the closing period.

Types of Fixed Asset Transactions

Transaction Type	Description	Timing
Initial recognition	The initial recordation of a fixed asset	On acquisition date or when posted from accounts payable at month-end
Interest capitalization	The inclusion of the interest costs associated with the construction of a fixed asset in the cost of that asset	At month-end
Asset retirement obligations	An obligation associated with the retirement of a fixed asset	At any time
Impairment	A reduction in the recorded book value of a fixed asset, based on a corresponding reduction in its value	On a scheduled date or when an event indicates impairment
Depreciation	The systematic charging to expense of a fixed asset	At month-end
Subsequent adjustments	A change in the book value of a fixed asset, based on incremental additions to or reductions of the asset	When there is a change to the fixed asset
Disposals	The sale, donation, or scrapping of a fixed asset	When a fixed asset is sold or otherwise disposed of

Of the fixed asset transactions shown in the preceding table, only depreciation and interest capitalization should be included in the closing process, while it may sometimes be necessary to also record the initial acquisition of fixed assets at that time. In this chapter, we address the accounting for those three items: initial asset recognition, the depreciation entry, and interest capitalization. Fixed asset impairment is not a direct part of the closing process, but is sometimes included in it, if only to ensure that impairment is considered at fixed intervals. For this reason, we also include a discussion of fixed asset impairment. The other fixed asset activities are not part of the closing process, and so are not described in this chapter.

Initial Asset Recognition

Fixed assets can be purchased and recorded in the accounting records at any time of the month. It is somewhat more likely that they will be recorded in the accounting records as part of the closing process, because they may have been initially recorded as expenses and are discovered during the closing process to actually be fixed assets. Consequently, we are describing here the basic rules for recording a fixed asset in the accounting records.

You should initially record a fixed asset at the historical cost of acquiring it, which includes the costs to bring it to the condition and location necessary for its intended use. If these preparatory activities will occupy a period of time, also include in the cost of the asset the interest costs related to the cost of the asset during the preparation period (see the Interest Capitalization section).

The activities involved in bringing a fixed asset to the condition and location necessary for its intended purpose include the following:

- Physical construction of the asset
- Demolition of any preexisting structures
- Renovating a preexisting structure to alter it for use by the buyer
- Administrative and technical activities during preconstruction for such activities as designing the asset and obtaining permits
- Administrative and technical work after construction commences for such activities as litigation, labor disputes, and technical problems

---

EXAMPLE

Lowry Locomotion constructs a new production facility. The facility costs $10 million to build. Also, Lowry takes out a loan for the entire $10 million amount of the facility, and pays $250,000 in interest costs during the six-month construction period. Further, the company incurs $500,000 in architectural fees and permit costs before work begins.

All of these costs can be capitalized into the cost of the facility asset, so Lowry records $1.75 million as the cost of the asset. The facility costs were originally compiled in a construction-in-progress account. The journal entry to initially recognize the production facility as a completed asset is:

	Debit	Credit
Buildings (asset)	1,750,000	
Construction in progress (asset)		1,750,000

The Depreciation Entry

Only record depreciation as part of the closing process, because it is based on the presence of all applicable fixed assets in the accounting records as of month-end, and you cannot reliably estimate depreciation in advance for fixed assets that may not yet have been purchased or recorded prior to month-end. Thus, depreciation is the primary closing activity related to fixed assets.

The basic depreciation entry is to debit the depreciation expense account (which appears in the income statement) and credit the accumulated depreciation account (which appears in the balance sheet as a contra account that reduces the amount of fixed assets). Over time, the accumulated depreciation balance will continue to increase as more depreciation is added to it, until such time as it equals the original cost of the asset. At that time, stop recording any depreciation expense, since the cost of the asset has now been reduced to zero.

The journal entry for depreciation can be a simple two-line entry designed to accommodate all types of fixed assets, or it may be subdivided into separate entries for each type of fixed asset.

EXAMPLE

Lowry Locomotion calculates that it should have $25,000 of depreciation expense in the current month. The entry is:

	Debit	Credit
Depreciation expense	25,000	
Accumulated depreciation		25,000

In the following month, Lowry's controller decides to show a higher level of precision at the expense account level, and instead elects to apportion the $25,000 of depreciation among different expense accounts, so that each class of asset has a separate depreciation charge. The entry is:

	Debit	Credit
Depreciation expense – Automobiles	4,000	
Depreciation expense – Computer equipment	8,000	
Depreciation expense – Furniture and fixtures	6,000	
Depreciation expense – Office equipment	5,000	
Depreciation expense – Software	2,000	
Accumulated depreciation		25,000

The journal entry to record the amortization of intangible assets is fundamentally the same as the entry for depreciation, except that the accounts used substitute the word "amortization" for depreciation. An intangible asset is a non-physical asset having a useful life greater than one year. Examples of intangible assets are trademarks, patents, and non-competition agreements.

EXAMPLE

Lowry Locomotion calculates that it should have $4,000 of amortization expense in the current month that is related to intangible assets. The entry is:

	Debit	Credit
Amortization expense	4,000	
Accumulated amortization		4,000

Interest Capitalization

Interest capitalization is the inclusion of any interest expense directly related to the construction of a fixed asset in the cost of that fixed asset. Interest is capitalized as part of the closing process, because you must wait until month-end for all expenditures related to fixed assets to be recorded, as well as to determine the interest rate to be applied to the capitalization calculation.

Follow these steps to calculate the amount of interest to be capitalized for a specific project:

1. Construct a table itemizing the amounts of expenditures made and the dates on which the expenditures were made.
2. Determine the date on which interest capitalization ends.
3. Calculate the capitalization period for each expenditure, which is the number of days between the specific expenditure and the end of the interest capitalization period.
4. Divide each capitalization period by the total number of days elapsed between the date of the first expenditure and the end of the interest capitalization period to arrive at the capitalization multiplier for each line item.
5. Multiply each expenditure amount by its capitalization multiplier to arrive at the average expenditure for each line item over the capitalization measurement period.
6. Add up the average expenditures at the line item level to arrive at a grand total average expenditure.
7. If there is project-specific debt, multiply the grand total of the average expenditures by the interest rate on that debt to arrive at the capitalized interest related to the debt.
8. If the grand total of the average expenditures exceeds the amount of the project-specific debt, multiply the excess expenditure amount by the weighted average of the company's other outstanding debt to arrive at the remaining amount of interest to be capitalized.
9. Add together both capitalized interest calculations. If the combined total is more than the total interest cost incurred by the company during the calculation period, reduce the amount of interest to be capitalized to the total interest cost incurred by the company during the calculation period.
10. Record the interest capitalization with a debit to the project's fixed asset account and a credit to the interest expense account.

EXAMPLE

Lowry Locomotion is building a company headquarters building. Lowry makes payments related to the project of $10,000,000 and $14,000,000 to a contractor on January 1 and July 1, respectively. The building is completed on December 31.

For the 12-month period of construction, Lowry can capitalize all of the interest on the $10,000,000 payment, since it was outstanding during the full period of construction. Lowry can capitalize the interest on the $14,000,000 payment for half of the construction period, since it was outstanding during only the second half of the construction period. The average expenditure for which the interest cost can be capitalized is calculated in the following table:

Date of Payment	Expenditure Amount	Capitalization Period*	Capitalization Multiplier	Average Expenditure
January 1	$10,000,000	12 months	12 ÷ 12 months = 100%	$10,000,000
July 1	14,000,000	6 months	6 ÷ 12 months = 50%	7,000,000
				$17,000,000

* In the table, the capitalization period is defined as the number of months that elapse between the expenditure payment date and the end of the interest capitalization period.

The only debt that Lowry has outstanding during this period is a line of credit, on which the interest rate is 8%. The maximum amount of interest that Lowry can capitalize into the cost of the building project is $1,360,000, which is calculated as:

8% Interest rate × $17,000,000 Average expenditure = $1,360,000

Lowry records the following journal entry:

	Debit	Credit
Buildings (asset)	1,360,000	
Interest expense		1,360,000

Tip: There may be an inordinate number of expenditures related to a larger project, which could result in a large and unwieldy calculation of average expenditures. To reduce the workload, consider aggregating these expenses by month, and then assume that each expenditure was made in the middle of the month, thereby reducing all of the expenditures for each month to a single line item.

You cannot capitalize more interest cost in an accounting period than the total amount of interest cost incurred by the business in that period. If there is a corporate parent, then this rule means that the amount capitalized cannot exceed the total amount of interest cost incurred by the business on a consolidated basis.

Interest capitalization may appear to be (and is) an unwieldy calculation that could significantly interfere with closing the books. This is true, but it only applies to situations where there is debt outstanding that specifically applies to the construction of a fixed asset, so you may never have to calculate interest capitalization in your entire accounting career.

Asset Impairment

Carrying amount is the recorded amount of an asset, net of any accumulated depreciation or accumulated impairment losses. Recognize an impairment loss on a fixed asset if its carrying amount is not recoverable and exceeds its fair value. Recognize this loss within income from continuing operations on the income statement.

The carrying amount of an asset is not recoverable if it exceeds the sum of the undiscounted cash flows you expect to result from the use of the asset over its remaining useful life and the final disposition of the asset. These cash flow estimates should incorporate assumptions that are reasonable in relation to the assumptions the entity uses for its budgets, forecasts, and so forth. If there are a range of possible cash flow outcomes, consider using a probability-weighted cash flow analysis.

The amount of an impairment loss is the difference between an asset's carrying amount and its fair value. Once you recognize an impairment loss, this reduces the carrying amount of the asset, so you may need to alter the amount of periodic depreciation being charged against the asset to adjust for this lower carrying amount (otherwise, you will incur an excessively large depreciation expense over the remaining useful life of the asset).

Test assets for impairment at the lowest level at which there are identifiable cash flows that are largely independent of the cash flows of other assets. In cases where there are no identifiable cash flows at all (as is common with corporate-level assets), place these assets in an asset group that encompasses the entire entity, and test for impairment at the entity level.

A reporting unit is an operating segment or one level below an operating segment. An operating segment is a component of a public entity that engages in business activities and whose results are reviewed by the chief operating decision maker, and for which discrete financial information is available. Only add goodwill to an asset group for impairment testing when the asset group is a reporting unit, or includes a reporting unit. Thus, you should not include goodwill in any asset groups below the reporting unit level.

You should test for the recoverability of an asset whenever the circumstances indicate that its carrying amount may not be recoverable. Examples of such situations are:

- *Cash flow.* There are historical and projected operating or cash flow losses associated with the asset.
- *Costs.* There are excessive costs incurred to acquire or construct the asset.
- *Disposal.* The asset is more than 50% likely to be sold or otherwise disposed of significantly before the end of its previously estimated useful life.
- *Legal.* There is a significant adverse change in legal factors or the business climate that could affect the asset's value.
- *Market price.* There is a significant decrease in the asset's market price.

- *Usage.* There is a significant adverse change in the asset's manner of use, or in its physical condition.

If there is an impairment at the level of an asset group, allocate the impairment among the assets in the group on a pro rata basis, based on the carrying amounts of the assets in the group. However, the impairment loss cannot reduce the carrying amount of an asset below its fair value.

EXAMPLE

Lowry Locomotion operates a toy manufacturing facility. Lowry considers the entire facility to be a reporting unit, so it conducts an impairment test on the entire operation. The test reveals that a continuing decline in the market for toy trains has caused a $2 million impairment charge. Lowry allocates the charge to the four assets in the facility as follows:

Asset	Carrying Amount	Proportion of Carrying Amounts	Impairment Allocation	Revised Carrying Amount
Finishing line	$8,000,000	67%	$1,340,000	$6,660,000
Paint booth	1,500,000	13%	260,000	1,240,000
Stamp press	2,000,000	16%	320,000	1,680,000
Trim line	500,000	4%	80,000	420,000
Totals	$12,000,000	100%	$2,000,000	$10,000,000

Under no circumstances are you allowed to reverse an impairment loss under GAAP. However, you can do so under IFRS. For a more detailed discussion of asset impairment under both GAAP and IFRS, see the author's *Fixed Asset Accounting* book.

Reconciling Fixed Assets

It is useful to match the fixed assets register report to the ending balance in the fixed asset accounts in the general ledger. It is quite possible that there will be a difference between the two, because there are a large number of transactions that can impact the general ledger, and which might not have been reflected in the fixed asset register report. Reconciling these differences can be time-consuming, so we recommend that this analysis be conducted several days prior to the end of the month. This may mean that some new reconciliation issues will arise in the final day or two of the month that you will not detect until the following month; nonetheless, reconciling fixed assets can be a laborious chore, even for an experienced accountant, and so should be handled outside of the most intensive part of the closing process.

Summary

The intent of this chapter has been to address only those aspects of fixed assets that specifically pertain to closing the books. As noted in the introduction, there are other activities related to fixed assets that can be separated from the closing process and handled at other times of the month. If you want to learn more about these other fixed asset activities, please refer to the author's *Fixed Asset Accounting* book, which contains a comprehensive treatment of the subject from the perspectives of both the GAAP and IFRS accounting frameworks.

Chapter 10
Closing Accounts Payable

Introduction

Accounts payable can be one of the worst closing bottlenecks, because of the inherent delay involved in waiting for supplier invoices to arrive. In some cases, this single issue can delay the issuance of financial statements by a week or more. In this chapter, we discuss the problems related to closing accounts payable, and the range of solutions available to you. In particular, we address accounts payable accruals, approvals, expense reports, suspense items, subcontractor billings, credit card statements, and reconciling accounts payable.

Related Podcast Episode: Episode 22 of the Accounting Best Practices Podcast discusses accounts payable in relation to closing the books. It is available at: **accountingtools.com/podcasts** or **iTunes**

Accounts Payable Accruals

Accounts payable can be a significant bottleneck in the closing process. The reason is that some suppliers only issue invoices at the end of each month when they are closing *their* books, so you will not receive their invoices until several days into the next month. This circumstance usually arises either when a supplier ships something near the end of the month or when it is providing a continuing service. There are several ways to deal with these items:

1. *Do nothing.* If you wait a few days, the invoices will arrive in the mail, and you can record the invoices and close the books. The advantage of this approach is a high degree of precision and perfect supporting evidence for all expenses. It is probably the best approach at year-end, if you plan to have the financial statements audited. The downside is that it can significantly delay the issuance of the financial statements.

2. *Accrue continuing service items.* As just noted, suppliers providing continuing services are more likely to issue invoices at month-end. When services are being provided on a continuing basis, you can estimate what the expense should be, based on prior invoices. Thus, it is not difficult to create reversing journal entries (see the Journal Entries chapter) for these items at the end of the month. It is likely that your accruals will vary somewhat from the amounts on the actual invoices, but the differences should be immaterial.

3. *Accrue based on purchase orders.* As just noted, suppliers issue invoices at month-end when they ship goods near that date. If you are using purchase orders to order these items, the supplier is supposed to issue an invoice containing the same price stated on the purchase order. Therefore, if an item is

received at the receiving dock but there is no accompanying invoice, use the purchase order to create a reversing journal entry that accrues the expense associated with the received item.

Tip: The last of the preceding options noted that you should accrue an expense for any received item for which there is no supplier invoice. This means that a key step in the closing process is to match the receipts listed on the receiving log to supplier invoices, to see if any invoices are missing. This is crucial, since an expensive item could otherwise be logged into the warehouse as an inventory asset without having any offsetting expense recorded against it.

In short, we strongly recommend using accruals to record expenses for supplier invoices that have not yet arrived. The sole exception is the end of the fiscal year, when the outside auditors may expect a greater degree of precision and supporting evidence, and will expect you to wait for actual invoices to arrive before closing the books.

Invoice Approval Delays

There may be a number of supplier invoices arriving at month-end, and there is a natural inclination to have them formally approved before you enter them into the accounts payable module of the accounting system. This inclination may seem reasonable, since there is always a chance that a manager does not want to pay an invoice, or that an invoice contains an incorrect amount, or is even a fraudulent invoice. Thus, the reasoning goes that you should obtain management approval of supplier invoices before entering them in the accounting system, to avoid the recordation of expenses that might be incorrect.

Unfortunately, obtaining invoice approvals can be a frustrating and lengthy process. Many managers give little priority to this task, and so bury invoices in their "in" boxes until all other tasks have been completed. This causes massive disruptions in the closing process, for the controller wants to issue financial statements as soon as possible, but knows that doing so without having recorded all supplier invoices will result in abnormally low expenses. You can eliminate or at least mitigate this problem using one of the following approaches, which can be used in combination:

1. *Record first.* Always record supplier invoices in the accounting system as soon as they are received, rather than recording them only after managers have approved them. This presents the risk that some invoices will be paid that should not be paid, but we deal with that problem by incorporating the next two improvements.

Tip: Contact all suppliers and direct them to send all invoices directly to the accounting department – not to their contacts elsewhere within the company. Doing so improves the speed with which invoices are recorded in the accounting system, and so improves the speed and accuracy of the closing process.

---

2. *Set approval rules*. Create a policy that any supplier invoice below a certain dollar limit does not require manager approval. This addresses the bulk of all invoices and therefore minimizes paperwork for managers, without seriously impacting the risk of making an incorrect payment. Further, skip approvals for all recurring invoices (such as utility bills), and for any invoices for which a formal contract already approves payments. We can assume that these invoices would probably have been approved.

3. *Require negative approval*. Of the remaining invoices that managers still have to approve, only send copies of the invoices to managers, and tell them that you only need a response if they *do not* approve an invoice. If the accounting staff does not receive a response from a manager, it assumes that an invoice should be paid. This approach reduces manager paperwork even further, while virtually ensuring that the accounting staff can close accounts payable in a timely manner. If you use this approach, it is better to send a scanned invoice copy to managers by e-mail, so that there is a record that the invoice was sent.

Tip: It is possible that one or more of the approval streamlining rules just noted will allow an invoice to slip through the company controls and be paid when it should not have been paid. To mitigate this risk, schedule an occasional meeting with each department manager to review a selection of invoices, and verify that they should be paid. By doing so, you can keep unnecessary payments from being made.

4. *Special handling*. There will be times when an invoice will be so large that it absolutely, positively must be approved by a manager before you can close the books and issue financial statements. In such cases, do not take the risk that it may be lost in the inter-office mail. Instead, have someone hand-deliver it to the relevant person or to the backup approver if the primary approver is not available, and wait for it to be approved. This approach is clearly labor-intensive, but is appropriate when the approval is likely to be a bottleneck keeping the financial statements from being released.

The preceding solutions should address all situations where invoice approvals are impeding the closing of the books. If you still have a situation where a delayed manager approval is interfering with the issuance of financial statements, refer the issue to a more senior manager and ask for a replacement approver who is more reliable. The key issue is to obtain a *permanent* replacement approver, since those managers who have had paperwork issues in the past will undoubtedly do so again in the future, and will therefore continue to interfere with the timely closing of the books.

> **Tip:** From the perspective of closing the books in a timely manner, it is rarely necessary to invest in an expensive workflow management system that routes invoices to approvers. Instead, the preceding rules avoid the need to send most invoices to anyone. A standard e-mail system is generally sufficient for the routing of any remaining invoices.

Expense Reports

It can be extremely difficult to obtain expense reports from some employees in a timely manner. Some expense reports are quite large, and so can have a material impact on the financial statements. Therefore, you cannot ignore this issue. There are two general approaches to how to handle expense reports, which are:

- *Require company credit cards.* If you mandate the use of company credit cards by employees, this means that you should receive credit card statements from the credit card company right at month-end, and can then charge these items to the correct department without much trouble. If you are particularly concerned about closing the books fast, arrange with the credit card company to close the credit card period a few days early; by doing so, the credit card statement will be received sooner, and the payables staff can have it fully processed before it interferes with other closing activities.
- *Allow personal credit cards.* If employees pay with their own credit cards, they will be quite interested in rapid reimbursement, so that they can pay for their credit cards in a timely manner. This built-in need for payment tends to mitigate the risk of having large overdue expense reports. However, there are usually a few employees who are extraordinarily late (sometimes several months late!) in submitting expense reports. Here are some options for dealing with them:
  - *Scheduled reminders.* Issue a general e-mail to all employees a few days before the end of the month, requesting that expense reports be submitted by a certain date.
  - *Performance reviews.* If an employee is persistently very late in submitting expense reports, include it as a discussion point in their performance reviews.
  - *Refuse payment.* You could institute a company policy that expense reports submitted past a certain date will not be paid. However, this is an extreme method for handling the situation, and may result in a very angry employee.

One option is to have someone personally review every submitted expense report to ensure that the correct receipts are attached, and that all company travel and entertainment policies have been followed. If not, the company may be justified in refusing reimbursement for some items in an expense report. While expense report auditing may seem to be a reasonable control over unwarranted employee expenditures, it can delay closing the books, since there can be quite a backlog in the accounting department at month-end, when most expense reports arrive.

The solution to the expense report backlog is to spot those employees with a history of expense report compliance problems, and review their expense reports in detail; all other expense reports are only audited occasionally. This approach massively reduces the amount of detailed review work and therefore eliminates the related accounting bottleneck. It also has a minimal impact on overpayments to employees, since compliance problems are usually quite rare, and centered on just those few employees who are already being audited.

A more expensive solution is to have employees enter their expense reports on-line, probably through an expense report processing service provided by a third party. These systems can import credit card charges and match them to receipts, as well as automatically apply audit rules to spot items that will not be reimbursed. This approach applies 100% auditing to all submitted expense reports, but it is also expensive. Thus, this solution presents a tradeoff of enhanced control at a higher cost.

In general, the best solution to keeping expense reports from interfering with the closing process is to require everyone to use company credit cards, and to have the statements for those cards delivered to the company shortly before the end of the month. See the next section for a discussion of an additional issue with company credit cards.

Issues with the Credit Card Close

The divisional controller of a publicly-traded multinational company asked AccountingTools for advice about problems he was having receiving expense reports on a timely basis. His company has a 4-4-5 close, so some months contain four weeks and others have five weeks. His comments are:

> "The killer item is American Express. Currently, AmEx cuts off around the 20th of the month. We get the invoices online on the 21st and send them out electronically to the individual cardholders. That way, they get it via e-mail, even when traveling. Users complete an expense report for their AmEx items and return them to us. This process often takes a week to get everything we need. Due to our odd month-end, a month can end as early as the 23rd or as late as the 31st. I'd prefer not to push back the AmEx statement cutoff, since that means we could be missing a half-month of expenses on the long months, but it creates a crunch in short months. I've looked at online expense processing from vendors like Concur. I'm choking a little on the expense, but beyond that, I'm not sure how much time it would actually save us, since the biggest problem is getting them from people."

> "We finally gave up on the stick approach and moved to a carrot and stick. Everyone who gets their AmEx in on time and complete gets entered for a monthly $50 AmEx gift card giveaway. Everyone not on time gets their name on a list that goes to the CEO."

Here are some possible solutions that we suggested:

- "We find that the carrot does not normally work, unless it is a BIG carrot. Unless you've seen an improvement from the $50 drawing, you might want to drop it, or improve the odds of winning by using multiple gift cards.
- There are usually repeat offenders every month, so target them for special treatment. We assume that they will not submit an expense report, so we immediately start hounding them as soon as they receive the statement. The normal escalation path is a direct e-mail, then a phone call, then the supervisor is contacted, and then the CEO. The total warning period is four days.
- The real problem for us is when people are gone for vacations during this time period, so we have everyone enter their vacation time in a company-wide Outlook calendar, and then ask them in advance who should complete the report if they are not available. Better yet, they can access a partial statement on-line at the AmEx site before they go on vacation, and send us the expense report in advance.
- If we do not receive an expense report, we charge the amounts on credit card statements to default expense accounts, which are then routed back to the department managers for review and correction in the next month. However, this might not work for you if these are re-billable expenses."

Accounts Payable Suspense Items

There are times when a supplier invoice arrives and the accounting staff does not know what to do with it; such invoices are stuffed into a payables suspense folder, and the accounting staff researches them when there is time. Examples of such situations are:
- An invoice is for an amount near the company's capitalization limit, which means that the accounting staff is not certain whether it should charge the item to expense or record it as a fixed asset.
- It is not clear which department should be charged for the expense.
- The invoice is for an unusual expense, and there is uncertainty about which account should be charged.
- The company has multiple locations, and it is not clear which location should be charged.
- The invoice appears to address multiple accounts or departments, so an allocation is needed for the expense.

The broad range of examples show that there will always be situations that cannot be resolved in advance with a policy or procedure – instead, someone needs to review an invoice and make a decision pertaining to that specific invoice. This involves a certain amount of research time by a senior accounting person, who may not have sufficient time available to address the issue. This, in turn, can impact the closing process, for these invoices may be of a sufficiently large dollar amount to impact the reported financial results if they are not recorded within the period.

Here are several possible options for dealing with accounts payable suspense items, particularly in regard to mitigating their impact on closing the books:

- *Scheduled review times.* The accounting department tends to have a lower work load at certain times of the month (usually after issuing financial statements and completing payroll cycles), and those are good times to schedule reviews of all outstanding suspense items. These scheduled reviews should be a formal meeting involving as many people as needed to reach a decision regarding a suspense item. After a few review sessions, it will be apparent how many people are needed to reach a decision, and you can schedule that group for future sessions.

- *Final review schedule.* There should be a final review of suspense items just *before* the end of the month. By doing so, there should be only a very small number of suspense items remaining *at* the end of the month that must still be addressed.

- *Adjustment policy.* The review group will occasionally make an incorrect decision regarding the disposition of a supplier invoice. If so, create an adjustment policy that allows these invoices to be re-assigned to the correct expense accounts. Doing so makes it easier for a small group to initially disposition suspense items quickly, knowing that they will not get in trouble for an incorrect coding.

- *Immateriality policy.* Create a policy that allows you to ignore any accounts payable suspense items still open as of the closing process if they are smaller than a designated amount. These items are immaterial to the results shown in the financial statements, and so can be dealt with after the financial statements have been issued.

In short, dealing with accounts payable suspense items is all about scheduling review meetings in advance of the closing process. By doing so, this becomes a minor issue during the close.

Reconciling Accounts Payable

The accounting software should have an accounts payable module that is used to enter supplier invoices. This module automatically populates the accounts payable account in the general ledger with transactions. When you reach the end of the month, you should be able to print the open accounts payable report and have the grand total on that report match the ending balance in the accounts payable general ledger account. Thus, there are no reconciling items between the open accounts payable report and the general ledger.

If there is a difference between the two numbers, it is almost certainly caused by the use of a journal entry that debited or credited the accounts payable account. *Never* create such a journal entry, because there is so much detail in the accounts payable account that it is very time-consuming to wade through it to ascertain the source of the variance.

The one transaction that will be a temptation to record in the accounts payable account is the accrued expense. Instead, create a current liability account in the general ledger called "Accrued Expenses" and enter the accruals in that account. By doing so, you are properly segregating normal accounts payable transactions from special month-end accrual transactions.

This differentiation is not a minor one. Accrual transactions require more maintenance than standard accounts payable transactions, because they may linger through multiple accounting periods, and you need to monitor them to know when to eliminate them from the general ledger. This problem can be addressed with reversing journal entries (see the Journal Entries chapter), but some accruals may not be designated as reversing entries, which calls for long-term tracking. If you were to lump accrued expenses into the accounts payable account, it would be very difficult to continually monitor the outstanding accruals.

In summary, restrict the accounts payable account to standard payables transactions, which makes it easier to reconcile at month-end. Any transactions related to accounts payable but which are entered via journal entries should be recorded in a separate account.

Summary

The key issue in closing accounts payable is the tradeoff between the relative degree of inaccuracy associated with accruing expenses and the offsetting benefit of closing the books several days sooner. This is a more difficult decision to make if you do not use purchase orders and regularly receive large amounts of materials, since it is more difficult to accrue an expense for any items received near month-end. Further, a really risk-averse controller may not want to take the chance of accruing for an expense that turns out to be substantially different when the invoice eventually arrives, and so will mandate a multi-day waiting period to ensure that all invoices have arrived before closing the books. In these cases, accounts payable may very well be the largest bottleneck interfering with closing the books.

Chapter 11
Closing Payroll

Introduction

A payroll cycle is the length of time between payrolls. Thus, if a business pays its employees every Friday, that is a one-week payroll cycle. Closing payroll does *not* involve the closing of an individual payroll cycle, which frequently occurs a day or two prior to the end of a month (see the author's *Payroll Management* book for more information about closing a payroll cycle). Instead, closing payroll centers on the proper accrual of any compensation expense incurred by the business near the end of the month. This expense should be accrued if it has been earned but not paid. In this chapter, we will discuss the accruals for wages, commissions, bonuses, payroll taxes, benefits, and vacations.

> **Related Podcast Episode:** Episode 24 of the Accounting Best Practices Podcast discusses payroll in relation to closing the books. It is available at: **accounting-tools.com/podcasts** or **iTunes**

The Wage Accrual

Create a salary and wage accrual entry when employees have worked some hours at the end of the accounting period for which they have not yet been paid. If a company pays on a weekly or biweekly basis, this entry will probably be required for both the salaried and hourly employees. If a company pays on a semi-monthly or monthly basis, this entry will probably only be needed for hourly employees, since salaried personnel will have been paid through the last day of the month. The following calendars illustrate the concept.

An example of a weekly payroll cycle is shown below, where employees are paid every Tuesday for the hours they worked in the preceding week. In this situation, accrue the wages of hourly employees from Sunday the 28th through Wednesday the 31st, since they would not have been paid for those days. Also, accrue the pay of salaried employees for Wednesday the 31st, since they would have been paid only through the pay date, which was the 30th day of the month.

Weekly Payroll Cycle

January						
S	M	T	W	T	F	S
	1	2	3	4	5	6
7	8	9	10	11	12	13
14	15	16	17	18	19	20
21	22	23	24	25	26	27
28	29	30	31			

An example of a biweekly payroll cycle is shown below, where employees are paid every other Tuesday for the hours worked in the preceding two weeks. In this situation, accrue wages and salaries for the same time periods just indicated for the weekly payroll cycle.

Biweekly Payroll Cycle

January						
S	M	T	W	T	F	S
	1	2	3	4	5	6
7	8	9	10	11	12	13
14	15	16	17	18	19	20
21	22	23	24	25	26	27
28	29	30	31			

An example of a semimonthly payroll cycle is shown below, where employees are paid on the 15th and last days of the month for the hours they worked through the end of the day three days prior to the pay date. In this situation, accrue the wages of hourly employees for the same time periods just indicated for the weekly and biweekly payroll cycles. However, there would be no accrual for the pay of salaried employees, because they are paid through the pay date, and the pay date is the last day of the month.

Semimonthly Payroll Cycle

January						
S	M	T	W	T	F	S
	1	2	3	4	5	6
7	8	9	10	11	12	13
14	15	16	17	18	19	20
21	22	23	24	25	26	27
28	29	30	31			

An example of a monthly payroll cycle is shown below, where employees are paid on the last day of the month. In this situation, the wage accrual matches the scenario just noted for the semimonthly payroll cycle.

Monthly Payroll Cycle

S	M	T	W	T	F	S
			January			
	1	2	3	4	5	6
7	8	9	10	11	12	13
14	15	16	17	18	19	20
21	22	23	24	25	26	27
28	29	30	31			

The information used for the wage accrual entry is most easily derived from an electronic spreadsheet that itemizes all employees to whom the calculation applies, the number of unpaid days, and the hourly rate of pay for each person.

EXAMPLE

The diesel locomotive division of Lowry Locomotion pays its employees on a semi-monthly basis, based on timesheets completed through the preceding weekend. Consequently, it must accrue for the unpaid wages of hourly personnel who worked any days between the end of the last reporting period and the end of the month. The division creates a wage accrual based on the following information, which assumes three unpaid days of work:

Employee Name	Unpaid Hours	Pay Rate	Extension
Abramson, Kyle	24	$17.50	$420.00
Bono, Allan	24	21.00	504.00
Chase, Susan	24	19.25	462.00
Dementieva, Oksana	24	16.00	384.00
Endo, William	24	15.75	378.00
Frederick, Martina	24	20.00	480.00
			$2,628.00

The related wage accrual is:

	Debit	Credit
Wage expense	2,628	
Accrued wages (liability)		2,628

The wage accrual should be entered in the accounting software as a reversing entry, so that the system automatically reverses itself at the beginning of the following month (see the Journal Entries chapter).

> **Tip:** It is generally not necessary to also compile actual or estimated overtime costs for earned but unpaid days, since it requires extra effort to compile the information and it is usually an immaterial amount.

131

Companies with predominantly salaried staffs may be able to avoid making the wage accrual entry at all, on the grounds that the wages payable to a small number of hourly personnel at the end of the reporting period have an immaterial impact on reported financial results.

The Commission Accrual

It will be necessary to accrue an expense for a commission in the same period as you record the sale generated by the salesperson, *and* when you can calculate the amount of the commission. This is a debit to the commission expense account and a credit to a commission liability account. The commission expense can be classified as part of the cost of goods sold, since it directly relates to the sale of goods or services. It is also acceptable to classify it as part of the expenses of the sales department.

EXAMPLE

Wes Smith sells a $1,000 item for Lowry Locomotion. Under the terms of his commission agreement, he receives a 5% commission on the revenue generated by the transaction, and will be paid on the 15th day of the following month. At the end of the accounting period in which Mr. Smith generates the sale, Lowry creates the following entry to record its liability for the commission:

	Debit	Credit
Commission expense	50	
Accrued commissions (liability)		50

Lowry then reverses the entry at the beginning of the following accounting period, because it is going to record the actual payment on the 15th of the month. Thus, the reversing entry is:

	Debit	Credit
Accrued commissions (liability)	50	
Commission expense		50

On the 15th day of the month, Lowry pays Mr. Smith his commission and records this entry:

	Debit	Credit
Commission expense	50	
Cash		50

The Bonus Accrual

A bonus expense should be accrued whenever there is an expectation that the financial or operational performance of a company at least equals the performance levels required in any active bonus plans.

The decision to accrue a bonus calls for considerable judgment, for the entire period of performance may encompass many future months, during which time a person may *not* continue to achieve his bonus plan objectives, in which case any prior bonus accrual should be reversed. Here are some alternative ways to treat a bonus accrual during the earlier stages of a bonus period:

- Accrue no expense at all until there is a reasonable probability that the bonus will be achieved.
- Accrue a smaller expense early in a performance period to reflect the higher risk of performance failure, and accrue a larger expense later if the probability of success improves.

One thing you should *not* do is accrue a significant bonus expense in a situation where the probability that the bonus will be awarded is low; such an accrual is essentially earnings management, since it creates a false expense that is later reversed when the performance period is complete.

EXAMPLE

The management team of Lowry Locomotion will earn a year-end group bonus of $240,000 if profits exceed 12 percent of revenues. There is a reasonable probability that the team will earn this bonus, so the controller records the following accrual in each month of the performance year:

	Debit	Credit
Bonus expense	20,000	
Accrued bonus liability		20,000

The management team does not quite meet the profit criteria required under the bonus plan, so the group instead receives a $150,000 bonus. This results in the following entry to eliminate the liability and pay out the bonus:

	Debit	Credit
Accrued bonus liability	240,000	
Bonus expense		90,000
Cash		150,000

Tip: Employee performance plans are usually maintained by the human resources department. You should summarize these plans into a format that the accounting staff can consult when calculating its estimates of bonus accruals.

The Payroll Tax Accrual

When accruing for wages, commissions, and bonuses, you should also accrue for the payroll taxes related to those forms of compensation. The reason is that payroll taxes are sufficiently large to be considered material to the results reported in the financial statements.

> **Tip:** Integrate the payroll tax accrual into the accruals for wages, commissions, and bonuses. By having payroll taxes listed in the journal entry templates for these expenses, it is difficult to forget to accrue for the taxes. Conversely, it is quite easy to forget the entry when the payroll tax accrual is an entirely separate entry.

In the interests of simplicity, accrue for payroll taxes using a single expense account for all types of payroll taxes. Thus, you should combine the accruals for social security, Medicare, and federal unemployment taxes in a single expense account. If you do not use this approach and forget to reverse a payroll tax accrual, it can be difficult to track down all of the various accruals in the individual payroll tax accounts.

The basic payroll tax accrual format is:

	Debit	Credit
Payroll tax expense	xxx	
Accrued payroll tax liability		xxx

The social security wage cap is the annual compensation level above which no additional social security tax is paid for an individual. It is possible that the compensation of highly-compensated employees will exceed the social security wage cap at some point later in the calendar year. If so, you need to decide whether to include this consideration in the formulation of the payroll tax accrual. Realistically, few employees earn enough compensation to exceed the wage cap, so it is not an issue in many companies. However, if that is not the case, the amount of social security tax that a company no longer pays may be large enough to warrant its consideration in the formulation of the payroll tax accrual, at least during the final months of the calendar year.

The Benefits Accrual

If there are employee benefit expenses that have been incurred during the reporting period, but for which no supplier invoice has yet been received, accrue the expense if it is material. This is a rare accrual, since most benefit suppliers issue invoices in advance, rather than in arrears.

The proper benefits accrual is a journal entry that charges the applicable expense account and an offsetting accrued benefit liability, and which automatically reverses itself in the following accounting period (when the supplier invoice presumably arrives and is recorded). The following sample shows a journal entry that could be used to accrue a number of types of benefit expenses.

Sample Benefits Accrual Entry

	Debit	Credit
Medical insurance expense	xxx	
Dental insurance expense	xxx	
Disability insurance expense	xxx	
Life insurance expense	xxx	
Accrued benefits liability		xxx

It is easiest to derive the benefits information for the accrual entry from the last supplier invoices. These invoices typically show benefit costs by individual, so you can estimate the amount needed for the accrual by using the preceding invoice as a baseline and adjusting it for any changes in headcount or benefits granted.

The Vacation Accrual

Accrued vacation pay is the amount of vacation time that an employee has earned as per a company's employee benefit manual, but which he has not yet used. The calculation of accrued vacation pay for each employee is:

1. Calculate the amount of vacation time earned through the beginning of the accounting period. This should be a roll-forward balance from the preceding period.
2. Add the number of hours earned in the current accounting period.
3. Subtract the number of vacation hours used in the current period.
4. Multiply the ending number of accrued vacation hours by the employee's hourly wage to arrive at the correct accrual that should be on the company's books.
5. If the amount already accrued for the employee from the preceding period is lower than the correct accrual, record the difference as an addition to the accrued liability. If the amount already accrued from the preceding period is higher than the correct accrual, record the difference as a reduction of the accrued liability.

A sample spreadsheet follows that uses the preceding steps, and which can be used to compile accrued vacation pay:

Sample Vacation Accrual Spreadsheet

Name	Vacation Roll-Forward Balance	+ New Hours Earned	- Hours Used	= Net Balance	× Hourly Pay	= Accrued Vacation $
Hilton, David	24.0	10	34.0	0.0	$25.00	$0.00
Idle, John	13.5	10	0.0	23.5	17.50	411.25
Jakes, Jill	120.0	10	80.0	50.0	23.50	1,175.00
Kilo, Steve	114.5	10	14.0	110.5	40.00	4,420.00
Linder, Alice	12.0	10	0.0	22.0	15.75	346.50
Mills, Jeffery	83.5	10	65.00	28.5	19.75	562.88
					Total	$6,915.63

It is not necessary to reverse the vacation pay accrual in each period if you choose to instead record just incremental changes in the accrual from month to month.

EXAMPLE

There is already an existing accrued balance of 40 hours of unused vacation time for Wes Smith on the books of Lowry Locomotion. In the most recent month that has just ended, Mr. Smith accrued an additional five hours of vacation time (since he is entitled to 60 hours of accrued vacation time per year, and $60 \div 12 = 5$ hours per month). He also used three hours of vacation time during the month. This means that, as of the end of the month, Lowry should have accrued a total of 42 hours of vacation time for him (calculated as 40 hours existing balance + 5 hours additional accrual − 3 hours used).

Mr. Smith is paid $30 per hour, so his total vacation accrual should be $1,260 (42 hours × $30/hour), so Lowry accrues an additional $60 of vacation liability.

What if a company has a "use it or lose it" policy? This means that employees must use their vacation time by a certain date (such as the end of the year), and can only carry forward a small number of hours (if any) into the next year. One issue is that this policy may be illegal, since vacation is an earned benefit that cannot be taken away (which depends on state law). If this policy is considered to be legal, it is acceptable to reduce the accrual as of the date when employees are supposed to have used their accrued vacation, thereby reflecting the reduced liability to the company as represented by the number of vacation hours that employees have lost.

What if an employee receives a pay raise? Then increase the amount of his entire vacation accrual by the incremental amount of the pay raise. This is because, if the employee were to leave the company and be paid all of his unused vacation pay, he would be paid at his most recent rate of pay.

Reconciling Compensation Accruals

As part of the closing process, verify the balances in the various accrued liability accounts. All accrued wages, commissions, payroll taxes, and benefits from the preceding period should have been reversed, leaving only the current-period accruals in these accounts. However, the bonus and vacation accruals should retain their balances from the preceding period, until such time as they are paid out.

Summary

If a company has a large number of employees who are paid on an hourly basis and there is a multi-day gap between the payroll calculation date and the pay date, the wage accrual may involve a large expense, and so is an important part of the closing process. Conversely, if a company employs mostly salaried individuals and pays them through the end of the month, there may be no compensation accrual at all. Thus, the expense accruals related to payroll depend upon a combination of the types of compensation paid and the amount of time at month-end that has been earned but not yet paid.

Chapter 12
The Income Statement

Introduction

In most organizations, the income statement is considered the most important of the financial statements, and may even be the only one of the financial statements that is produced (though we do not recommend doing so). Given its importance, we spend extra time in this chapter addressing different income statement formats, and then walk through the steps needed to create an income statement.

Income Statement Overview

The income statement is an integral part of an entity's financial statements, and contains the results of its operations during an accounting period, showing revenues and expenses, and the resulting profit or loss.

There are two ways to present the income statement. One method is to present all items of revenue and expense for the reporting period in a statement of comprehensive income. Alternatively, you can split this information into an income statement and a statement of comprehensive income. Other comprehensive income contains all changes that are not permitted in the main part of the income statement. These items include unrealized gains and losses on available-for-sale securities, cash flow hedge gains and losses, foreign currency translation adjustments, and pension plan gains or losses. Smaller companies tend to ignore the distinction and simply aggregate the information into a document that they call the income statement; this is sufficient for internal reporting, but auditors will require the expanded version before they will certify a company's financial statements.

There are no specific requirements for the line items to include in the income statement, but the following line items are typically used, based on general practice:
- Revenue
- Tax expense
- Post-tax profit or loss for discontinued operations and their disposal
- Profit or loss
- Other comprehensive income, subdivided into each component thereof
- Total comprehensive income

A key additional item is to present an analysis of the expenses in profit or loss, using a classification based on their nature or functional area; the goal is to maximize the relevance and reliability of the presented information. If you elect to present expenses by their nature, the format looks similar to the following:

Sample Presentation by Nature of Items

Revenue		$xxx
Expenses		
Direct materials	$xxx	
Direct labor	xxx	
Salaries expense	xxx	
Payroll taxes	xxx	
Employee benefits	xxx	
Depreciation expense	xxx	
Telephone expense	xxx	
Other expenses	xxx	
Total expenses		$xxx
Profit before tax		$xxx

Alternatively, if you present expenses by their functional area, the format looks similar to the following, where most expenses are aggregated at the department level:

Sample Presentation by Function of Items

Revenue	$xxx
Cost of goods sold	xxx
Gross profit	xxx
Administrative expenses	$xxx
Distribution expenses	xxx
Research and development expenses	xxx
Sales and marketing expenses	xxx
Other expenses	xxx
Total expenses	$xxx
Profit before tax	$xxx

Of the two methods, presenting expenses by their nature is easier, since it requires no allocation of expenses between functional areas. Conversely, the functional area presentation may be more relevant to users of the information, who can more easily see where resources are being consumed.

Add additional headings, subtotals, and line items to the items noted above if doing so will increase the user's understanding of the entity's financial performance.

An example follows of an income statement that presents expenses by their nature, rather than by their function.

EXAMPLE

Lowry Locomotion presents its results in two separate statements by their nature, resulting in the following format, beginning with the income statement:

Lowry Locomotion
Income Statement
For the years ended December 31

(000s)	20x2	20x1
Revenue	$900,000	$850,000
Expenses		
Direct materials	$270,000	$255,000
Direct labor	90,000	85,000
Salaries	300,000	275,000
Payroll taxes	27,000	25,000
Depreciation expense	45,000	41,000
Telephone expense	30,000	20,000
Other expenses	23,000	22,000
Finance costs	29,000	23,000
Other income	-25,000	-20,000
Profit before tax	$111,000	$124,000
Income tax expense	38,000	43,000
Profit from continuing operations	$73,000	$81,000
Loss from discontinued operations	42,000	0
Profit	$31,000	$81,000

Lowry Locomotion then continues with the following statement of comprehensive income:

Lowry Locomotion
Statement of Comprehensive Income
For the years ended December 31

(000s)	20x2	20x1
Profit	$31,000	$81,000
Other comprehensive income		
Exchange differences on translating foreign operations	$5,000	$9,000
Available-for-sale financial assets	10,000	-2,000
Actuarial losses on defined benefit pension plan	-2,000	-12,000
Other comprehensive income, net of tax	$13,000	-$5,000
Total comprehensive income	$18,000	$76,000

The Single-Step Income Statement

The simplest format in which you can construct an income statement is the single-step income statement. In this format, present a single subtotal for all revenue line items, and a single subtotal for all expense line items, with a net gain or loss appearing at the bottom of the report. A sample single-step income statement follows:

Sample Single-Step Income Statement

Revenues	$1,000,000
Expenses:	
Cost of goods sold	350,000
Advertising	30,000
Depreciation	20,000
Rent	40,000
Payroll taxes	28,000
Salaries and wages	400,000
Supplies	32,000
Travel and entertainment	50,000
Total expenses	950,000
Net income	$50,000

The single-step format is not heavily used, because it forces the reader of an income statement to separately summarize information for subsets of information within the income statement. For a more readable format, try the following multi-step approach.

The Multi-Step Income Statement

The multi-step income statement involves the use of multiple sub-totals within the income statement, which makes it easier for readers to aggregate selected types of information within the report. The usual subtotals are for the gross margin, operating expenses, and other income, which allow readers to determine how much the company earns just from its manufacturing activities (the gross margin), what it spends on supporting operations (the operating expense total) and which components of its results do not relate to its core activities (the other income total). A sample format for a multi-step income statement follows:

Sample Multi-Step Income Statement

Revenues	$1,000,000
Cost of goods sold	350,000
Gross margin	$650,000
Operating expenses	
Advertising	30,000
Depreciation	20,000
Rent	40,000
Payroll taxes	28,000
Salaries and wages	380,000
Supplies	32,000
Travel and entertainment	50,000
Total operating expenses	$580,000
Other income	
Interest income	-5,000
Interest expense	25,000
Total other income	$20,000
Net income	$50,000

The Condensed Income Statement

A condensed income statement is simply an income statement with many of the usual line items condensed down into a few lines. Typically, this means that all revenue line items are aggregated into a single line item, while the cost of goods sold appears as one line item, and all operating expenses appear in another line item. A typical format for a condensed income statement is:

Sample Condensed Income Statement

Revenues	$1,000,000
Cost of goods sold	350,000
Sales, general, and administrative expenses	580,000
Financing income and expenses	20,000
Net income	$50,000

A condensed income statement is typically issued to those external parties who are less interested in the precise sources of a company's revenues or what expenses it incurs, and more concerned with its overall performance. Thus, bankers and investors may be interested in receiving a condensed income statement.

The Contribution Margin Income Statement

A contribution margin income statement is an income statement in which all variable expenses are deducted from sales to arrive at a contribution margin, from which all fixed expenses are then subtracted to arrive at the net profit or loss for the period. This income statement format is a superior form of presentation, because the contribution margin clearly shows the amount available to cover fixed costs and generate a profit (or loss).

In essence, if there are no sales, a contribution margin income statement will have a zero contribution margin, with fixed costs clustered beneath the contribution margin line item. As sales increase, the contribution margin will increase in conjunction with sales, while fixed costs remain approximately the same.

A contribution margin income statement varies from a normal income statement in the following three ways:

- Fixed production costs are aggregated lower in the income statement, after the contribution margin;
- Variable selling and administrative expenses are grouped with variable production costs, so that they are a part of the calculation of the contribution margin; and
- The gross margin is replaced in the statement by the contribution margin.

Thus, the format of a contribution margin income statement is:

Sample Contribution Margin Income Statement

+	Revenues
-	Variable production expenses (such as materials, supplies, and variable overhead)
-	Variable selling and administrative expenses
=	Contribution margin
-	Fixed production expenses (including most overhead)
-	Fixed selling and administrative expenses
=	Net profit or loss

In many cases, direct labor is categorized as a fixed expense in the contribution margin income statement format, rather than a variable expense, because this cost does not always change in direct proportion to the amount of revenue generated. Instead, management needs to keep a certain minimum staffing in the production area, which does not vary even if there are lower production volumes.

The key difference between the gross margin and contribution margin is that fixed production costs are included in the cost of goods sold to calculate the gross margin, whereas they are not included in the same calculation for the contribution margin. This means that the contribution margin income statement is sorted based on the variability of the underlying cost information, rather than by the functional areas or expense categories found in a normal income statement.

It is useful to create an income statement in the contribution margin format when you want to determine that proportion of expenses that truly varies directly with revenues. In many businesses, the contribution margin will be substantially higher than the gross margin, because such a large proportion of production costs are fixed and few of its selling and administrative expenses are variable.

The Multi-Period Income Statement

A variation on any of the preceding income statement formats is to present them over multiple periods, preferably over a trailing 12-month period. By doing so, readers of the income statement can see trends in the information, as well as spot changes in the trends that may require investigation. This is an excellent way to present the income statement, and is highly recommended. The following sample shows the layout of a multi-period income statement over a four-quarter period.

Sample Multi-Period Income Statement

	Quarter 1	Quarter 2	Quarter 3	Quarter 4
Revenues	$1,000,000	$1,100,000	$1,050,000	$1,200,000
Cost of goods sold	350,000	385,000	368,000	**480,000**
Gross margin	$650,000	$715,000	$682,000	$720,000
Operating expenses				
Advertising	30,000	**0**	**60,000**	30,000
Depreciation	20,000	21,000	22,000	24,000
Rent	40,000	40,000	**50,000**	50,000
Payroll taxes	28,000	28,000	28,000	26,000
Salaries and wages	380,000	385,000	385,000	370,000
Supplies	32,000	30,000	31,000	33,000
Travel and entertainment	50,000	45,000	40,000	60,000
Total operating expenses	$580,000	$549,000	$616,000	$593,000
Other income				
Interest income	-5,000	-5,000	-3,000	-1,000
Interest expense	25,000	25,000	30,000	**39,000**
Total other income	$20,000	$20,000	$27,000	$38,000
Net income	$50,000	$146,000	$39,000	$89,000

The report shown in the sample reveals several issues that might not have been visible if the report had only spanned a single period. These issues are:

- *Cost of goods sold.* This cost is consistently 35% of sales until Quarter 4, when it jumps to 40%.
- *Advertising.* There was no advertising cost in Quarter 2 and double the amount of the normal $30,000 quarterly expense in Quarter 3. The cause could be a missing supplier invoice in Quarter 2 that was received and recorded in Quarter 3.
- *Rent.* The rent increased by $10,000 in Quarter 3, which may indicate a scheduled increase in the rent agreement.
- *Interest expense.* The interest expense jumps in Quarter 3 and does so again in Quarter 4, while interest income declined over the same periods. This indicates a large increase in debt.

In short, the multi-period income statement is an excellent tool for spotting anomalies in the presented information from period to period.

The Statement of Activities

The primary intent of a nonprofit organization is (as the name implies) something other than earning a profit. Consequently, a nonprofit does not issue an income statement, as does a for-profit business. Instead, a nonprofit issues an alternative called a *statement of activities*. This statement quantifies the revenue and expenses of a nonprofit for a reporting period. These revenues and expenses are broken down into unrestricted, temporarily restricted, and permanently restricted classifications, and are divided into separate columns across the statement. The rows in the statement reveal revenues and expenses. Though it is possible to compress these rows down to just a few line items, it is customary to be more expansive in detailing revenues and expenses. For example, line items that may be separately presented for nonprofit revenues can include:

- Contributions
- Fundraising events
- Gain on sale of investments
- Grants
- Investment income
- Member dues
- Program fees

In addition, nonprofit revenues can include net assets released from restriction. This is funds received in an earlier period that had temporary restrictions placed on them, and for which the restrictions have now been lifted. When these funds are shifted from the temporarily restricted column to the unrestricted column, the net effect on revenues during the reporting period is always zero, since this is just a change in classification.

Line items for expenses may also be separately presented, and in considerable detail. At a minimum, the statement of activities usually includes the following line items:

- *Program expenses.* Those expenses incurred in order to deliver specific programs in accordance with the mission of the nonprofit. The presentation may include additional line items to break out the expenses associated with each individual program.
- *Support services expenses.* Those expenses used to manage the organization and raise funds.

The net effect of all revenues and expenses is a change in net assets, rather than the profit or loss figure found in the income statement of a for-profit entity. A sample statement of activities format follows:

The Income Statement

Archimedes Education
Statement of Activities
For the month ended June 30, 20X1

	Unrestricted	Temporarily Restricted	Permanently Restricted	Totals
Revenues:				
Contributions	$48,000		$10,000	$58,000
Net unrealized and realized gains on long-term investments	2,000			2,000
Net assets released from restrictions	12,000	-$12,000		
Total revenues	$62,000	-$12,000	$10,000	$60,000
Expenses:				
Program expenses	$29,000			$29,000
Management and administration expenses	11,000			11,000
Fundraising expenses	6,000			6,000
Total expenses	$46,000			$46,000
Change in net assets	$16,000	-$12,000	$10,000	$14,000
+ Beginning net assets	32,000	12,000	0	44,000
= Ending net assets	$48,000	$0	$10,000	$58,000

In the sample, Archimedes has obtained $48,000 of unrestricted revenues that it is allowed to use in any way, such as to pay for current operations. In addition, a temporary restriction on revenues received in an earlier period has been lifted, allowing Archimedes to spend $12,000 that had been contributed in a prior period; this involves a reclassification from the temporarily restricted category to the unrestricted category. In addition, $10,000 of contributions have been received, and for which there is a permanent restriction. There are also unrealized gains of $2,000 on investments.

Despite the implication that a nonprofit is not supposed to earn a profit, it may need to generate substantial profits, in order to guard against shortfalls in donor funding or unexpected increases in expenses. Consequently, the results appearing in the statement of activities are closely perused by the managers of a nonprofit, to see if the business is generating sufficient profit to guard against future financial difficulties.

The ending net assets figure in the statement of activities should tie back to the information in the statement of financial position (see The Balance Sheet chapter). This is the beginning amount of net assets, net of any changes in net assets during the reporting period.

How to Construct the Income Statement

If you use an accounting software package, it is quite easy to construct an income statement. Just access the report writing module, select the time period for which you want to print the income statement, and print it.

> **Tip:** If you have used a report writer to create an income statement in your accounting software, there is a good chance that the first draft of the report will be wrong, due to some accounts being missed or duplicated. To ensure that the income statement is correct, compare it to the default income statement report that is usually provided with the accounting software, or compare the net profit or loss on the report to the current year earnings figure listed in the equity section of the balance sheet. If there is a discrepancy, you have an incorrect income statement report.

The situation is more complex if you choose to create the income statement by hand. This involves the following steps:
1. Create the trial balance report (see the Trial Balance chapter).
2. List each account pertaining to the income statement in a separate column of the trial balance.
3. Aggregate these line items into those you want to report in the income statement as a separate line item.
4. Shift the result into the format of the income statement that you prefer.

The following example illustrates the construction of an income statement.

EXAMPLE

The accounting software for Lowry Locomotion breaks down at the end of July, and the controller has to create the financial statements by hand. He has a copy of Lowry's trial balance, which is shown below. He transfers this information to an electronic spreadsheet, creates separate columns for accounts to include in the income statement, and copies those balances into these columns. This leaves a number of accounts related to the balance sheet, which he can ignore for the purposes of creating the income statement.

Lowry Locomotion Extended Trial Balance

	Adjusted Trial Balance		Income Statement		Aggregation	
	Debit	Credit	Debit	Credit	Debit	Credit
Cash	$60,000					
Accounts receivable	230,000					
Inventory	300,000					
Fixed assets (net)	210,000					
Accounts payable		$90,000				
Accrued liabilities		75,000				
Notes payable		420,000				
Equity		350,000				
Revenue		450,000		$450,000		$450,000
Cost of goods sold	290,000		$290,000		$290,000	
Salaries expense	225,000		225,000		245,000	
Payroll tax expense	20,000		20,000			
Rent expense	35,000		35,000			
Other expenses	15,000		15,000		50,000	
Totals	$1,385,000	$1,385,000	$585,000	$450,000	$585,000	$450,000

In the "Aggregation" columns of the extended trial balance, the controller has aggregated the expenses for salaries and payroll taxes into the salaries expense line, and aggregated the rent expense and other expenses into the other expenses line. He then transfers this information into the following condensed income statement:

Lowry Locomotion
Income Statement
For the month ended July 31, 20X1

Revenue	$450,000
Cost of goods sold	290,000
Salaries expenses	245,000
Other expenses	50,000
Net loss	-$135,000

Other Income Statement Topics

The following additional topics relate to the income statement, and can be of use to someone new to the creation of this report, who wants to understand the types of information contained within it.

What is a Cash Basis Income Statement?

A *cash basis income statement* is an income statement that only contains revenues for which cash has been received from customers, and expenses for which cash expenditures have been made. Thus, it is formulated under the guidelines of cash basis accounting (which is not compliant with GAAP or IFRS).

A cash basis income statement can contain results that are substantially different from those of an accrual basis income statement, since the recognition of revenue is delayed by the time required for customers to pay for billed amounts, and the recognition of expenses is delayed until such time as the company elects to pay its bills to suppliers. As an example of this difference, if a company were to issue 30-day payment terms to its customers and had similar terms with its suppliers, the results shown in its income statement would effectively be those that would have been reported under the accrual basis of accounting in the immediately preceding month.

Because of the important timing difference between a cash basis income statement and an accrual basis income statement, always prominently label the income statement using a format similar to the following:

ABC Company
Cash Basis Income Statement
for the month ended xx/xx/xxxx

To be even more clear for any reader of the income statement who did not see the revised header, re-label the "Net income" line with "Cash basis net income." Better yet, add a footer to the income statement, stating:

Cash Basis Income Statement - Not Prepared Under
Generally Accepted Accounting Principles

The key steps involved in adjusting a cash basis income statement to an accrual basis income statement include the following:

Revenue adjustments:

- Subtract any billings for which cash was received from customers
- Subtract any cash deposits received from customers that have not been earned
- Add billings to customers during the period
- Add earned but unbilled products/services

Expense adjustments:

- Subtract payments made for expenses incurred in a prior period
- Subtract any deposits paid for which the expense has not yet been recognized

- Add expenses accrued during the period for which there are not yet any supplier invoices
- Add supplier invoices received during the period, relating to the current period
- Add depreciation and amortization expense, as well as other non-cash expenses

What is a Partial Income Statement?

A partial income statement can refer to two types of income statements. It may mean "partial" in that it reports information for only part of a normal accounting period.

For example, a full income statement would report the results for all of February, whereas a partial income statement might only report the company's results for the period from February 21 to February 28. However, this is not the best usage of the term "partial," since the income statement is still reporting all results in full, but for just a limited time period. Thus, the header for such an income statement might be:

ABC Company
Income Statement
For the period February 21-28, 20X1

A more accurate use of the term "partial income statement" is when only a portion of an income statement is presented. For example, you might want to emphasize only the top half of the income statement, showing revenues less the cost of goods sold, and arriving at the gross margin. Alternatively, you may only want to present selling and administrative expenses, or only other comprehensive income, or only the results associated with discontinued operations.

It can be extremely misleading to present such snippets of information, so be sure to state which line items are being disclosed, preferably in the header of the partial income statement.

A partial income statement should only be used for very specific purposes, where you are trying to make a point about certain line items in the income statement. It should never be included in an otherwise full set of financial statements without complete disclosure. A partial income statement will never be certified by an auditor, since it does not comprise a complete income statement.

What are Headline Earnings?

Headline earnings is a subset of the profits reported by a business. When a business reports headline earnings, it is only including the following earnings:

- Profits or losses generated by operations
- Profits or losses generated by investment activities

The headline earnings concept does not include the following types of earnings:

- Profits or losses caused by the sale of assets

- Profits or losses caused by the termination of discontinued operations
- Profits or losses caused by write-downs in the value of assets
- Profits or losses caused by reductions in the number of employees

Headline earnings are useful for a financial analyst who wants to determine the earnings level of the core day-to-day operations of a business, without other ancillary transactions cluttering up the earnings information. It is also useful for comparing the results of the core operations of similar businesses within the same industry.

However, the presentation of headline earnings is not allowed under GAAP or IFRS, and so is not allowed within a company's financial statements. Thus, it is more of a public relations or financial analysis concept than an accounting concept.

For example, ABC International reports $100,000 of earnings in its most recent quarter, which includes a $10,000 gain on the sale of fixed assets and a $30,000 impairment charge on other fixed assets. The headline earnings for ABC would be $120,000, which factors out the two transactions just noted.

Summary

Of the income statement formats presented in this chapter, the most commonly used is the sample shown for the multi-step income statement. This format reveals expenses by nature, not by department. It is customary to create additional department-level statements that break down the expenditures for individual departments, so that department managers can see the results of the entire business on the income statement, and then review the results pertaining only to their departments on a separate document. The sales manager may also want to see additional detail for the types of revenue generated.

The contribution margin income statement certainly makes theoretical sense, but is rarely used, because outside users of financial statements are more accustomed to seeing a gross margin format on the income statement. Thus, if you plan to use it, prepare it for internal consumption and have a second, more traditional version available to distribute outside of the company.

Chapter 13
The Balance Sheet

Introduction

In most organizations, the balance sheet is considered the second most important of the financial statements, after the income statement. A common financial reporting package is to issue the income statement and balance sheet, along with supporting materials. This does not comprise a complete set of financial statements, but it is considered sufficient for internal reporting purposes in many organizations.

In this chapter, we explore several possible formats for the balance sheet, and also describe how to create it.

Overview of the Balance Sheet

A balance sheet (also known as a statement of financial position) presents information about an entity's assets, liabilities, and shareholders' equity, where the compiled result must match this formula:

$$\text{Total assets} = \text{Total liabilities} + \text{Equity}$$

The balance sheet reports the aggregate effect of transactions as of a specific date. The balance sheet is used to assess an entity's liquidity and ability to pay its debts.

There is no specific requirement for the line items to be included in the balance sheet. The following line items, at a minimum, are normally included in it:

Current Assets:

- Cash and cash equivalents
- Trade and other receivables
- Investments
- Inventories
- Assets held for sale

Non-Current Assets:

- Property, plant, and equipment
- Intangible assets
- Goodwill

Current Liabilities:

- Trade and other payables

- Accrued expenses
- Current tax liabilities
- Current portion of loans payable
- Other financial liabilities
- Liabilities held for sale

Non-Current Liabilities:

- Loans payable
- Deferred tax liabilities
- Other non-current liabilities

Equity:

- Capital stock
- Additional paid-in capital
- Retained earnings

Here is an example of a balance sheet which presents information as of the end of two fiscal years:

Lowry Locomotion
Balance Sheet
As of December 31, 20X2 and 20X1

(000s)	12/31/20X2	12/31/20X1
ASSETS		
Current assets		
Cash and cash equivalents	$270,000	$215,000
Trade receivables	147,000	139,000
Inventories	139,000	128,000
Other current assets	15,000	27,000
Total current assets	$571,000	$509,000
Non-current assets		
Property, plant, and equipment	551,000	529,000
Goodwill	82,000	82,000
Other intangible assets	143,000	143,000
Total non-current assets	$776,000	$754,000
Total assets	$1,347,000	$1,263,000
LIABILITIES AND EQUITY		
Current liabilities		
Trade and other payables	$217,000	$198,000

(000s)	12/31/20X2	12/31/20X1
Short-term borrowings	133,000	202,000
Current portion of long-term borrowings	5,000	5,000
Current tax payable	26,000	23,000
Accrued expenses	9,000	13,000
Total current liabilities	$390,000	$441,000
Non-current liabilities		
Long-term debt	85,000	65,000
Deferred taxes	19,000	17,000
Total non-current liabilities	$104,000	$82,000
Total liabilities	$494,000	$523,000
Shareholders' equity		
Capital	100,000	100,000
Additional paid-in capital	15,000	15,000
Retained earnings	738,000	625,000
Total equity	$853,000	$740,000
Total liabilities and equity	$1,347,000	$1,263,000

An asset on the balance sheet should be classified as current when an entity expects to sell or consume it during its normal operating cycle or within 12 months after the reporting period. If the operating cycle is longer than 12 months, use the longer period to judge whether an asset can be classified as current. Classify all other assets as non-current.

Classify all of the following as current assets:

- *Cash.* This is cash available for current operations, as well as any short-term, highly liquid investments that are readily convertible to known amounts of cash and which are so near their maturities that they present an insignificant risk of value changes. Do not include cash whose withdrawal is restricted, to be used for other than current operations, or segregated for the liquidation of long-term debts; such items should be classified as longer-term.

- *Accounts receivable.* This includes trade accounts, notes, and acceptances that are receivable. Also, include receivables from officers, employees, affiliates, and others if they are collectible within a year. Do not include any receivable that you do not expect to collect within 12 months; such items should be classified as longer-term.

- *Marketable securities.* This includes those securities representing the investment of cash available for current operations, including trading securities.

- *Inventory*. This includes merchandise, raw materials, work-in-process, finished goods, operating supplies, and maintenance parts.
- *Prepaid expenses*. This includes prepayments for insurance, interest, rent, taxes, unused royalties, advertising services, and operating supplies.

A liability is classified as current when the entity expects to settle it during its normal operating cycle or within 12 months after the reporting period, or if it is scheduled for settlement within 12 months. Classify all other liabilities as non-current.

Classify all of the following as current liabilities:

- *Payables*. This is all accounts payable incurred in the acquisition of materials and supplies that are used to produce goods or services.
- *Prepayments*. This is amounts collected in advance of the delivery of goods or services by the entity to the customer. Do not include a long-term prepayment in this category.
- *Accruals*. This is accrued expenses for items directly related to the operating cycle, such as accruals for compensation, rentals, royalties, and various taxes.
- *Short-term debts*. This is debts maturing within the next 12 months.

Current liabilities include accruals for amounts that can only be determined approximately, such as bonuses, and where the payee to whom payment will be made cannot initially be designated, such as a warranty accrual.

The Common Size Balance Sheet

A common size balance sheet presents not only the standard information contained in a balance sheet, but also a column that notes the same information as a percentage of the total assets (for asset line items) or as a percentage of total liabilities and shareholders' equity (for liability or shareholders' equity line items).

It is extremely useful to construct a common size balance sheet that itemizes the results as of the end of multiple time periods, so that you can construct trend lines to ascertain changes over longer time periods. The common size balance sheet is also useful for comparing the proportions of assets, liabilities, and equity between different companies, particularly as part of an industry or acquisition analysis.

For example, if you were comparing the common size balance sheet of your company to that of a potential acquiree, and the acquiree had 40% of its assets invested in accounts receivable versus 20% by your company, this may indicate that aggressive collection activities might reduce the acquiree's receivables if your company were to acquire it.

The common size balance sheet is not required under the GAAP or IFRS accounting frameworks. However, being a useful document for analysis purposes, it is commonly distributed within a company for review by management.

There is no mandatory format for a common size balance sheet, though percentages are nearly always placed to the right of the normal numerical results. If you are reporting balance sheet results as of the end of many periods, you may even dispense with numerical results entirely, in favor of just presenting the common size percentages.

EXAMPLE

Lowy Locomotion creates a common size balance sheet that contains the balance sheet as of the end of its fiscal year for each of the past two years, with common size percentages to the right:

Lowry Locomotion
Common Size Balance Sheet
As of 12/31/20x02 and 12/31/20x1

	($) 12/31/20x2	($) 12/31/20x1	(%) 12/31/20x2	(%) 12/31/20x1
Current assets				
Cash	$1,200	$900	7.6%	7.1%
Accounts receivable	4,800	3,600	30.4%	28.3%
Inventory	3,600	2,700	22.8%	21.3%
Total current assets	$9,600	$7,200	60.8%	56.7%
Total fixed assets	6,200	5,500	39.2%	43.3%
Total assets	$15,800	$12,700	100.0%	100.0%
Current liabilities				
Accounts payable	$2,400	$41,800	15.2%	14.2%
Accrued expenses	480	360	3.0%	2.8%
Short-term debt	800	600	5.1%	4.7%
Total current liabilities	$3,680	$2,760	23.3%	21.7%
Long-term debt	9,020	7,740	57.1%	60.9%
Total liabilities	$12,700	$10,500	80.4%	82.7%
Shareholders' equity	3,100	2,200	19.6%	17.3%
Total liabilities and equity	$15,800	$12,700	100.0%	100.0%

The Comparative Balance Sheet

A comparative balance sheet presents side-by-side information about an entity's assets, liabilities, and shareholders' equity as of multiple points in time. For example, a comparative balance sheet could present the balance sheet as of the end of each year for the past three years. Another variation is to present the balance sheet as of the end of each month for the past 12 months on a rolling basis. In both cases, the intent is to provide the reader with a series of snapshots of a company's financial condition over a period of time, which is useful for developing trend line analyses.

The comparative balance sheet is not required under the GAAP accounting framework for a privately-held company, but the Securities and Exchange Commission (SEC) does require it in numerous circumstances for the reports issued by publicly-held companies, particularly the annual Form 10-K and the quarterly Form 10-Q. The usual SEC requirement is to report a comparative balance sheet for the past two years, with additional requirements for quarterly reporting.

There is no standard format for a comparative balance sheet. It is somewhat more common to report the balance sheet as of the least recent period furthest to the right, though the reverse is the case when you are reporting balance sheets in a trailing twelve months format.

The following is a sample of a comparative balance sheet that contains the balance sheet as of the end of a company's fiscal year for each of the past three years.

Sample Comparative Balance Sheet

	as of 12/31/20X3	as of 12/31/20X2	as of 12/31/20X1
Current assets			
Cash	$1,200,000	$900,000	$750,000
Accounts receivable	4,800,000	3,600,000	3,000,000
Inventory	3,600,000	2,700,000	2,300,000
Total current assets	$9,600,000	$7,200,000	$6,050,000
Total fixed assets	6,200,000	5,500,000	5,000,000
Total assets	$15,800,000	$12,700,000	$11,050,000
Current liabilities			
Accounts payable	$2,400,000	$1,800,000	$1,500,000
Accrued expenses	480,000	360,000	300,000
Short-term debt	800,000	600,000	400,000
Total current liabilities	$3,680,000	$2,760,000	$2,200,000
Long-term debt	9,020,000	7,740,000	7,350,000
Total liabilities	$12,700,000	$10,500,000	$9,550,000
Shareholders' equity	3,100,000	2,200,000	1,500,000
Total liabilities and equity	$15,800,000	$12,700,000	$11,050,000

The sample comparative balance sheet reveals that the company has increased the size of its current assets over the past few years, but has also recently invested in a large amount of additional fixed assets that have likely been the cause of a significant boost in its long-term debt.

The Nonprofit Balance Sheet

A nonprofit organization needs to report the state of its assets and liabilities as of the end of each reporting period. In a for-profit business, the financial statement used to report this information is the balance sheet. A nonprofit entity reports similar information in the statement of financial position. The main difference between a balance sheet and a nonprofit's statement of financial position is that the balance sheet contains a shareholders' equity section, which is replaced by a net assets section in the statement of financial position.

A simplified statement of financial position format follows:

Archimedes Education
Statement of Financial Position
As of April 30, 20X1

ASSETS		LIABILITIES AND NET ASSETS	
Cash and cash equivalents	$25,000	Accounts payable	$12,000
Accounts and pledges receivable	63,000	Accrued expenses	5,000
Prepaid expenses	5,000	Grants payable	14,000
Investments	10,000	Deferred revenue	8,000
Fixed assets	180,000	Debt	10,000
		Net assets:	
		Unrestricted net assets	114,000
		Temporarily restricted net assets	75,000
		Permanently restricted net assets	45,000
Total assets	$283,000	Total liabilities and net assets	$283,000

The main intent of reporting this information is to show to donors that the entity is relatively liquid, and so will not go out of business after a large donation is made. If a nonprofit is borrowing money from a lender, the lender may examine this statement to see if the nonprofit is liquid enough to pay back borrowed funds.

The net asset classification in the statement of financial position is the equivalent of retained earnings in the balance sheet of a for-profit business. When contributing assets, a donor may impose no restrictions, temporary restrictions, or permanent restrictions on their use. The result is three types of net assets, which are classified as unrestricted, temporarily restricted, and permanently restricted. The accounting for these different types of net assets varies, depending on which type of restriction is imposed. The differences are noted in the following sub-sections.

Unrestricted Net Assets

When a donor imposes no restriction on a contribution made to a nonprofit, the nonprofit records the contribution as an asset and as unrestricted contribution revenue. These funds are used to pay for the general operations of a nonprofit. The fundraising staff strongly encourages donors to make unrestricted donations, since these funds can be put to the broadest possible range of uses. Since this contribution revenue also creates a profit, the profit appears in the statement of financial position as an increase in unrestricted net assets.

Temporarily Restricted Net Assets

When a donor imposes a temporary restriction on a contribution made to a nonprofit, the nonprofit records the contribution as an asset and as temporarily restricted contribution revenue. Since this revenue also creates a profit, the profit appears in the statement of financial position as an increase in temporarily restricted net assets. Only the donor can change this designation; a nonprofit's board of directors is not allowed to do so.

The intent when using this type of account is for the funds recorded within it to gradually be used up, so that the balance trends toward zero over time, unless replenished by additional contributions.

There may be a number of sub-accounts within a temporarily restricted net asset, for those situations in which donors want to contribute to specific aspects of a project, or to release funds for use over a period of time. For example, when a museum is being built, donors may only want to contribute to certain exhibits or rooms within the museum. Or, donors may want their contributions to be spent evenly over the next five years.

Permanently Restricted Net Assets

When a donor imposes a permanent restriction on the use of donated funds, this means that the asset must continue to be held by the nonprofit in perpetuity, usually allowing the nonprofit to only spend any interest income derived from the funds. The income from these funds is likely to be unrestricted. In this case, the initial contribution is recorded as an asset and as permanently restricted contribution revenue. Again, since this revenue also generates a profit, the profit appears in the statement of financial position as an increase in permanently restricted net assets.

The balance in this account tends to increase over time, since the entity is prevented from using the underlying contribution, and additional donations may be made.

How to Construct the Balance Sheet

When using an accounting software package, it is quite easy to construct the balance sheet. Just access the report writing module, select the time period for which you want to print the balance sheet, and print it.

Tip: It is generally not necessary to create a custom version of the balance sheet in the accounting software package, since the default version is usually sufficient. If you choose to do so, test it by verifying that the total of all asset line items equals the total of all liability and equity line items. An error is usually caused by some accounts not being included in the custom report, or added to the custom report multiple times.

If you choose to construct the balance sheet manually, follow these steps:

1. Create the trial balance report (see the Trial Balance chapter).
2. List each account pertaining to the balance sheet in a separate column of the trial balance.
3. Add the difference between the revenue and expense line items on the trial balance to a separate line item in the equity section of the balance sheet.
4. Aggregate these line items into those you want to report in the balance sheet as a separate line item.
5. Shift the result into the format of the balance sheet that you prefer.

The following example illustrates the construction of a balance sheet.

EXAMPLE

The accounting software for Lowry Locomotion breaks down at the end of July, and the controller has to create the financial statements by hand. He has a copy of Lowry's trial balance, which is shown below. He transfers this information to an electronic spreadsheet, creates separate columns for accounts to include in the balance sheet, and copies those balances into the designated columns. This leaves a number of accounts related to the income statement, which he can ignore for the purposes of creating the balance sheet. However, he *does* include the net loss for the period in the "Current year profit" row, which is included in the equity section of the balance sheet.

Lowry Locomotion Extended Trial Balance

	Adjusted Trial Balance		Balance Sheet		Aggregation	
	Debit	Credit	Debit	Credit	Debit	Credit
Cash	$60,000		$60,000		$60,000	
Accounts receivable	230,000		230,000		230,000	
Inventory	300,000		300,000		300,000	
Fixed assets (net)	210,000		210,000		210,000	
Accounts payable		$90,000		$90,000		$165,000
Accrued liabilities		75,000		75,000		
Notes payable		420,000		420,000		420,000
Equity		350,000		350,000		215,000
Current year profit			135,000			
Revenue		450,000				
Cost of goods sold	290,000					
Salaries expense	225,000					
Payroll tax expense	20,000					
Rent expense	35,000					
Other expenses	15,000					
Totals	$1,385,000	$1,385,000	$935,000	$935,000	$800,000	$800,000

In the "Aggregation" columns of the extended trial balance, the controller has aggregated the liabilities for accounts payable and accrued liabilities in the accounts payable line, and aggregated equity and current year profit into the equity line. He then transfers this information into the following condensed balance sheet:

Lowry Locomotion
Income Statement
For the month ended July 31, 20X1

Assets	
Cash	$60,000
Accounts receivable	230,000
Inventory	300,000
Fixed assets	210,000
Total assets	**$800,000**
Liabilities	
Accounts payable	$165,000
Notes payable	420,000
Total liabilities	$585,000
Equity	$215,000
Total liabilities and equity	**$800,000**

Other Balance Sheet Topics

The following additional topics relate to the balance sheet, and can be of use to someone new to the creation of this report who wants to understand the types of information contained within it.

Does an Expense Appear on the Balance Sheet?

When you record an expense, it most obviously appears within a line item on the income statement. It also appears more indirectly on the balance sheet. For example, an expense reduces profits, so when you record an expense, the retained earnings line item within the equity section of the balance sheet will always decline by the same amount as the expense. In addition, either the asset side of the balance sheet will decline or the liabilities side will increase by the amount of the expense, thereby keeping the balance sheet in balance. Here are examples of where the changes may occur:

- *Assets*. Cash declines if you paid the expense item in cash, or inventory declines if you wrote off some inventory.
- *Contra asset accounts*. The accumulated depreciation contra account increases if you created a depreciation charge.
- *Liabilities*. Accrued expenses increase if you created an expense accrual, or accounts payable increase if you recorded a supplier invoice that is not yet paid.

163

Where do Accruals Appear on the Balance Sheet?

If you record an accrual for an expense, you are debiting the expense account and crediting an accrued liability account. Since an accrued expense is usually only for a very limited period of time (such as to record an expense for a supplier invoice that will probably arrive next month), this is a current liability. Therefore, when you accrue an expense, it appears in the current liabilities portion of the balance sheet.

It is possible, but not likely, that an accrued expense might appear in the balance sheet under long-term liabilities, but only if you do not plan to settle the liability for more than a year.

If you record an accrual for revenue that has not yet been billed, you are crediting the revenue account and debiting an unbilled revenue account. The unbilled revenue account should appear in the current assets portion of the balance sheet.

What is Order of Liquidity?

Order of liquidity is the presentation of assets in the balance sheet in order of the amount of time it would usually take to convert them into cash. Thus, cash is always presented first, followed by marketable securities, then accounts receivable, then inventory, and then fixed assets. Goodwill is listed last. The approximate amount of time required to convert each type of asset into cash is noted below:

- *Cash*. No conversion is needed.
- *Marketable securities*. A few days may be required to convert to cash in most cases.
- *Accounts receivable*. Will convert to cash in accordance with the company's normal credit terms, or can be converted to cash immediately through factoring the receivables.
- *Inventory*. Could require multiple months to convert to cash, depending on turnover levels and the proportion of inventory items for which there is not a ready resale market. It may even be impossible to convert to cash without accepting a significant discount.
- *Fixed assets*. Conversion to cash depends entirely on the presence of an active after-market for these items.
- *Goodwill*. This can only be converted to cash upon the sale of the business for an adequate price, and so should be listed last.

The order of liquidity concept is not used for the revenues or expenses in the income statement, since the liquidity concept does not apply to them.

Summary

Though a number of formats for the balance sheet were shown in this chapter, the most common one by far for internal reporting purposes is to present it only as of the end of the accounting period being reported – comparative balance sheets are usually only used by publicly-held companies or in situations where a business is specifically issuing financial statements meant to cover multiple reporting periods.

In the author's opinion, a better approach than single-period reporting is to configure the report writer in the accounting software to automatically issue a multi-period balance sheet that shows the balance sheet as of the end of each of the last 12 months. This gives management an excellent view of trends for key assets and liabilities. This format is superior to the single-period balance sheet, and should replace it when possible.

Chapter 14
The Statement of Cash Flows

Introduction

The statement of cash flows is the least used of the financial statements, and may not be issued at all for internal financial reporting purposes. The recipients of financial statements seem to be mostly concerned with the profit information on the income statement, and to a lesser degree with the financial position information on the balance sheet. Nonetheless, the cash flows on the statement of cash flows can provide valuable information, especially when combined with the other elements of the financial statements. At a minimum, be prepared to construct a statement of cash flows for the annual financial statements, which will presumably be issued outside of the company.

This chapter addresses the two formats used for the statement of cash flows, as well as how to assemble the information needed for the statement.

Overview of the Statement of Cash Flows

The statement of cash flows contains information about the flows of cash into and out of a company; in particular, it shows the extent of those company activities that generate and use cash and cash equivalents. It is particularly useful for assessing the differences between net income and the related cash receipts and payments.

> **Note:** A cash equivalent is a highly liquid investment having a maturity of three months or less. It should be at minimal risk of a change in value. Examples of cash equivalents are marketable securities, money market funds, and short-term government bonds. To be classified as a cash equivalent, an item must be unrestricted, so that it is available for immediate use.

The statement of cash flows does not replace the income statement. The income statement measures the revenues, expenses, and profit or loss generated during a reporting period. The cash flows that appear on the statement of cash flows do not necessarily match the income and loss information on the income statement, so both statements are needed to provide the most complete picture of the results generated by an entity.

Statement Objectives

The reader of an entity's financial statements should be able to assess the following when the statement of cash flows is included in the reporting package:
- The ability of the entity to generate positive cash flows in the future.

166

- The ability of the entity to pay its obligations.
- The ability of the entity to obtain financing.
- The reasons why there are differences between reported net income and cash flows.
- The impact of investing and financing activities on the entity's financial position.

Statement Requirements

The following general requirements apply to the statement of cash flows:
- *Cash balance matching.* The beginning and ending amounts of cash and cash equivalents shown in the statement of cash flows should match the amounts of cash and cash equivalents shown in the balance sheet for the same dates.
- *Format.* Entities are encouraged to use the direct method of report presentation (see the next section).
- *Reconciliation.* There shall be a reconciliation of the net income of a business to its net cash flow from operating activities, which shall report all major classes of reconciling items in separate line items. If the direct method is used (see the next section), the reconciliation shall be provided in a separate schedule. If the indirect method is used (see the Indirect Method section), the reconciliation can be integrated into the statement of cash flows, or provided as a separate schedule.
- *Gross reporting.* Cash inflows related to a financing or investing event should be separately reported from cash outflows. For example, the amounts spent to acquire fixed assets should be stated separately from the amounts received from the sale of fixed assets.

EXAMPLE

Teton Helicopter Rescue sells a helicopter and uses the proceeds to buy another helicopter. The proceeds from the sale of the old helicopter should be presented separately from the funds used to buy the replacement.

Territorial Lease Corporation issues bonds, and uses the proceeds to pay off an existing debt obligation. The proceeds from the bond issuance should be reported separately from the funds used to pay off the old debt.

Reporting Classifications

In the statement of cash flows, cash flow information is to be reported within three separate classifications. The use of classifications is intended to improve the quality of the information presented. These classifications are:
- *Operating activities.* These are an entity's primary revenue-producing activities. Operating activities is the default classification, so if a cash flow

does not belong in either of the following two classifications, it belongs in this classification. Operating cash flows are generally associated with revenues and expenses. Examples of cash inflows from operating activities are cash receipts from the sale of goods or services, accounts receivable, lawsuit settlements, normal insurance settlements, and supplier refunds. Examples of cash outflows for operating activities are for payments to employees and suppliers, fees and fines, lawsuit settlements, cash payments to lenders for interest, contributions to charity, cash refunds to customers, and the settlement of asset retirement obligations. Sample operating activities are segregated into cash inflows and outflows in the following table.

Sample Operating Activity Cash Inflows and Outflows

Cash Inflows	Cash Outflows
Cash receipts from the sale of goods and services	Cash payments to employees
Cash receipts from the collection of receivables	Cash payments to suppliers
Cash receipts from lawsuit settlements	Cash payment of fines
Cash receipts from settlement of insurance claims	Cash payments to settle lawsuits
Cash receipts from supplier refunds	Cash payments of taxes
Cash receipts from licensees	Cash refunds to customers
	Cash payments to settle asset retirement obligations
	Cash payment of interest to creditors
	Cash payment of contributions

- *Investing activities.* These are investments in productive assets, as well as in the debt and equity securities issued by other entities. These cash flows are generally associated with the purchase or sale of assets. Examples are cash receipts from the sale or collection of loans, the sale of securities issued by other entities, the sale of long-term assets, and the proceeds from insurance settlements related to damaged property. Examples of cash outflows from investing activities are cash payments for loans made to other entities, the purchase of the debt or equity of other entities, and the purchase of fixed assets (including capitalized interest). Sample investing activities are segregated into cash inflows and outflows in the following table.

Sample Investing Activity Cash Inflows and Outflows

Cash Inflows	Cash Outflows
Cash receipts from the sale of equity investments	Cash payments made to acquire equity investments
Cash receipts from the collection of principal on a loan	Cash payments made to acquire debt securities
Cash receipts from the sale of fixed assets	Cash payments made to acquire fixed assets

- *Financing activities*. These are the activities resulting in alterations to the amount of contributed equity and an entity's borrowings. These cash flows are generally associated with liabilities or equity, and involve transactions between the reporting entity and its providers of capital. Examples are cash receipts from the sale of an entity's own equity instruments or from issuing debt, and proceeds from derivative instruments. Examples of cash outflows from financing activities are cash outlays for dividends, share repurchases, payments for debt issuance costs, and the pay down of outstanding debt. Sample financing activities are segregated into cash inflows and outflows in the following table.

Sample Financing Activity Cash Inflows and Outflows

Cash Inflows	Cash Outflows
Cash receipts from the sale of company shares	Cash payments to pay dividends
Cash receipts from the issuance of debt instruments	Cash payments to buy back company shares
Cash receipts from a mortgage	Cash payments for debt issuance costs
Cash receipts from derivative instruments	Cash payments to pay down principal on debt

The order of presentation in the statement of cash flows is as just described – operating activities, followed by investing activities, and then financing activities.

Some types of cash flows could be classified as being in more than one of the preceding classifications. If so, the designated classification should be based on the activity most likely to provide the majority of cash flows for an item.

EXAMPLE

Mole Industries has a rent-to-purchase feature on its line of trench digging equipment, where customers can initially rent the equipment and then apply the rental payments to an outright purchase. The rental of equipment could be considered an investing activity. However, since the company earns the bulk of its cash flow from the sale of equipment, the cash flows are placed within the operating activities classification.

The *direct method* or the *indirect method* can be used to present the statement of cash flows. The direct method shows cash inflows and outflows in the operating section. The indirect method derives operating cash flows by modifying the net income figure. No matter which method is used, the total amount of cash provided or used by operations is the same. These methods are described in the following sections.

The Direct Method

The direct method of presenting the statement of cash flows presents the specific cash flows associated with items that affect cash flow. Items that typically do so include:

- Cash collected from customers
- Interest and dividends received
- Cash paid to employees
- Cash paid to suppliers
- Interest paid
- Income taxes paid

Though additional disclosures can be made, entities tend to limit their reporting to the preceding line items. The format of the direct method appears in the following example. Also included in the example is a reconciliation of net income to cash from operating activities, which is required when the direct method is used.

EXAMPLE

Lowry Locomotion constructs the following statement of cash flows using the direct method:

Lowry Locomotion
Statement of Cash Flows
For the year ended 12/31/20X1

Cash flows from operating activities		
Cash receipts from customers	$45,800,000	
Cash paid to suppliers	-29,800,000	
Cash paid to employees	-11,200,000	
Cash generated from operations	4,800,000	
Interest paid	-310,000	
Income taxes paid	-1,700,000	
Net cash from operating activities		$2,790,000
Cash flows from investing activities		
Purchase of fixed assets	-580,000	
Proceeds from sale of equipment	110,000	
Net cash used in investing activities		-470,000
Cash flows from financing activities		
Proceeds from issuance of common stock	1,000,000	

Proceeds from issuance of long-term debt	500,000	
Principal payments under capital lease obligation	-10,000	
Dividends paid	-450,000	
Net cash used in financing activities		1,040,000
Net increase in cash and cash equivalents		3,360,000
Cash and cash equivalents at beginning of period		1,640,000
Cash and cash equivalents at end of period		$5,000,000

Reconciliation of net income to net cash provided by operating activities:

Net income		$2,665,000
Adjustments to reconcile net income to net cash provided by operating activities:		
Depreciation and amortization	$125,000	
Provision for losses on accounts receivable	15,000	
Gain on sale of equipment	-155,000	
Increase in interest and income taxes payable	32,000	
Increase in deferred taxes	90,000	
Increase in other liabilities	18,000	
Total adjustments		125,000
Net cash provided by operating activities		$2,790,000

The standard-setting bodies encourage the use of the direct method, but it is rarely used, for the excellent reason that the information in it is difficult to assemble; companies simply do not collect and store information in the manner required for this format. Instead, they use the indirect method, which is described in the following section.

The Indirect Method

Under the indirect method of presenting the statement of cash flows, the presentation begins with net income or loss, with subsequent additions to or deductions from that amount for non-cash revenue and expense items, resulting in cash provided by operating activities. Adjustments to the net income figure that are needed to derive cash flows from operating activities include:

- Accrued revenue
- Accrued expenses, such as a provision for bad debt losses
- Noncash expenses, such as depreciation, amortization, and depletion
- Gains and losses from the sale of assets

- Change in accounts receivable
- Change in inventory
- Change in accounts payable

The format of the indirect method appears in the following example. Note that the indirect method does not include cash inflows and outflows in the cash flows from operating activities section, but rather a derivation of cash flows based on adjustments to net income.

EXAMPLE

Puller Corporation constructs the following statement of cash flows using the indirect method:

Puller Corporation
Statement of Cash Flows
For the year ended 12/31/20X3

Cash flows from operating activities		
Net income		$3,000,000
Adjustments for:		
Depreciation and amortization	$125,000	
Provision for losses on accounts receivable	20,000	
Gain on sale of facility	-65,000	
		80,000
Increase in trade receivables	-250,000	
Decrease in inventories	325,000	
Decrease in trade payables	-50,000	
		25,000
Cash generated from operations		3,105,000
Cash flows from investing activities		
Purchase of fixed assets	-500,000	
Proceeds from sale of equipment	35,000	
Net cash used in investing activities		-465,000
Cash flows from financing activities		
Proceeds from issuance of common stock	150,000	
Proceeds from issuance of long-term debt	175,000	
Dividends paid	-45,000	

Net cash used in financing activities	<u>280,000</u>
Net increase in cash and cash equivalents	2,920,000
Cash and cash equivalents at beginning of period	<u>2,080,000</u>
Cash and cash equivalents at end of period	<u>$5,000,000</u>

When the indirect method is used, the reporting entity should separately disclose the amounts of interest paid and income taxes paid during the period.

The key difference between the direct and indirect methods is the derivation of the cash flows from operating activities section, where the direct method requires the reporting of specific operating activity cash inflows and outflows, while the indirect method backs into this information.

When considering which presentation method to use, consider that the indirect method provides some information that does not relate to cash flows, such as depreciation and loss provisions. The presence of non-cash items in an ostensibly cash-focused report can be confusing to some readers. In addition, a large number of reconciling items can make it difficult to understand the presented information.

The indirect method is very popular, because the information required for it is relatively easily assembled from the accounts that a business normally maintains.

Presentation Variations

The preceding discussions of the direct and indirect methods involved variations on the presentation of the operating activities section of the statement of cash flows. There are also variations on how the information in the investing activities and financing activities sections can be presented. The presentation can employ *grouped activities* or *combined activities*. When activities are *grouped*, related cash inflows and outflows are clustered together. The following sample illustration of a partial statement of cash flows shows the concept.

Grouped Activities in a Partial Statement of Cash Flows

Cash flows from investing activities	
Payments for purchases of investments	-$70,000
Receipts from sale of investments	35,000
Payments for purchases of fixed assets	-300,000
Receipts from sale of fixed assets	28,000
Payments for purchases of businesses	-1,850,000
Receipts from sale of businesses	695,000
Other investing activities	-45,000
Net cash used in investing activities	-$1,507,000
Cash flows from financing activities	
Receipts from long-term debt issuances	1,500,000
Payments on long-term debt issuances	-125,000
Receipts from issuance of common stock	500,000
Payments to buy back common stock	-40,000
Payment of dividends to shareholders	-80,000
Net cash provided by financing activities	$1,755,000

In the sample illustration, note how payments and receipts are paired for each investing and financing activity. For example, payments for the purchase of investments are paired with receipts from the sale of investments. This approach allows the reader to easily determine the net cash flows of paired items.

When activities are *combined*, all cash inflow line items are clustered together, followed by a clustering of all cash outflow items. The following sample illustration of a partial statement of cash flows shows the concept.

Combined Activities in a Partial Statement of Cash Flows

Cash flows from investing activities		
Cash inflows from the sale of investments		
Real estate sales	$2,000,000	
Machinery and equipment sales	425,000	
Liquidation of marketable securities	100,000	
		$2,525,000
Cash outflows for the purchase of investments		
Real estate purchases	-$1,450,000	
Machinery and equipment purchases	-710,000	
Marketable security purchases	-40,000	
		-2,200,000
Net cash provided by investing activities		$325,000
Cash flows from financing activities		
Cash inflows from:		
Long-term debt issuances	$500,000	
Common stock issuances	200,000	
		$700,000
Cash outflows from:		
Principal payments on debt	-$210,000	
Treasury stock purchased	-18,000	
Dividends paid	-30,000	
		-258,000
Net cash provided by financing activities		$442,000

Because of the use of subtotals, the combined activities approach results in a lengthier presentation than the grouped activities approach.

Information Sources

The most commonly used format for the statement of cash flows is the indirect method (as described in a preceding section). The general layout of an indirect method statement of cash flows is shown next, along with an explanation of the sources of the information in the statement.

Company Name
Statement of Cash Flows
For the year ended 12/31/20X1

Line Item	Derivation
Cash flows from operating activities	
Net income	From the net income line on the income statement
Adjustment for:	
Depreciation and amortization	From the corresponding line items in the income statement
Provision for losses on accounts receivable	From the change in the allowance for doubtful accounts in the period
Gain/loss on sale of facility	From the gain/loss accounts in the income statement
Increase/decrease in trade receivables	Change in trade receivables during the period, from the balance sheet
Increase/decrease in inventories	Change in inventories during the period, from the balance sheet
Increase/decrease in trade payables	Change in trade payables during the period, from the balance sheet
Cash generated from operations	Summary of the preceding items in this section
Cash flows from investing activities	
Purchase of fixed assets	Itemized in the fixed asset accounts during the period
Proceeds from sale of fixed assets	Itemized in the fixed asset accounts during the period
Net cash used in investing activities	Summary of the preceding items in this section
Cash flows from financing activities	
Proceeds from issuance of common stock	Net increase in the common stock and additional paid-in capital accounts during the period
Proceeds from issuance of long-term debt	Itemized in the long-term debt account during the period
Dividends paid	Itemized in the retained earnings account during the period
Net cash used in financing activities	Summary of the preceding items in this section
Net change in cash and cash equivalents	Summary of all preceding subtotals

The general layout of the direct method of presentation is shown next, along with an explanation of the sources of the information in the statement.

Company Name
Statement of Cash Flows
For the year ended 12/31/20X1

Line Item	Derivation
Cash flows from operating activities	
Cash receipts from customers	Summary of the cash receipts journal for the period
Cash paid to suppliers	Summary of the cash disbursements journal for the period (less the financing and income tax payments noted below)
Cash paid to employees	Summary of the payroll journal for the period
Cash generated from operations	Summary of the preceding items in this section
Interest paid	Itemized in the cash disbursements journal
Income taxes paid	Itemized in the cash disbursements journal
Net cash from operating activities	Summary of the preceding items in this section
Cash flows from investing activities	
Purchase of fixed assets	Itemized in the fixed asset accounts during the period
Proceeds from sale of fixed assets	Itemized in the fixed asset accounts during the period
Net cash used in investing activities	Summary of the preceding items in this section
Cash flows from financing activities	
Proceeds from issuance of common stock	Net increase in the common stock and additional paid-in capital accounts during the period
Proceeds from issuance of long-term debt	Itemized in the long-term debt account during the period
Principal payment under capital leases	Itemized in the capital leases liability account during the period
Dividends paid	Itemized in the retained earnings account during the period
Net cash used in financing activities	Summary of the preceding items in this section
Net change in cash and cash equivalents	Summary of all preceding subtotals

As can be seen from the explanations for both methods, the statement of cash flows is much more difficult to create than the income statement and balance sheet. In fact, a complete statement may require a substantial supporting spreadsheet that shows the details for each line item in the statement.

If an entity's accounting software contains a template for the statement of cash flows, then use it! The information may not be aggregated quite correctly, and it may not contain all of the line items required for the statement, but it *will* produce most of the needed information, and is much easier to modify than the alternative of creating the statement entirely by hand.

Illustration of the Preparation of a Statement of Cash Flows

In this section, we present a sample business, Prickly Corporation, along with selected information from its income statement and balance sheet. We then describe how this information is converted into a statement of cash flows.

Selected financial information for Prickly is as follows:

Condensed Income Statement

Revenue		$1,000,000
Cost of goods sold	$575,000	
Administrative expenses	300,000	
Depreciation expense	25,000	
Total expenses		900,000
Net income		$100,000

Change in Certain Balance Sheet Accounts

Cash	+$15,000
Accounts receivable	+30,000
Inventory	+80,000
Fixed assets	+45,000
Accounts payable	+35,000
Common stock	+10,000

Based on the preceding financial information, we can derive the following statement of cash flows for Prickly, using the direct method of presentation. In the following statement, we note the explanation for each line item calculation in the "Explanation" column.

The Statement of Cash Flows

Prickly Corporation
Statement of Cash Flows
For the Year Ended December 31, 20X1

Cash flows from operating activities		Explanation
Cash receipts from customers	$970,000	Revenue – receivable increase
Cash paid to suppliers	-620,000	Cost of sales + inventory increase – payables increase
Administrative expenses	-300,000	Taken from the income statement
Net cash from operating activities	50,000	
Cash flows from investing activities		
Purchase of fixed assets	-45,000	Change in fixed assets in the period
Cash flows from financing activities		
Sale of common stock	10,000	Change in common stock in the period
Net increase in cash	$15,000	Calculated from preceding subtotals

We can also use the preceding financial information to derive a statement of cash flows using the indirect method, which is presented next. Again, we note the explanation for each line item in the "Explanation" column.

Prickly Corporation
Statement of Cash Flows
For the Year Ended December 31, 20X1

Cash flows from operating activities		Explanation
Net income	$100,000	Taken from the income statement
Adjustments to reconcile net income to net cash provided by operating activities:		
Depreciation	25,000	Taken from the income statement
Increase in receivables	-30,000	Change in receivables in the period
Increase in inventory	-80,000	Change in inventory in the period
Increase in payables	35,000	Change in payables in the period
Cash generated from operations	50,000	
Cash flows from investing activities		
Purchase of fixed assets	-45,000	Change in fixed assets in the period
Cash flows from financing activities		
Sale of common stock	10,000	Change in common stock in the period
Net increase in cash	$15,000	Calculated from preceding subtotals

Note that the total change in cash stated in the final line item is the same, no matter which method is used.

Summary

The statement of cash flows is a useful ancillary statement that sometimes accompanies the income statement and balance sheet. It can be difficult to assemble, unless it is available as an accounting software template, which is why it tends to be treated as an occasional add-on to the other elements of the financial statements. If you plan to issue it, we strongly recommend using the indirect method, since it can be much more easily assembled from the general ledger than the direct method.

Chapter 15
The Statement of Retained Earnings

Introduction

The statement of retained earnings, also known as the statement of shareholders' equity, is essentially a reconciliation of the beginning and ending balances in a company's equity during an accounting period. It is not considered an essential part of the monthly financial statements, and so is the most likely of all the financial statements not to be issued. However, it is a common part of the annual financial statements. This chapter discusses the format of the statement and how to create it.

Overview of the Statement of Retained Earnings

The statement of retained earnings reconciles changes in the retained earnings account during an accounting period. The statement starts with the beginning balance in the retained earnings account, and then adds or subtracts such items as profits and dividend payments to arrive at the ending retained earnings balance. The general calculation structure of the statement is:

Beginning retained earnings + Net income − Dividends +/- Other changes
= Ending retained earnings

The statement of retained earnings is most commonly presented as a separate statement, but can also be added to another financial statement. The following example shows a simplified format for the statement.

EXAMPLE

The controller of Lowry Locomotion assembles the following statement of retained earnings to accompany his issuance of the financial statements of the company:

Lowry Locomotion
Statement of Retained Earnings
For the year ended 12/31/20X1

Retained earnings at December 31, 20X0	$150,000
Net income for the year ended December 31, 20X1	40,000
Dividends paid to shareholders	-25,000
Retained earnings at December 31, 20X1	$165,000

It is also possible to provide a greatly expanded version of the statement of retained earnings that discloses the various elements of retained earnings. For example, it could separately identify the par value of common stock, additional paid-in capital, retained earnings, and treasury stock, with all of these elements then rolling up into the total just noted in the last example. The following example shows what the format could look like.

EXAMPLE

The controller of Lowry Locomotion creates an expanded version of the statement of retained earnings in order to provide more visibility into activities involving equity. The statement follows:

Lowry Locomotion
Statement of Retained Earnings
For the year ended 12/31/20X1

	Common Stock, $1 par	Additional Paid-in Capital	Retained Earnings	Total Shareholders' Equity
Retained earnings at December 31, 20X0	$10,000	$40,000	$100,000	$150,000
Net income for the year ended December 31, 20X1			40,000	40,000
Dividends paid to shareholders			-25,000	-25,000
Retained earnings at December 31, 20X1	$10,000	$40,000	$115,000	$165,000

How to Prepare the Statement of Retained Earnings

A simplified version of the statement of retained earnings was shown in the first of the examples in this chapter. This format works well if there are few equity transactions during the year. However, a more active environment calls for a considerable amount of detail in the statement. In the latter case, consider following these steps:

1. Create separate accounts in the general ledger for each type of equity. Thus, there are different accounts for the par value of stock, additional paid-in capital, and retained earnings. Each of these accounts is represented by a separate column in the statement.
2. Transfer every transaction within each equity account to a spreadsheet, and identify it in the spreadsheet.
3. Aggregate the transactions within the spreadsheet into similar types, and transfer them to separate line items in the statement of retained earnings.

4. Complete the statement, and verify that the beginning and ending balances in it match the general ledger, and that the aggregated line items within it add up to the ending balances for all columns.

If you do not use the spreadsheet recommended in the preceding steps, you may find it difficult to compile the aggregated line items in the statement, resulting in incorrect subtotals and totals within the statement.

Summary

The statement of retained earnings is nothing more than a reconciliation of the equity accounts, and so is not a key part of the monthly financial statements. Instead, only issue it as part of the annual financial statements. However, if you only create it once a year, you may find that even a small number of equity transactions can be surprisingly difficult to convert into the format of the statement. Consequently, consider maintaining on a spreadsheet an informal running total of changes in the equity accounts. This makes it easier to assemble the final statement of retained earnings at the end of the year.

Chapter 16
Financial Statement Disclosures

Introduction

Financial statement disclosures are explanatory and supplemental notes that accompany the financial statements issued by a business. The exact nature of these footnotes varies, depending upon the framework used to construct the financial statements (such as GAAP or IFRS). Financial statement disclosures are an integral part of the financial statements, so you must issue them under some circumstances to users along with the financial statements.

There are an enormous number of detailed disclosures that may be required, depending upon the types of business transactions that a company engages in, and the industry in which it does business. An even more extensive set of footnotes are required by the Securities and Exchange Commission of any publicly-held company when they issue their annual financial statements on the Form 10-K and quarterly financial statements on the Form 10-Q.

In this chapter, we provide a sampling of the types of disclosures that you may need to append to the financial statements, along with pertinent examples.

Accounting Disclosures

The number of possible footnote disclosures is extremely large. The following list touches upon the more common footnotes, and is by no means even remotely comprehensive. If your company is in a specialized industry, there may be a number of additional disclosures required that are specific to that industry. A representative set of financial statement disclosures include:

- *Accounting policies*. Describe significant accounting principles followed. For example:

  Cash and Cash Equivalents

  We consider all highly liquid instruments purchased with an original maturity of three months or less to be cash equivalents. We continually monitor our positions with, and the credit quality of, the financial institutions with which we invest. As of the balance sheet dates, and periodically throughout the year, we have maintained balances in various operating accounts in excess of federally insured limits.

  Concentrations of Credit Risk

  We grant credit in the normal course of business, primarily consisting of accounts receivable and subscriptions receivable. We periodically perform credit analyses and monitor the financial condition of our major customers to reduce credit risk.

Trade Accounts Receivable

At the time accounts receivable originate, we consider the need for an allowance for doubtful accounts. We continually review the provision for uncollectible amounts; we adjust it to maintain the allowance at a level considered adequate to cover future losses. The allowance is our best estimate of uncollectible amounts; we determine it based on historical performance which we track on an ongoing basis. The losses we ultimately incur may differ materially in the near term from the amounts estimated in determining the allowance.

Identifiable Intangible Assets and Goodwill

We account for our business acquisitions using the acquisition method of accounting, which allocates the total cost of an acquisition to the underlying net assets based on their respective estimated fair values. As part of this allocation process, we identify and attribute values and estimated lives to the intangible assets acquired. We amortize identifiable intangible assets with finite lives on a straight-line basis over their respective lives.

- *Bad debts.* Note the method used to derive bad debt reserves, and the reserve amount as of the balance sheet date. For example:

   The company derives an allowance for doubtful accounts based on its actual bad debt losses over the preceding year, divided by the average accounts receivable balance in the measurement period. In addition, management believes that general economic conditions are worsening, and so has increased this reserve percentage from the calculated amount of 1.9% to 2.5% of outstanding receivables. In addition, the company recognizes a 100% bad debt reserve for any receivables that are more than 120 days old. These policies resulted in an ending allowance for doubtful accounts of $329,000.

- *Business combinations.* Describe the type of combination, the reason for the acquisition, the payment price, liabilities assumed, goodwill incurred, acquisition-related costs, and many other factors. For example:

   The company acquired T-Rex Construction in July 20x4 by paying $17.25 per share for all of the common shares of T-Rex outstanding. T-Rex rents cranes and ditch-digging equipment to construction contractors on a short-term basis. The company funded this acquisition with a long-term loan for $12,000,000 and $4,500,000 from its cash reserves. The purchase was allocated to the assets acquired and liabilities assumed, based on the estimated fair value of T-Rex as of the acquisition date. As a result of the transaction, the company recorded $1,000,000 of goodwill, as well as $2,900,000 of intangible assets that are attributable to customer relationships and non-competition agreements that have useful lives of four years. The operating results of T-Rex are included in the company's consolidated financial statements as of the effective date of the acquisition.

- *Cash.* Note any uninsured cash balances or restrictions on the use of cash. For example:

  (1) The board of directors has authorized the restriction of $500,000 as a reserve in anticipation of a groundwater pollution settlement with the Environmental Protection Agency. This left approximately $2,400,000 in restricted cash as of the balance sheet date.

  (2) The company uses cash concentration systems to maximize its investment strategy. Doing so routinely results in cash investments exceeding Federal Deposit Insurance Corporation (FDIC) insurance limits. As of the balance sheet date, $2,000,000 held as cash reserves exceeded the FDIC insurance limits.

  (3) The company maintains a $350,000 compensating balance arrangement with Bank Eastern (Eastern) under the terms of its line of credit with Eastern. The terms allow Eastern to segregate this amount in a separate account, and prohibit use of the cash unless the line of credit balance is lower than $1,000,000.

- *Contingencies and commitments.* Describe the nature of any reasonably possible losses, and any guarantees, including maximum liabilities. For example:

  (1) The company has a contingent liability related to a groundwater contamination claim at its Stillwater facility. A settlement of $15,000,000 has been established through judicial hearings, but the company's insurance provider is claiming that it has no obligation to reimburse the company for the amount of the settlement. Company counsel believes that the claim of the insurance company is not valid, and that it will be forced to pay the company for the full amount of the settlement.

  (2) The company has guaranteed a term loan held by a key supplier, under which the company is liable for both the unpaid balance of the loan and any unpaid interest, though only after the lender has made a good-faith effort to collect these amounts from the supplier. The unpaid amount of principal and interest on the loan as of the balance sheet date was $1,400,000.

- *Customers.* State whether any customers comprise a significant proportion of the company's total business, and the amount of that proportion. For example:

The company transacts a significant amount of its business with two customers. One customer comprises 20% of net revenues for the entire business, and 40% of the revenues for the Agricultural Products segment. The second customer comprises 24% of net revenues for the entire business, and 70% of the revenues for the Government Products business.

- *Debt.* Describe loans payable, interest rates, and maturities occurring over the next five years. For example:

    (1) The company has obtained an unsecured fixed-rate loan from Bank Eastern. Under the terms of the loan, the company pays a fixed 8.0% interest rate on $3,500,000 of debt. The loan requires principal payments of $500,000 at the end of each of the first three years of the loan, with the remaining principal balance due in a balloon payment on the termination date of the loan, which is December 15, 20x4.

    (2) The company has entered into a line of credit arrangement with Bank Eastern (Eastern). Under the terms of the agreement, the company pays an interest rate equal to the Eastern prime lending rate plus one percent, which equates to a 7.25% borrowing rate as of the date of the arrangement. The company can borrow up to $3,000,000 under the line of credit, and has used $400,000 of the facility as of the balance sheet date. There are no covenants associated with the line of credit.

- *Endowments.* Note the total amount of any deficiencies in donor-restricted endowment funds, where the fair value is less than the amount required by donors or the law. For example:

    The entity's endowment management policy stipulates that any changes in the consumer price index that deflate the value of an endowment be added back into the endowment, thereby preserving the inflation-adjusted value of the endowment. After this adjustment is made, all remaining funds earned from investment activities are made available for appropriation. In the presented year of results, the entity earned $50,000 on its investment activities, returned $15,000 to the endowment funds to preserve their value, and appropriated the remaining $35,000 for current needs.

- *Fixed assets.* Note the investments in various types of fixed assets, methods of depreciation used, the amount of capitalized interest, asset retirement obligations, and impairments. A simplified summary example is:

    We state property and equipment at cost. For all property and equipment, we calculate depreciation utilizing the straight-line method over the estimated useful lives for owned assets or to the estimated salvage value, where appropriate, or over the related lease terms for leasehold improvements. Useful lives range from 1 to 7 years. Property and equipment include the following approximate amounts:

	December 31, 20x3
Computer equipment	$580,000
Software	429,000
Furniture and fixtures	161,000
Office equipment	23,000
Leasehold improvements	78,000
Less: Accumulated depreciation	-213,000
Fixed assets, net	$1,058,000

- *Goodwill and intangibles.* Reconcile any changes in goodwill during the period, and any impairment losses. For example:

  (1) The company recorded $1,000,000 of intangible assets related to the patents that it acquired as part of the J.C. Fellows acquisition. The company is amortizing these patents over ten years, which matches the remaining term of the acquired patents.

  (2) The company has written down its goodwill asset by $900,000. The reason for the write-down is that the company has elected to exit the cellphone tower market, and the $900,000 write-down is associated with the company's purchase of the MicroTower Company, which will be closed as a result of this decision.

- *Hedging.* State the objective and strategies for using a hedging instrument, as well as the risks being hedged. For example:

  The company designates selected futures contracts as fair value hedges of firm commitments to purchase sugar cane for ethanol production. Changes in the fair value of a derivative that is highly effective and that is classified and qualified as a fair value hedge, as well as the gain or loss on the hedged item that is attributable to the hedged risk are recorded in the results of the current period.

  An ineffective hedge results from a change in the fair value of the hedge that differs from fair value changes for the hedged item. The recorded amount of ineffectiveness related to the company's designated fair value hedges was insignificant during the fiscal year.

- *Impairments.* Describe any assets that have been impaired and the amount of the impairment. For example:

  The company has written down the value of the tanning beds used in its tanning salons, on the grounds that federal regulations have significantly reduced the resale prices of these units. The company hired an independent appraiser to determine the fair market values to which the book values of the tanning beds were reduced. The impairment loss was $320,000, and was recorded within the Other Gains and Losses line item in the income statement. Following the impairment charge, the book value of the tanning beds was $800,000.

- *Inventories.* Describe any cost flow assumptions used, as well as any lower of cost or market losses. For example:

  The company uses the last in, first out (LIFO) valuation method to calculate the cost of its inventories. The company experienced a loss of $150,000 during the period that was caused by the elimination of LIFO inventory layers. The company also recorded a loss of $100,000 during the period that was caused by the write-down of the cost of inventories to market, under the lower of cost or market rule.

- *Investments.* Note the fair value and unrealized gains and losses on investments. For example:

  (1) The company uses quoted market prices for similar instruments to derive the fair value of its investments, or it estimates the fair value based on the discounted cash flows using interest rates available for similar instruments having approximately the same remaining maturities. Based on these derivations, the company has unrealized gains of approximately $180,000 on investments having an aggregate fair value of $4,300,000.

  (2) The company liquidated $5,000,000 of securities from its held-to-maturity portfolio in order to raise cash to pay off a debt whose covenants had been breached. This liquidation resulted in the recognition of a $50,000 gain.

- *Leases.* Itemize future minimum lease payments. For example:

  The company has entered into a variety of leases for office equipment, furniture and fixtures, all of which are recorded as operating leases. The future minimum lease payments for these leases follow:

20x1	$150,000
20x2	135,000
20x3	70,000
20x4	65,000
20x5	22,000
	$442,000

- *Liabilities.* Describe any larger accrued liabilities. For example:

  The company accrues a liability for the amount of any vacation and sick time earned but not used by its employees. The company allows employees to accumulate up to four weeks of vacation time, while the potential amount of sick time that may be accrued is not limited. The company has accrued $620,000 for this liability.

- *Pensions.* Reconcile various elements of the company pension plan during the period, and describe investment policies. For example:

  (1) The investment policy of the pension plan is to balance the maintenance of a productive capital base with superior investment results. To do so, the plan invests approximately 50% in equities and 50% in debt securities. These proportions are altered over time in reaction to market conditions related to interest rates, inflation, and other factors.

  (2) The changes in the projected benefit obligation of plan assets for the year ended December 31 were as follows:

	December 31, 20x1
Net benefit obligation – beginning of year	$472,000
Service costs incurred	5,000
Employee contributions	20,000
Interest costs on projected benefit obligations	12,000
Actuarial gain	-14,000
Gross benefits paid	-28,000
Plan amendment	1,000
Foreign currency exchange rate change	7,000
Net benefit obligation – end of year	$475,000

- *Receivables.* Note the carrying amount of any financial instruments that are used as collateral for borrowings, and concentrations of credit risk. For example:

  The company has entered into a short-term loan arrangement with Bank Eastern (Eastern). Under the terms of this arrangement, the company has pledged the full amount of its accounts receivable as collateral on a line of credit. The amount loaned by Eastern is limited to 80% of all accounts receivable less than 90 days old. As of the balance sheet date, the amount of accounts receivable subject to this arrangement was $1,400,000.

- *Related parties.* State the nature of the relationship with a related party, and the amounts due to or from the other party. For example:

  > Mr. Ray Osborne is a director of the company and is also the landlord from which the company leases its headquarters building. The annual total of these lease payments is $1,200,000, which the board of directors has determined is comparable to the current market rate. The lease expires on July 31, 20x5.

- *Revenue recognition.* Note the company's revenue recognition policies. For example:

  (1) The company sells home security monitoring services along with its electronic home security systems. Monitoring revenue is recognized ratably over the term of the monitoring agreements, which varies from 24 to 48 months. As of the balance sheet date, the company had not recognized $3,700,000 of monitoring revenues.

  (2) The company sells solar panel arrays to customers at cost, and also earns 10% of any cost savings experienced by customers for the first three years following installation. The amounts of these savings are difficult to ascertain in advance, since they are strongly impacted by weather conditions. Thus, the company only recognizes its share of cost savings after the actual savings have been calculated, which is done in the month following each calendar quarter.

  (3) The company recognizes revenue under the specific performance method, where revenue is only recognized after customers have approved specific project milestones to which billable amounts are attached in the project contract.

  (4) The company sells its products through consignment arrangements with a variety of retail stores. Under the terms of these consignment agreements, the company records revenue only after it receives notification of a sale transaction from a consignee.

- *Risks and uncertainties.* Note the use of significant estimates in accounting transactions, as well as various business vulnerabilities. For example:

  (1) Due to the large number of hurricanes that have made landfall in the Louisiana area in the past few years, it is not possible to obtain flood insurance for the company's main processing facility in Louisiana. The company has built drainage systems around the facility and also stockpiled sandbags in case of flooding. Given these risk mitigation steps, management believes that the risk of loss from a hurricane has been reduced.

191

(2) A key component of the company's products is tungsten, which it buys under several long-term contracts from suppliers located in central Africa. These suppliers are based in locations where civil unrest has resulted in rioting over the past few years. In the event of a complete breakdown in tungsten supplies, management believes that it can obtain adequate supplies on the spot market, but at prices approximately 40% higher than those at which it purchases tungsten under its long-term contracts.

- *Segment data.* Identify company segments and the operational results of each one. For example:

  The company has determined that it has two reportable segments, which are direct-to-consumer and pro shops. Other unreported segments include the company's product servicing and warranty insurance businesses. The following table reveals the operations of the company's reportable segments:

	Direct to Consumers	Pro Shops	Other Segments	Total
Revenues	$3,200,000	$4,700,000	$600,000	$8,500,000
Interest revenue	200,000	100,000	0	300,000
Interest expense	50,000	300,000	150,000	500,000
Depreciation	150,000	70,000	20,000	240,000
Segment profit	175,000	200,000	-20,000	355,000
Segment assets	750,000	350,000	100,000	1,200,000

- *Stockholders' equity.* Describe any changes in equity during the period, as well as the terms of any convertible equity and dividends in arrears. For example:

  (1) As of December 31, 20x1, the capital structure of the company consisted of 5,000,000 shares of common stock authorized and 3,250,000 shares outstanding, as well as 1,000,000 shares of preferred stock authorized and 125,000 shares outstanding. Both classes of stock have par values of $0.01 per share. The preferred stockholders are entitled to a $2.50 cumulative recurring dividend by the end of each calendar year, and are entitled to the payback of their original investments in the event of the sale of the business, and before dividends are paid to common stockholders.

  (2) On October 15, 20x2, the board of directors authorized the amendment of the company's articles of incorporation to increase the number of authorized shares of preferred stock to 2,000,000 from the prior level of 1,000,000.

(3) On November 14, 20x2, the board of directors declared a cash dividend of $2.00 per share, payable on December 29, 20x2, to shareholders of record on November 29, 20x2. The distribution of this dividend does not violate any of the company's loan covenants.

(4) The board of directors deferred the payment of $1.00 per share of dividends declared on November 14, 20x2, totaling $500,000, due to a cash shortfall caused by the delayed repatriation of cash from a foreign subsidiary.

- *Subsequent events.* Disclose the nature of subsequent events and estimate their financial effect. For example:

  (1) Subsequent to the reporting period, the company issued 25,000 shares of preferred stock at an average price of $15 per share. This resulted in receipts, net of transactional fees, of $350,000. Management intends to use the funds for a possible acquisition.

  (2) From January 30 through February 12, the company repurchased 2,000,000 shares of its common stock at an average price of $9.90. The total expenditure related to this activity was $19,800,000.

  (3) The company has evaluated subsequent events through April 4, 20x1, the date when the financial statements were issued. The company is not aware of any subsequent events that would require recognition or disclosure in the financial statements.

Clearly, the sheer volume of disclosures can overshadow the financial statements themselves. This can present a considerable problem from the perspective of issuing the footnotes in a timely manner, since they are manually generated separately from the financial statements. Thus, if you make a change in the financial statements, it may impact a number of disclosures in the footnotes that must be altered by hand.

Summary

If you are only issuing financial statements for consumption within the company, there is no need to append *any* disclosures to them, which can save an enormous amount of work. Instead, reserve the use of disclosures for the audited or reviewed financial statements, which should not be necessary more than once a year for privately-held companies, and quarterly for publicly-held firms.

If you have hired an auditor to conduct an audit of the financial statements, that person will conduct just as thorough an investigation of the disclosures as of the financial statements, and will base his or her opinion of the financial statements partially on the information contained within the footnotes. Consequently, if you *do* need to include disclosures, spend a considerable amount of time ensuring that they are complete, and that the information in them agrees with the financial statements.

The disclosure examples provided in this chapter are by no means comprehensive. On the contrary, they only provide a taste of the extraordinary range of disclosures that may be required. To make matters more difficult, disclosure requirements change with great regularity. Consequently, consult with your certified public accountant when assembling a complete set of disclosures to accompany your financial statements.

Chapter 17
Segment Reporting

Introduction

If a company is publicly-held, it needs to report segment information, which is part of the disclosures attached to the financial statements. This information is supposedly needed to give the readers of the financial statements more insights into the operations and prospects of a business, as well as to allow them to make more informed judgments about a public entity as a whole. In this chapter, we describe how to determine which business segments to report separately, and how to report that information. The information provided in this chapter does not apply to the following:

- Nonpublic entities
- Not-for-profit entities
- Subsidiaries, unless publicly-held and their financial statements are issued separately
- Joint ventures, unless publicly-held and their financial statements are issued separately

Overview of Segment Reporting

An operating segment is a component of a public entity, and which possesses the following characteristics:

- *Business activities*. It has business activities that can generate revenues and cause expenses to be incurred. This can include revenues and expenses generated by transactions with other operating segments of the same public entity. It can also include activities that do not yet include revenues, such as a start-up business.
- *Results reviewed*. The chief operating decision maker of the public entity regularly reviews its operating results, with the intent of assessing its performance and making decisions about allocating resources to it.
- *Financial results*. Financial results specific to it are available.

Generally, an operating segment has a manager who is accountable to the chief operating decision maker, and who maintains regular contact with that person, though it is also possible that the chief operating decision maker directly manages one or more operating segments.

If a company has a matrix form of organization, where some managers are responsible for geographic regions and others are responsible for products and services, then the results of the products and services are considered to be operating segments.

Some parts of a business are not considered to be reportable business segments under the following circumstances:

- *Corporate overhead.* The corporate group does not usually earn outside revenues, and so is not considered a segment.
- *Post-retirement benefit plans.* A benefit plan can earn income from investments, but it has no operating activities, and so is not considered a segment.
- *One-time events.* If an otherwise-insignificant segment has a one-time event that boosts it into the ranks of reportable segments, do not report it, since there is no long-term expectation for it to remain a reportable segment.

The primary issue with segment reporting is determining which business segments to report. The rules for this selection process are quite specific. Report segment information if a business segment passes any one of the following three tests:

1. *Revenue.* The revenue of the segment is at least 10% of the consolidated revenue of the entire business; or
2. *Profit or loss.* The absolute amount of the profit or loss of the segment is at least 10% of the greater of the combined profits of all the operating segments reporting a profit, or of the combined losses of all operating segments reporting a loss (see the following example for a demonstration of this concept); or
3. *Assets.* The assets of the segment are at least 10% of the combined assets of all the operating segments of the business.

If you run the preceding tests and arrive at a group of reportable segments whose combined revenues are not at least 75% of the consolidated revenue of the entire business, add more segments until the 75% threshold is surpassed.

If you have a business segment that used to qualify as a reportable segment and does not currently qualify, but which you expect to qualify in the future, continue to treat it as a reportable segment.

If there are operating segments that have similar economic characteristics, their results can be aggregated into a single operating segment, but only if they are similar in all of the following areas:

- The nature of their products and services
- The nature of their systems of production
- The nature of their regulatory environments (if applicable)
- Their types of customers
- Their distribution systems

The number of restrictions on this type of reporting makes it unlikely that you would be able to aggregate reportable segments.

After all of the segment testing has been completed, it is possible that there will be a few residual segments that do not qualify for separate reporting. If so, combine the information for these segments into an "other" category and include it in the segment report for the entity. Be sure to describe the sources of revenue included in this "other" category.

Finally, if an operating segment does not meet any of the preceding criteria, it can still be treated as a reportable segment if management decides that information about the segment may be of use to readers of the company's financial statements.

Tip: The variety of methods available for segment testing makes it possible that you will have quite a large number of reportable segments. If so, it can be burdensome to create a report for so many segments, and it may be confusing for the readers of the company's financial statements. Consequently, consider limiting the number of reportable segments to ten; you can aggregate the information for additional segments for reporting purposes.

EXAMPLE

Lowry Locomotion has six business segments whose results it reports internally. Lowry's controller needs to test the various segments to see which ones qualify as being reportable. He collects the following information:

Segment	(000s) Revenue	(000s) Profit	(000s) Loss	(000s) Assets
Diesel locomotives	$120,000	$10,000	$--	$320,000
Electric locomotives	85,000	8,000	--	180,000
Maglev cars	29,000	--	-21,000	90,000
Passenger cars	200,000	32,000		500,000
Toy trains	15,000	--	-4,000	4,000
Trolley cars	62,000	--	-11,000	55,000
	$511,000	$50,000	-$36,000	$1,149,000

In the table, the total profit exceeds the total loss, so the controller uses the total profit for the 10% profit test. The controller then lists the same table again, but now with the losses column removed and with test thresholds at the top of the table that are used to determine which segments are reported. An "X" mark below a test threshold indicates that a segment is reportable. In addition, the controller adds a new column on the right side of the table, which is used to calculate the total revenue for the reportable segments.

Segment	(000s) Revenue	(000s) Profit	(000s) Assets	75% Revenue Test
Reportable threshold (10%)	**$51,100**	**$5,000**	**$114,900**	
Diesel locomotives	X	X	X	$120,000
Electric locomotives	X	X	X	85,000
Maglev cars				
Passenger cars	X	X	X	200,000
Toy trains				
Trolley cars	X			62,000
			Total	$467,000

This analysis shows that the diesel locomotive, electric locomotive, passenger car, and trolley car segments are reportable, and that the combined revenue of these reportable segments easily exceeds the 75% reporting threshold. Consequently, the company does not need to separately report information for any additional segments.

Segment Disclosure

This section contains the disclosures for various aspects of segment reporting that are required under GAAP. At the end of each set of requirements is a sample disclosure containing the more common elements of the requirements.

Segment Disclosure

The key requirement of segment reporting is that the revenue, profit or loss, and assets of each segment be separately reported for any period for which an income statement is presented. In addition, reconcile this segment information back to the company's consolidated results, which requires the inclusion of any adjusting items. Also disclose the methods by which you determined which segments to report. The essential information to include in a segment report includes:
- The types of products and services sold by each segment
- The basis of organization (such as by geographic region or product line)
- Revenues from external customers
- Revenues from inter-company transactions
- Interest income
- Interest expense
- Depreciation, depletion, and amortization expense
- Material expense items
- Income tax expense or income
- Other material non-cash items
- Profit or loss

If an operating segment only has minimal financial operations, it is not necessary to report any information about interest income or interest expense.

The following two items must also be reported if they are included in the determination of segment assets, or are routinely provided to the chief operating decision maker:

- Equity method interests in other entities.
- The total expenditure for additions to fixed assets. Expenditures for most other long-term assets are excluded from this requirement.

The preceding disclosures should be presented along with the following reconciliations, which are separately identified and described:

Category	Reconciliation
Revenues	Total company revenues to reportable segment revenues
Profit or loss	Total consolidated income before income taxes and discontinued operations to reportable segment profit or loss
Assets	Consolidated assets to reportable segment assets
Other items	Consolidated amounts to reportable segment amounts for every other significant item of disclosed segment information

If an operating segment qualifies for the first time as being reportable, also report the usual segment information for it in any prior period segment data that may be presented for comparison purposes, even if the segment was not reportable in the prior period. An exemption is allowed for this prior period reporting if the required information is not available, or if it would be excessively expensive to collect the information.

The operating segment information reported should be the same information reported to the chief operating decision maker for purposes of assessing segment performance and allocating resources. This may result in a difference between the information reported at the segment level and in the public entity's consolidated financial results. If so, disclose the differences between the two figures. This may include a discussion of any policies for the allocation of costs that have been centrally incurred, or the allocation of jointly-used assets.

The following additional items should also be included in the disclosure of operating segment information:

- The basis of accounting for any inter-segment transactions.
- Any changes in the methods used to measure segment profit or loss from the prior period, and the effect of those changes on the reported amount of segment profit or loss.
- A discussion of any asymmetrical allocations, such as the allocation of depreciation expense to a segment without a corresponding allocation of assets.

If a business is reporting condensed financial statements for interim periods, it must disclose the following information for each reportable segment:

- Revenues from external customers for the current quarter and year-to-date, with comparable information for the preceding year
- Revenues from inter-company transactions for the current quarter and year-to-date, with comparable information for the preceding year
- Profit or loss for the current quarter and year-to-date, with comparable information for the preceding year
- Total assets for which there has been a material change from the last annual disclosure
- A description of any differences in the basis of segmentation from the last annual disclosure, or in the method of measuring segment profit or loss
- A reconciliation of the aggregate segment profit or loss to the consolidated income before income taxes and discontinued operations for the public company

If a public entity alters its internal structure to such an extent that the composition of its operating segments is altered, restate its reported results for earlier periods, as well as interim periods, to match the results and financial position of the new internal structure. This requirement is waived if it is impracticable to obtain the required information. The result may be the restatement of some information, but not all of the segment information. If an entity does alter its internal structure, it should disclose whether there has also been a restatement of its segment information for earlier periods. If the entity does not change its prior period information, it must report segment information in the current period under both the old basis and new basis of segmentation, unless it is impracticable to do so.

EXAMPLE

The controller of Lowry Locomotion produces the following segment report for the segments identified in the preceding example:

(000s)	Diesel	Electric	Passenger	Trolley	Other	Consolidated
Revenues	$120,000	$85,000	$200,000	$62,000	$44,000	$511,000
Interest income	11,000	8,000	28,000	8,000	2,000	57,000
Interest expense	--	--	--	11,000	39,000	50,000
Depreciation	32,000	18,000	50,000	6,000	10,000	116,000
Income taxes	4,000	3,000	10,000	-3,000	-7,000	7,000
Profit	10,000	8,000	32,000	-11,000	-25,000	14,000
Assets	320,000	180,000	500,000	55,000	94,000	1,149,000

Products, Services, and Customer Disclosure

A publicly-held entity must report the sales garnered from external customers for each product and service or group thereof, unless it is impracticable to compile this information.

The entity must also describe the extent of its reliance on its major customers. In particular, if revenues from a single customer exceed 10% of the entity's revenues, this fact must be disclosed, along with the total revenues garnered from each of these customers and the names of the segments in which these revenues were earned.

It is not necessary to disclose the name of a major customer.

If there is a group of customers under common control (such as different departments of the federal government), the revenues from this group should be reported in aggregate as though the revenues were generated from a single customer.

EXAMPLE

Armadillo Industries reports the following information about its major customers:

Revenues from one customer of Armadillo's home security segment represented approximately 12% of the company's consolidated revenues in 20X2, and 11% of consolidated revenues in 20X1.

Geographic Area Disclosure

A publicly-held entity must disclose the following geographic information, unless it is impracticable to compile:

- *Revenues*. All revenues generated from external customers, and attributable to the entity's home country, and all revenues attributable to foreign countries. Foreign-country revenues by individual country shall be stated if these country-level sales are material. There must also be disclosure of the basis under which revenues are attributed to individual countries.
- *Assets*. All long-lived assets (for which the definition essentially restricts reporting to fixed assets) that are attributable to the entity's home country, and all such assets attributable to foreign countries. Foreign-country assets by individual country shall be stated if these assets are material.

It is also acceptable to include in this reporting subtotals of geographic information by groups of countries.

Geographic area reporting is waived if providing it is impracticable. If so, the entity must disclose the fact.

201

EXAMPLE

Armadillo Industries reports the following geographic information about its operations:

	Revenues	Long-Lived Assets
United States	$27,000,000	$13,000,000
Mexico	23,000,000	11,000,000
Chile	14,000,000	7,000,000
Other foreign countries	8,000,000	2,000,000
Total	$72,000,000	$33,000,000

Summary

The determination of whether a business has segments is, to a considerable extent, based upon whether you track information internally at the segment level. Thus, if a company's accounting systems are sufficiently primitive, or if management is sufficiently disinterested to not review information about business segments, it is entirely possible that even a publicly-held company will have no reportable business segments.

If you *do* have a number of reportable segments, consider using the report writing software in your accounting system to create a standard report that automatically generates the entire segment report for your disclosures. By using this approach, you will not waste time manually compiling the information, and will avoid running the risk of making a mistake while doing so. However, if the reportable segments change over time, you will need to modify the report structure to match the new group of segments.

Chapter 18
Interim Reporting

Introduction

If a company is publicly-held, the Securities and Exchange Commission (SEC) requires that the business file a variety of quarterly information on the Form 10-Q. This information is a reduced set of the requirements for the more comprehensive annual Form 10-K. The requirement to issue these additional financial statements may appear to be simple enough, but you must consider whether to report information assuming that quarterly results are stand-alone documents, or part of the full-year results of the business. This chapter discusses the disparities that these different viewpoints can cause in the financial statements, as well as how to report changes in accounting principle and estimate.

Overview of Interim Reporting

A business will periodically create financial statements for shorter periods than the fiscal year, which are known as *interim periods*. The most common examples of interim periods are monthly or quarterly financial statements, though any period of less than a full fiscal year can be considered an interim period. The concepts related to interim periods are most commonly applicable to the financial statements of publicly-held companies, since they are required to issue quarterly financial statements that must be reviewed by their outside auditors; these financials must account for certain activities in a consistent manner, as well as prevent readers from being misled about the results of the business on an ongoing basis.

General Interim Reporting Rule

The general rule for interim period reporting is that the same accounting principles and practices be applied to interim reports that are used for the preparation of annual financial statements. The following bullet points illustrate revenues and expenses that follow the general rule, and therefore do not change for interim reporting:

- *Revenue.* Revenue is recognized in the same manner that is used for annual reporting, with no exceptions.
- *Costs associated with revenue.* If a cost is typically assigned to a specific sale (such as cost of goods sold items), expense recognition is the same as is used for annual reporting.
- *Direct expenditures.* If an expense is incurred in a period and relates to that period, it is recorded as an expense in that period. An example is salaries expense.

- *Accruals for estimated expenditures.* If there is an estimated expenditure to be made at a later date but which relates to the current period, it is recorded as an expense in the current period. An example is accrued wages.
- *Depreciation and amortization.* If there is a fixed asset, depreciation (for tangible assets) or amortization (for intangible assets) is ratably charged to all periods in its useful life.

In addition, there are cases where a company is accustomed to only making a year-end adjustment, such as to its reserves for doubtful accounts, obsolete inventory, and/or warranty claims, as well as for year-end bonuses. Where possible, these adjustments should be made in the interim periods, thereby reducing the amount of any residual adjustments still required in the year-end financial statements.

Variations from the Interim Reporting Rule

There are other cases in which the treatment of certain transactions will vary for interim periods. The following rules should be applied in these cases:

- *Expense allocation.* Non-product expenses should be allocated among interim periods based on time expired, usage, or benefits received. In most cases, this means that expenses will simply be charged to expense in the current period, with no allocation to other interim periods. However, it could result in spreading expense recognition over several months or quarters.
- *Arbitrary assignments.* It is not allowable to make arbitrary assignments of costs to certain interim periods.
- *Gains and losses.* Gains and losses that arise in an interim period shall be recognized at once, and not be deferred to any later interim periods.

EXAMPLE

Armadillo Industries incurs an annual property tax charge of $60,000. Also, Armadillo has historically earned an annual volume discount of $30,000 per year, based on its full-year purchases from a major supplier.

Since the property tax charge is applicable to all months in the year, the controller accrues a $5,000 monthly charge for this expense. Similarly, the volume discount relates back to volume purchases throughout the year, not just the last month of the year, in which the discount is retroactively awarded. Accordingly, the controller creates a monthly credit of $2,500 to reflect the expected year-end volume discount of $30,000.

The concepts of recognizing expenses are more thoroughly discussed in the next two sections, which address the integral view and the discrete view of how to handle interim expense recognition.

There are several specific areas in which the accounting for interim reporting can differ from what is used for annual reporting. In particular:

- *Estimated inventory.* It is acceptable to use the gross profit method or other methods to estimate the cost of goods sold during interim periods. This is allowed in order to reduce the amount of time required to derive the cost of goods sold using a formal count of the ending inventory.
- *LIFO layers.* If a company uses the last in, first out (LIFO) method of calculating inventory, existing inventory cost layers may be liquidated during an interim period. If such a cost layer is expected to be replaced by the end of the fiscal year, the cost of sales for the interim period can include the expected replacement cost of that LIFO cost layer.
- *Lower of cost or market.* If there is a reduction in the market value of inventory, the difference between the market value and its cost should be charged to expense in an interim period. However, you are allowed to offset the full amount of these losses with any market value gains in subsequent periods within the same fiscal year on the same inventory items. Alternatively, you are allowed to avoid recognizing these losses in an interim period if there are seasonal price fluctuations that are expected to result in an offsetting increase in market prices by the end of the year.
- *Purchase price and volume variances.* If a company uses a standard costing system to assign costs to its inventory items, it is acceptable to defer the recognition of any variances from standard cost in interim periods, if it has already been planned that these variances will have been absorbed by the end of the fiscal year. However, if there are unexpected purchase price or volume variances, recognize them in the interim period in which they occur.

EXAMPLE

Pianoforte International writes down the value of its mahogany wood holdings, due to a crash in world mahogany prices. The amount of the first-quarter write down is $100,000. By year-end, the market price has stabilized at a higher level, allowing Pianoforte to reverse $62,000 of the original write down and report the change in its fiscal year-end results.

Changes in Accounting Principle in Interim Periods

An accounting principle is an acceptable method for recording and reporting an accounting transaction. There is a change in accounting principle when:

- There are several accounting principles that apply to a situation, and you switch to a principle that you have not used in the past; or
- When the accounting principle that formerly applied to the situation is no longer generally accepted; or
- You change the method of applying the principle.

Only change an accounting principle when doing so is required by GAAP, or you can justify that it is preferable to use the new principle. If you elect to proceed with a change in accounting principle, apply it retrospectively to all prior periods, including all interim reporting, unless it is impractical to do so. To complete a retrospective application of a change in accounting principle, do the following:

1. Include the cumulative effect of the change on periods prior to those presented in the carrying amount of assets and liabilities as of the beginning of the first period in which you are presenting financial statements; and
2. Enter an offsetting amount in the beginning retained earnings balance of the first period in which you are presenting financial statements; and
3. Adjust all presented financial statements to reflect the change to the new accounting principle.

From a reporting perspective, a change in accounting principle requires disclosure of the change in principle from those applied in the comparable interim period of the prior annual period, as well as the preceding interim periods in the current fiscal year, and in the annual report for the prior fiscal year.

Changes in Accounting Estimate in Interim Periods

There is a change in accounting estimate when there is a change that affects the carrying amount of an existing asset or liability, or that alters the subsequent accounting for existing or future assets or liabilities. A change in estimate arises from the appearance of new information that alters the existing situation.

Changes in estimate are a normal part of accounting, and an expected part of the ongoing process of reviewing the current status and future benefits and obligations related to assets and liabilities. All of the following are situations where there is likely to be a change in accounting estimate:

- Allowance for doubtful accounts
- Reserve for obsolete inventory
- Changes in the useful life of depreciable assets
- Changes in the salvage values of depreciable assets
- Changes in the amount of expected warranty obligations
- Changes in the estimated effective annual tax rate

When there is a change in estimate, account for it in the period of change. You do *not* need to restate earlier financial statements; thus, there is no need to restate any prior-period interim reporting. There should be disclosure in the current and subsequent interim periods of the effect on earnings of the change in estimate, if material in relation to any of the reporting periods presented. This disclosure should continue to be made for as long as necessary, to avoid any misleading comparisons between periods.

Tip: Where possible, adopt accounting changes during the first interim period of a fiscal year. Doing so eliminates any comparability problems between the interim periods for the remainder of the fiscal year.

Error Correction in Interim Periods

When determining the materiality of an error, relate the amount to the estimated profit for the entire fiscal year and the effect on the earnings trend, rather than for the current interim period. Otherwise, a disproportionate number of error corrections will be separately reported within the financial statements.

If an error correction is considered material at the interim period level but not for the full fiscal year, disclose the error in the interim report.

EXAMPLE

Armadillo Industries has profits of $1,000,000 in its first quarter, and expects to generate $4,000,000 of profits for the entire fiscal year. The company has historically considered materiality to be 5% of its profits. In the first quarter, the accounting department uncovers a $100,000 error. Though this amount is 10% of first-quarter profits, it is only 2.5% of full-year expected profits. Given the minimal impact on full-year profits, Armadillo does not have to segregate this information for reporting purposes in its first quarter interim reporting, though it must still disclose the information.

Adjustments to Prior Interim Periods

If an item impacting a company's profits occurs during an interim period other than the first interim period of the fiscal year, and some portion or all of it is an adjustment relating to a prior interim period of the current fiscal year, report the item as follows:

- Include that portion of the item that relates to the current interim period in the results of the current interim period
- Restate the results of prior interim periods to include that portion of the item relating to each interim period
- If there are any portions of the item relating to activities in prior fiscal years, include the change in a restatement of the first interim period of the current fiscal year

The Integral View

Under the integral view of producing interim reports, the assumption is that the results reported in interim financial statements are an integral part of the full-year financial results (hence the name of this concept). This viewpoint produces the following accounting issues:

- *Accrue expenses not arising in the period*. If you know that an expense will be paid later in the year that is incurred at least partially in the reporting period, accrue some portion of the expense in the reporting period. Here are several examples:
  - *Advertising*. If you pay in advance for advertising that is scheduled to occur over multiple time periods, recognize the expense over the entire range of time periods.

- o *Bonuses.* If there are bonus plans that may result in bonus payments later in the year, accrue the expense in all accounting periods. Only accrue this expense if you can reasonably estimate the amount of the bonus, which may not always be possible during the earlier months covered by a performance contract.
  - o *Contingencies.* If there are contingent liabilities that will be resolved later in the year, and which are both probable and reasonably estimated, then accrue the related expense.
  - o *Profit sharing.* If employees are paid a percentage of company profits at year-end, and the amount can be reasonably estimated, then accrue the expense throughout the year as a proportion of the profits recognized in each period.
  - o *Property taxes.* A local government entity issues an invoice to the company at some point during the year for property taxes. These taxes are intended to cover the entire year, so accrue a portion of the expense in each reporting period.
- *Tax rate.* A company is usually subject to a graduated income tax rate that incrementally escalates through the year as the business generates more profit. Under the integral view, use the expected tax rate for the entire year in every reporting period, rather than the incremental tax rate that applies only to the profits earned for the year to date.

EXAMPLE

The board of directors of Lowry Locomotion approves a senior management bonus plan for the upcoming year that could potentially pay the senior management team a maximum of $240,000. It initially seems probable that the full amount will be paid, but by the third quarter it appears more likely that the maximum amount to be paid will be $180,000. In addition, the company pays $60,000 in advance for a full year of advertising in *Locomotive Times* magazine. Lowry recognizes these expenses as follows:

	Quarter 1	Quarter 2	Quarter 3	Quarter 4	Full Year
Bonus expense	$60,000	$60,000	$30,000	$30,000	$180,000
Advertising	15,000	15,000	15,000	15,000	60,000

The accounting staff spreads the recognition of the full amount of the projected bonus over the year, but then reduces its recognition of the remaining expense starting in the third quarter, to adjust for the lowered bonus payout expectation.

The accounting staff initially records the $60,000 advertising expense as a prepaid expense, and recognizes it ratably over all four quarters of the year, which matches the time period over which the related advertisements are run by *Locomotive Times*.

One problem with the integral view is that it tends to result in a significant number of expense accruals. Since these accruals are usually based on estimates, it is entirely possible that adjustments should be made to the accruals later in the year, as the company obtains more precise information about the expenses that are being accrued. Some of these adjustments could be substantial, and may materially affect the reported results in later periods.

The Discrete View

Under the discrete view of producing interim reports, the assumption is that the results reported for a specific interim period are *not* associated with the revenues and expenses arising during other reporting periods. Under this view, record the entire impact of a transaction within the reporting period, rather than ratably over the entire year. The following are examples of the situations that can arise under the discrete method:

- *Reduced accruals.* A substantially smaller number of accruals are likely under the discrete method, since the assumption is that you should not anticipate the recordation of transactions that have not yet arisen.
- *Gains and losses.* Do not spread the recognition of a gain or loss across multiple periods. If you were to do so, it would allow a company to spread a loss over multiple periods, thereby making the loss look smaller on a per-period basis than it really is.

Comparison of the Integral and Discrete Views

The integral view is clearly the better method from a theoretical perspective, since the causes of some transactions can span an entire year. For example, a manager may be awarded a bonus at the end of December, but he probably had to achieve specific results throughout the year to earn it. Otherwise, if you were to adopt the discrete view, interim reporting would yield exceedingly varied results, with some periods revealing inordinately high or low profitability.

However, you should adopt the integral view from the perspective of accounting efficiency; that is, it is very time-consuming to maintain a mass of revenue and expense accruals, their ongoing adjustments, and documentation of the reasons for them throughout a year. Instead, use the integral view only for the more material transactions that are anticipated, and use the discrete view for smaller transactions. Thus, you could accrue the expense for property taxes throughout the year if the amount were significant, or simply record it in the month when the invoice is received, if the amount is small.

Disclosures for Interim Reporting

The level of financial reporting contained within the interim reports of publicly-held companies is lower than the requirements for annual financial statements, which is necessary in order to release interim reports on an accelerated schedule. To prevent an excessive reduction in the level of reporting, GAAP requires the following minimum content in the financial statements:

- *Financial statement items.* Includes sales, provision for income taxes, net income, and comprehensive income.
- *Earnings per share.* Includes both basic and diluted earnings per share.

The following additional disclosures are specific to interim reports:
- *Cost of goods sold derivation.* If a different method is used during an interim period than at year-end to derive the cost of goods sold, this different method must be disclosed, as well as any significant adjustments resulting from a reconciliation with the annual physical inventory count.
- *Expenses charged wholly within current period.* If there are costs wholly charged to expense within an interim period, and for which there are no comparable expenses in the corresponding interim period of the preceding year, the nature and amount of the expense should be disclosed.
- *Prior period adjustment.* If there is a material retroactive prior period adjustment made during any interim period, disclosure must be made of the effect on net income and earnings per share of any prior period included in the report, as well as on retained earnings.
- *Seasonality.* When there are seasonal variations in a business, disclose the seasonal nature of its activities, thereby avoiding confusion about unusually high or low results in an interim period. It may also be necessary to supplement interim reports with financial results for the 12-month periods ended at the interim date for the current and preceding years.

Tip: The Securities and Exchange Commission allows line items in the balance sheet to be aggregated if a line item is less than 10% of total assets and the amount has not changed by more than 25% since the end of the preceding fiscal year. The same concept applies to the income statement, except that the thresholds are 15% of average net income for the last three fiscal years (not including loss years) and the change limit is 20% from the corresponding interim period of the preceding fiscal year. For the statement of cash flows, the threshold is 10% of the average of net cash flows from operating activities for the last three years.

The SEC requires that the disclosures in interim reports not be misleading. This means that a material change from any disclosure in the most recent annual report should be noted in the next interim report. However, even if there is no significant change in a material contingency, the matter must continue to be disclosed until resolved.

Summary

When creating interim financial statements, you should judiciously apply the integral and discrete views to the statements – that is, the integral method is more accurate, but the discrete view is more efficient. Thus, restrict the integral view to material transactions, and apply the discrete view to all other transactions.

The other area that can cause extra work when closing the books is the concept of changes in accounting principle, since it calls for the restatement of financial statements. You should certainly avoid this whenever possible, so only make a change in accounting principle if there is a very good reason for doing so. Or, if it is absolutely necessary to make the change, it is better to do so at the end of the fiscal year, when you are no longer reporting any interim results, only full-year results.

Chapter 19
Earnings per Share

Introduction

Earnings per share is a company's net income divided by the weighted-average number of shares outstanding. This calculation is subject to a number of additional factors involving preferred shares, convertible instruments, and dividends. If a company is publicly-held, it is required to report two types of earnings per share information within the financial statements. These can be complex calculations, and so may slow down the closing process. In this chapter, we describe how to calculate both basic and diluted earnings per share, as well as how to present this information within the financial statements.

Basic Earnings per Share

Basic earnings per share is the amount of a company's profit or loss for a reporting period that is available to the shares of its common stock that are outstanding during a reporting period. If a business only has common stock in its capital structure, it presents only its basic earnings per share for income from continuing operations and net income. This information is reported on its income statement.

The formula for basic earnings per share is:

$$\frac{\text{Profit or loss attributable to common equity holders of the parent business}}{\text{Weighted average number of common shares outstanding during the period}}$$

In addition, subdivide this calculation into the following:
- The profit or loss from continuing operations attributable to the parent company
- The total profit or loss attributable to the parent company

When calculating basic earnings per share, incorporate in the numerator an adjustment for dividends. Deduct from the profit or loss the after-tax amount of any dividends declared on non-cumulative preferred stock, as well as the after-tax amount of any preferred stock dividends, even if the dividends are not declared; this does not include any dividends paid or declared during the current period that relate to previous periods.

Also, incorporate the following adjustments into the denominator of the basic earnings per share calculation:
- *Contingent stock.* If there is contingently issuable stock, treat it as though it were outstanding as of the date when there are no circumstances under which the shares would *not* be issued.

212

- *Issuance date.* Include shares under any of the following circumstances:
  - A liability is settled in exchange for shares
  - An acquisition paid for with shares is recognized
  - Any shares related to a mandatorily convertible instrument as of the contract date
  - Cash is receivable for sold shares
  - Dividends are reinvested
  - Interest stops accruing on convertible debt instruments on which shares can be issued
  - Services are paid for with shares
- *Weighted-average shares.* Use the weighted-average number of shares during the period in the denominator. This is done by adjusting the number of shares outstanding at the beginning of the reporting period for common shares repurchased or issued in the period. This adjustment is based on the proportion of the days in the reporting period that the shares are outstanding.

EXAMPLE

Lowry Locomotion earns a profit of $1,000,000 net of taxes in Year 1. In addition, Lowry owes $200,000 in dividends to the holders of its cumulative preferred stock. Lowry calculates the numerator of its basic earnings per share as follows:

$1,000,000 Profit - $200,000 Dividends = $800,000

Lowry had 4,000,000 common shares outstanding at the beginning of Year 1. In addition, it sold 200,000 shares on April 1 and 400,000 shares on October 1. It also issued 500,000 shares on July 1 to the owners of a newly-acquired subsidiary. Finally, it bought back 60,000 shares on December 1. Lowry calculates the weighted-average number of common shares outstanding as follows:

Date	Shares	Weighting (Months)	Weighted Average
January 1	4,000,000	12/12	4,000,000
April 1	200,000	9/12	150,000
July 1	500,000	6/12	250,000
October 1	400,000	3/12	100,000
December 1	-60,000	1/12	-5,000
			4,495,000

Lowry's basic earnings per share is:

$800,000 adjusted profits ÷ 4,495,000 weighted-average shares = $0.18 per share

---

Diluted Earnings per Share

Diluted earnings per share is the profit for a reporting period per share of common stock outstanding during that period; it includes the number of shares that would have been outstanding during the period if the company had issued common shares for all potential dilutive common stock outstanding during the period.

If a company has more types of stock than common stock in its capital structure, it must present both basic earnings per share and diluted earnings per share information; this presentation must be for both income from continuing operations and net income. This information is reported on the company's income statement.

To calculate diluted earnings per share, include the effects of all dilutive potential common shares. This means that you increase the number of shares outstanding by the weighted average number of additional common shares that would have been outstanding if the company had converted all dilutive potential common stock to common stock. This dilution may affect the profit or loss in the numerator of the dilutive earnings per share calculation. The formula is:

(Profit or loss attributable to common equity holders of parent company
+ After-tax interest on convertible debt + Convertible preferred dividends)
(Weighted average number of common shares outstanding during the period
+ All dilutive potential common stock)

You may need to make two adjustments to the *numerator* of this calculation. They are:

- *Interest expense*. Eliminate any interest expense associated with dilutive potential common stock, since you assume that these shares are converted to common stock. The conversion would eliminate the company's liability for the interest expense.
- *Dividends*. Adjust for the after-tax impact of dividends or other types of dilutive potential common shares.

You may need to make additional adjustments to the *denominator* of this calculation. They are:

- *Anti-dilutive shares*. If there are any contingent stock issuances that would have an anti-dilutive impact on earnings per share, do not include them in the calculation. This situation arises when a business experiences a loss, because including the dilutive shares in the calculation would reduce the loss per share.
- *Dilutive shares*. If there is potential dilutive common stock, add all of it to the denominator of the diluted earnings per share calculation. Unless there is more specific information available, assume that these shares are issued at the beginning of the reporting period.
- *Dilutive securities termination*. If a conversion option lapses during the reporting period for dilutive convertible securities, or if the related debt is extinguished during the reporting period, the effect of these securities should

still be included in the denominator of the diluted earnings per share calculation for the period during which they were outstanding.

In addition to these adjustments to the denominator, also apply all of the adjustments to the denominator already noted for basic earnings per share.

> **Tip:** The rules related to diluted earnings per share appear complex, but they are founded upon one principle – that you are trying to establish the absolute worst-case scenario to arrive at the smallest possible amount of earnings per share. If you are faced with an unusual situation involving the calculation of diluted earnings per share and are not sure what to do, that rule will likely apply.

In addition to the issues just noted, here are a number of additional situations that could impact the calculation of diluted earnings per share:

- *Most advantageous exercise price.* When you calculate the number of potential shares that could be issued, do so using the most advantageous conversion rate from the perspective of the person or entity holding the security to be converted.
- *Settlement assumption.* If there is an open contract that could be settled in common stock or cash, assume that it will be settled in common stock, but only if the effect is dilutive. The presumption of settlement in stock can be overcome if there is a reasonable basis for expecting that settlement will be partially or entirely in cash.
- *Effects of convertible instruments.* If there are convertible instruments outstanding, include their dilutive effect if they dilute earnings per share. Consider convertible preferred stock to be anti-dilutive when the dividend on any converted shares is greater than basic earnings per share. Similarly, convertible debt is considered anti-dilutive when the interest expense on any converted shares exceeds basic earnings per share. The following example illustrates the concept.

EXAMPLE

Lowry Locomotion earns a net profit of $2 million, and it has 5 million common shares outstanding. In addition, there is a $1 million convertible loan that has an eight percent interest rate. The loan may potentially convert into 500,000 of Lowry's common shares. Lowry's incremental tax rate is 35 percent.

Lowry's basic earnings per share is $2,000,000 ÷ 5,000,000 shares, or $0.40/share. The following calculation shows the compilation of Lowry's diluted earnings per share:

Net profit	$2,000,000
+ Interest saved on $1,000,000 loan at 8%	80,000
- Reduced tax savings on foregone interest expense	-28,000
= Adjusted net earnings	$2,052,000
Common shares outstanding	5,000,000
+ Potential converted shares	500,000
= Adjusted shares outstanding	5,500,000
Diluted earnings per share ($2,052,000 ÷ 5,500,000)	**$0.37/share**

- *Option exercise.* If there are any dilutive options and warrants, assume that they are exercised at their exercise price. Then, convert the proceeds into the total number of shares that the holders would have purchased, using the average market price during the reporting period. Then use in the diluted earnings per share calculation the difference between the number of shares assumed to have been issued and the number of shares assumed to have been purchased. The following example illustrates the concept.

EXAMPLE

Lowry Locomotion earns a net profit of $200,000, and it has 5,000,000 common shares outstanding that sell on the open market for an average of $12 per share. In addition, there are 300,000 options outstanding that can be converted to Lowry's common stock at $10 each.

Lowry's basic earnings per share is $200,000 ÷ 5,000,000 common shares, or $0.04 per share.

Lowry's controller wants to calculate the amount of diluted earnings per share. To do so, he follows these steps:
1. *Calculate the number of shares that would have been issued at the market price.* Thus, he multiplies the 300,000 options by the average exercise price of $10 to arrive at a total of $3,000,000 paid to exercise the options by their holders.
2. *Divide the amount paid to exercise the options by the market price to determine the number of shares that could be purchased.* Thus, he divides the $3,000,000 paid to exercise the options by the $12 average market price to arrive at 250,000 shares that could have been purchased with the proceeds from the options.
3. *Subtract the number of shares that could have been purchased from the number of options exercised.* Thus, he subtracts the 250,000 shares potentially purchased from the 300,000 options to arrive at a difference of 50,000 shares.

4. *Add the incremental number of shares to the shares already outstanding.* Thus, he adds the 50,000 incremental shares to the existing 5,000,000 to arrive at 5,050,000 diluted shares.

Based on this information, the controller arrives at diluted earnings per share of $0.0396, for which the calculation is:

$200,000 Net profit ÷ 5,050,000 Common shares

- *Put options.* If there are purchased put options, only include them in the diluted earnings per share calculation if the exercise price is higher than the average market price during the reporting period.
- *Written put options.* If there is a written put option that requires a business to repurchase its own stock, include it in the computation of diluted earnings per share, but only if the effect is dilutive. If the exercise price of such a put option is above the average market price of the company's stock during the reporting period, this is considered to be "in the money," and the dilutive effect is to be calculated using the following method, which is called the *reverse treasury stock method*:
  1. Assume that enough shares were issued by the company at the beginning of the period at the average market price to raise sufficient funds to satisfy the put option contract.
  2. Assume that these proceeds are used to buy back the required number of shares.
  3. Include in the denominator of the diluted earnings per share calculation the difference between the numbers of shares issued and purchased in steps 1 and 2.

EXAMPLE

A third party exercises a written put option that requires Armadillo Industries to repurchase 1,000 shares from the third party at an exercise price of $30. The current market price is $20. Armadillo uses the following steps to compute the impact of the written put option on its diluted earnings per share calculation:
1. Armadillo assumes that it has issued 1,500 shares at $20.
2. The company assumes that the "issuance" of 1,500 shares is used to meet the repurchase obligation of $30,000.
3. The difference between the 1,500 shares issued and the 1,000 shares repurchased is added to the denominator of Armadillo's diluted earnings per share calculation.

- *Call options.* If there are purchased call options, only include them in the diluted earnings per share calculation if the exercise price is lower than the market price.

> **Tip:** There is only a dilutive effect on the diluted earnings per share calculation when the average market price is greater than the exercise prices of any options or warrants.

- *Contingent shares in general.* Treat common stock that is contingently issuable as though it was outstanding as of the beginning of the reporting period, but only if the conditions have been met that would require the company to issue the shares. If the conditions were not met by the end of the period, then include in the calculation, as of the beginning of the period, any shares that would be issuable if the end of the reporting period were the end of the contingency period, and the result would be dilutive.
- *Contingent shares dependency.* If there is a contingent share issuance that is dependent upon the future market price of the company's common stock, include the shares in the diluted earnings per share calculation, based on the market price at the end of the reporting period; however, only include the issuance if the effect is dilutive. If the shares have a contingency feature, do not include them in the calculation until the contingency has been met.
- *Issuances based on future earnings and stock price.* There may be contingent stock issuances that are based on future earnings and the future price of a company's stock. If so, the number of shares to include in diluted earnings per share should be based on the earnings to date and the current market price as of the end of each reporting period. If both earnings and share price targets must be reached in order to trigger a stock issuance and both targets are not met, do not include any related contingently issuable shares in the diluted earnings per share calculation.
- *Compensation in shares.* If employees are awarded shares that have not vested or stock options as forms of compensation, treat these grants as options when calculating diluted earnings per share. Consider these grants to be outstanding on the grant date, rather than any later vesting date.

Always calculate the number of potential dilutive common shares independently for each reporting period presented in the financial statements.

Presentation of Earnings per Share

The basic and diluted earnings per share information is normally listed at the bottom of the income statement for every period included in the income statement. Also, if diluted earnings per share information is reported in *any* of the periods included in a company's income statement, it must be reported for *all* of the periods included in the statement. The following sample illustrates the concept.

Sample Presentation of Earnings per Share

Earnings per Share	20x3	20x2	20x1
From continuing operations			
Basic earnings per share	$1.05	$0.95	$0.85
Diluted earnings per share	1.00	0.90	0.80
From discontinued operations			
Basic earnings per share	$0.20	$0.17	$0.14
Diluted earnings per share	0.15	0.08	0.07
From total operations			
Basic earnings per share	$1.25	$1.12	$0.99
Diluted earnings per share	1.15	0.98	0.87

Note that, if the company reports a discontinued operation, it must present the basic and diluted earnings per share amounts for these items. The information can be included either as part of the income statement or in the accompanying notes. The preceding sample presentation includes a disclosure for earnings per share from discontinued operations.

Tip: If the amounts of basic and diluted earnings per share are the same, it is allowable to have a dual presentation of the information in a single line item on the income statement.

In addition to the earnings per share reporting format just noted, a company is also required to report the following information:

- *Reconciliation.* State the differences between the numerators and denominators of the basic and diluted earnings per share calculations for income from continuing operations.
- *Preferred dividends effect.* State the effect of preferred dividends on the computation of income available to common stockholders for basic earnings per share.
- *Potential effects.* Describe the terms and conditions of any securities not included in the computation of diluted earnings per share due to their antidilutive effects, but which could potentially dilute basic earnings per share in the future.
- *Subsequent events.* Describe any transactions occurring after the latest reporting period but before the issuance of financial statements that would have a material impact on the number of common or potential common shares if they had occurred prior to the end of the reporting period.

Summary

It will have been evident from the discussions of basic and diluted earnings per share that the calculation of diluted earnings per share can become quite complex if there is a correspondingly complex equity structure. It is relatively simple to calculate basic earnings per share in the midst of the closing process, but that is certainly not the case for diluted earnings per share. Instead, create an electronic spreadsheet that calculates diluted earnings per share for you. Further, save the calculation for each reporting period on a separate page of the spreadsheet; by doing so, there will be an excellent record of how these calculations were managed in the past. Finally, consider running a preliminary calculation of diluted earnings per share just before the end of the reporting period, which can be used to incorporate and test the impact of any recent changes in the company's equity structure.

Chapter 20
The Public Company Close

Introduction

Closing the books for a publicly held company is considerably more involved than it is for a privately held company, because several parties have to examine and approve the financial statements, and because the disclosures that accompany the financial statements are substantial. In this chapter, we will address unique aspects of the closing process that apply to public companies, as well as describe the more common features of the quarterly Form 10-Q and annual Form 10-K filings.

> **Related Podcast Episode:** Episode 77 of the Accounting Best Practices Podcast discusses closing the books for a public company. It is available at: **accounting-tools.com/podcasts** or **iTunes**

The Public Company Closing Process

A publicly held company is required by the Securities and Exchange Commission (SEC) to file a large report concerning its financial condition at the end of each quarter. These are the Form 10-Q (for quarterly filings) and Form 10-K (for annual filings). The contents of both reports are discussed in the following sections.

There are a number of time-consuming steps involved in the production of the Forms 10-Q and 10-K. In fact, though there may be an excellent system in place for producing reliable financial statements within a few days of month-end, the additional steps are so onerous that you may find it difficult to file the reports with the SEC in a timely manner, even though the filing dates are a number of weeks later.

> **Tip:** If your company is a small one with a minimal public valuation, consider outsourcing the construction of the Forms 10-Q and 10-K to outside specialists. These reports require particular types of knowledge that the accounting staff of a small business is unlikely to have, which makes outsourcing a good option. However, since these specialists are overwhelmed with work from all of their clients following the end of each quarter, your reports may be filed near or on the last allowable date.

The additional steps needed to close the books for a publicly held company include all of the following:

1. *Auditor investigation.* The outside auditors must conduct a review of the company's financial statements and disclosures for its quarterly results, and

a full audit of its annual results. A *review* is a service under which an auditor obtains limited assurance that there are no material modifications that need to be made to an entity's financial statements for them to be in conformity with the applicable financial reporting framework. An *audit* is the review and verification of an entity's accounting records, as well as the physical inspection of its assets. The auditor then attests to the fairness of presentation of the financial statements and related disclosures. An audit is more time-consuming and expensive than a review. The auditor investigation is the most time-consuming of the public company requirements. The company can reduce the amount of time required for a review or audit by providing full staff support to the audit team, as well as by having all requested information available as of the beginning of the audit or review work.

2. *Legal review.* It would be extremely unwise to issue the financial statement package without first having legal counsel review the statements and (especially) the disclosures to ensure that all required disclosures have been made, and to verify that all statements made are correct and fully supportable. This review is usually completed near or after the end of the work done by the auditors, but can be scheduled slightly sooner if you believe the disclosures to be substantially complete at that time.

Tip: The auditors can waste a considerable amount of time double-checking and triple-checking the accuracy of the disclosures that accompany the financial statements. Doing so delays the closing process, as well as increasing the fees charged by the auditors. To reduce the auditor time spent reviewing the disclosures, have one or more in-house personnel review them in advance.

---

3. *Officer certification.* Depending upon what type of form is being issued, different company officers are required to certify that the information in the financial statements presents fairly the financial condition and results of operations of the business. Since there are substantial penalties and jail time involved if an officer were to make a false certification, it should be no surprise that the signing officers will want to spend time reviewing the complete set of financial statements and disclosures. This review can be done before the auditors have completed their work, so officer certification does not usually increase the duration of the closing process.

4. *Audit committee and board approvals.* The audit committee must approve every Form 10-Q, and the board of directors must approve every Form 10-K. Given the number of people involved, schedule review and approval meetings well in advance, to be conducted a few days prior to the required filing date of the applicable Form. Scheduling the review slightly early gives you time to make adjustments, in case anyone expresses concerns during the review, and wants changes to be made prior to filing.

Issue the complete set of financial statements and disclosures to the audit committee or board members at least one full day in advance of a review and approval meeting, so that they have sufficient time to examine the material.

> **Tip:** It is customary to use conference calls for review and approval meetings, rather than in person; doing so works well if people are located far apart. Also, the company may have an arrangement where audit committee or board members are paid less if they attend meetings by phone, so this approach can save the company money.

5. *EDGARize and file.* Once the Form 10-Q or Form 10-K is complete and fully approved, file it with the SEC. The filing is done using the Electronic Data Gathering, Analysis, and Retrieval (EDGAR) system that is operated by the SEC. The information can be submitted in various formats, but you will almost certainly have to convert it from the format in which the documents were originally prepared. This means hiring someone to convert the reports to the applicable format, which is a process known as *EDGARizing*. Not only is the conversion specialist responsible for converting the financial statements, but this person also files the statements with the SEC on behalf of the company. The conversion process usually takes one or two days, but also factor in additional time for the auditors to review the converted format – the auditors must give their approval before you can file with the SEC.

> **Tip:** Spend as much time as possible reviewing the financial statement package in advance before sending it to the EDGARizing firm, because they charge significant fees if you want to make subsequent changes to the converted documents.

Of all the issues noted in this section, the largest factor standing in the way of closing the books is likely to be the work schedule of the auditors. If they have other clients scheduled ahead of your company, the review or audit work may not even begin until several weeks after you have closed the books in all other respects. Consequently, it is extremely useful to work with the audit partner to move the company to the head of the auditors' work queue. Of course, if you are scheduled first by the auditors, this means that you must also have financial statements and all supporting schedules prepared at a very early date – so be ready before lobbying for a scheduling change.

The Form 10-Q

A publicly held company is required to issue the Form 10-Q to report the results of its first, second, and third fiscal quarters. The Form 10-Q includes not just the financial statements, but also a number of disclosures. The following table itemizes the more common disclosures:

Selection of Form 10-Q Disclosures

Item Header	Description
Item 1A. Risk factors	A thorough listing of all risks that the company may experience. It warns investors of what could reduce the value of their investments in the company.
Item 3. Legal proceedings	Describe any legal proceedings currently involving the company, and its estimate of the likely outcome of those proceedings.
Item 4. Submission of matters to a vote of security holders	Describe matters submitted to the shareholders for a vote during the most recent quarter of the fiscal year.
Item 7. Management's discussion and analysis (MD&A)	Describe opportunities, challenges, risks, trends, future plans, and key performance indicators, as well as changes in revenues, the cost of goods sold, other expenses, assets, and liabilities.
Item 7A. Quantitative and qualitative disclosures about market risk	Quantify the market risk at the end of the last fiscal year for the company's market risk-sensitive instruments.
Item 8. Financial statements and supplementary data	Make all disclosures required by GAAP, including descriptions of: • Accrued liabilities • Acquisitions • Discontinued operations • Fixed assets • Income taxes • Related party transactions • Segment information • Stock options
Item 9A. Controls and procedures	Generally describe the system of internal controls, testing of controls, changes in controls, and management's conclusions regarding the effectiveness of those controls.
Item 15. Exhibits and financial statement schedules	Item 601 of Regulation S-K requires that a business attach a number of exhibits to the Form 10-K, including (but not limited to): • Code of ethics • Material contracts • Articles of incorporation • Bylaws • Acquisition purchase agreements

Before filing, the Form 10-Q must be signed by an authorized officer, as well as the principal financial or chief accounting officer.

A *large accelerated filer* is a company having an aggregate market value owned by investors who are not affiliated with the company of a minimum of $700 million.

An *accelerated filer* is a company having an aggregate market value owned by investors who are not affiliated with the company of less than $700 million, but more than $75 million. You must file the Form 10-Q within 40 days of the end of the fiscal quarter if the company is either a large accelerated filer or an accelerated filer. If that is not the case, file it within 45 days of the end of the fiscal quarter.

The Form 10-K

A publicly held company is required to issue the Form 10-K to report the results of its fiscal year. The Form 10-K includes not just the financial statements, but also a number of additional disclosures. The following table itemizes the more common disclosures:

Selection of Form 10-K Disclosures

Item Header	Description
Item 1. Business	Provide a description of the company's purpose, history, operating segments, customers, suppliers, sales and marketing operations, customer support, intellectual property, competition, and employees. It should tell readers what the company does and describe its business environment.
Item 1A. Risk factors	A thorough listing of all risks that the company may experience. It warns investors of what could reduce the value of their investments in the company.
Item 1B. Unresolved staff comments	Disclose all unresolved comments received from the SEC if they are material. (only applies to written comments from the SEC received at least 180 days before the fiscal year-end by an accelerated or large accelerated filer)
Item 2. Properties	Describe the leased or owned facilities of the business, including square footage, lease termination dates, and lease amounts paid per month.
Item 3. Legal proceedings	Describe any legal proceedings currently involving the company, and its estimate of the likely outcome of those proceedings.
Item 4. Submission of matters to a vote of security holders	Describe matters submitted to the shareholders for a vote during the fourth quarter of the fiscal year.
Item 5. Market for company stock	Describe where the company's stock trades and the number of holders of record, as well as the high and low closing prices per share, by quarter.
Item 6. Selected financial data	For the last five years, state selected information from the company's income statement and balance sheet (should be in tabular comparative format).

Item Header	Description
Item 7. Management's discussion and analysis (MD&A)	Describe opportunities, challenges, risks, trends, future plans, and key performance indicators, as well as changes in revenues, the cost of goods sold, other expenses, assets, and liabilities.
Item 7A. Quantitative and qualitative disclosures about market risk	Quantify the market risk at the end of the last fiscal year for the company's market risk-sensitive instruments.
Item 8. Financial statements and supplementary data	Make all disclosures required by GAAP, including descriptions of: • Accrued liabilities • Acquisitions • Discontinued operations • Fixed assets • Income taxes • Related party transactions • Segment information • Stock options
Item 9. Changes in and disagreements with accountants on accounting and financial disclosure	Describe any disagreements with the auditors when management elects to account for or disclose transactions in a manner different from what the auditors want.
Item 9A. Controls and procedures	Generally describe the system of internal controls, testing of controls, changes in controls, and management's conclusions regarding the effectiveness of those controls.
Item 10. Directors, executive officers and corporate governance	Identify the executive officers, directors, promoters, and individuals classified as control persons.
Item 11. Executive compensation	Itemize the types of compensation paid to company executives.
Item 12. Security ownership of certain beneficial owners and management and related stockholder matters	State the number of shares of all types owned or controlled by certain individuals classified as beneficial owners and/or members of management.
Item 13. Certain relationships and related transactions, and director independence	If there were transactions with related parties during the past fiscal year, and the amounts involved exceeded $120,000, describe the transactions.

Item Header	Description
Item 14. Principal accountant fees and services	State the aggregate amount of any fees billed in each of the last two fiscal years for professional services rendered by the company's auditors for: • Reviews and audits; • Audit-related activities; • Taxation work; and • All other fees.
Item 15. Exhibits and financial statement schedules	Item 601 of Regulation S-K requires that a business attach a number of exhibits to the Form 10-K, including (but not limited to): • Code of ethics • Material contracts • Articles of incorporation • Bylaws • Acquisition purchase agreements

Before filing, the Form 10-K must be signed by *all* of the following:
- Principal executive officer
- Principal financial officer
- Controller
- A majority of the board of directors

The Form 10-K must be filed within 60 days of the end of the fiscal year if the company is a large accelerated filer or an accelerated filer, or within 75 days of the end of the fiscal year if the company is an accelerated filer. If the company does not have either designation, file it within 90 days of the end of the fiscal year.

Summary

The disclosures to include in the Forms 10-Q and 10-K are only briefly summarized here, and do not include any disclosures that are required for specific industries. Refer to Regulation S-K of the Securities and Exchange Commission for a complete set of required disclosures. Also, do not skip the review by legal counsel! An experienced attorney can spot incorrect or missing disclosures that an auditor might not be aware of.

In summary, it is extremely difficult to reduce the amount of time required to file reports with the SEC, because it requires the cooperation of many parties outside of the accounting department – and over whom the controller has no control.

Chapter 21
Controls for Closing the Books

Introduction

Closing the books is a complicated process that requires the successful completion of a large number of steps to ensure that the reported results fairly represent the actual financial status of a business – and even then, an outlier event that the accounting staff has never seen before can throw off the reported results. Consequently, it is critical to have a strong system of controls integrated into the closing process to mitigate the risk of issuing incorrect financial statements. This chapter describes a variety of basic controls for closing the books, as well as additional controls that are imposed on public companies.

Related Podcast Episode: Episode 78 of the Accounting Best Practices Podcast discusses controls for financial statements. It is available at: **accounting-tools.com/podcasts** or **iTunes**

Preventive and Detective Controls

When considering the proper balance of controls used for closing the books, consider the types of controls being installed. A *preventive control* is one that keeps a financial statement error from ever occurring. Another type of control is the *detective control*. This control is useful, but only detects an error after it has occurred; thus, its main use is in making management aware of a problem that must be fixed.

A control system needs to have a mix of preventive and detective controls. Even though preventive controls are considered more valuable, they also tend to be more intrusive in the functioning of key business processes. Also, they are installed to address specific control issues that management is already aware of. Management also needs a liberal helping of detective controls, which can be used to spot new types of financial statement errors. Thus, a common occurrence is to throw out a web of detective controls that occasionally haul in a new type of problem, for which management installs a preventive control.

In short, a mix of the two types of controls is needed, where there may be no ideal solution. Instead, there may be a range of possible configurations within which a controller would consider a control system to be effective. In the following section, we describe a large number of controls for closing the books, most of which are of the detective variety.

Basic Controls

There are a number of financial statement controls worth considering. You can select just one control to address a specific risk, or adopt a larger number of controls that provide multiple ways to mitigate the same risk. We discuss how many controls to implement in the Balance Controls against Speed section. Here are a number of controls to consider:

Financial Statement Controls

Area	Description
General	*Closing checklist.* The most important control by far is a simple checklist of closing activities, which the controller monitors. This is a good way to verify that all steps required to close the books have been taken.
General	*Supporting documentation.* Anyone involved in the closing process should document the more complex journal entries, and have a second person review them for errors prior to entering them in the general ledger.
General	*Responsible person.* Assign responsibility for the entire closing process to one person, and assign responsibility for individual activities to those people assigned to the closing team.
General	*Limit journal entry authority.* It is more likely that an inexperienced person will incorrectly enter a journal entry in the general ledger, or not enter it at all, or enter it twice. Consequently, password-protect the journal entry screen in the accounting software and limit access to a trained general ledger accountant.
General	*Reconcile accounts.* There should be a mandatory reconciliation of all general ledger accounts that have ending balances larger than a predetermined amount, and which have had activity during the accounting period. This control may include a review of reconciled accounts by a supervisor. If some accounts persistently contain errors, consider requiring a preliminary review of them prior to the month-end close, when the accounting staff has more time for a thorough review.
General	*Analytical review.* Compare the preliminary financial statements to the results for the past few periods to see if there are any anomalies in the various line items, and investigate as necessary. This could be a simple search for blips in the trend line of results, or a more quantitatively-precise approach where changes over a specific dollar amount or percentage are investigated. A sample analytical review is shown after this list of controls.
General	*Retain spreadsheets.* If the information used to construct a journal entry was compiled in an electronic spreadsheet, lock down the spreadsheet to prevent it from being cleared out and used again in the next month. By doing so, you retain a historical record of the

Area	Description
	justifications for journal entries.
General	*Review spreadsheets.* There may be calculation errors in the spreadsheets used to create journal entries, so periodically review the calculations to verify that they are correct.
Disclosures	*Independent review.* If disclosures are to be issued along with the financial statements, consider hiring a third party, such as a CPA firm, to review the disclosures for adequacy.
Disclosures	*Match disclosures to financial statements.* A huge problem area is that the information in the disclosures does not match the financial statements. Someone should match the information in every disclosure to the same information in the financial statements, and adjust the disclosures as necessary.
Report structure	*Match default to custom reports.* When a company creates a special version of the financial statements provided with the accounting software package, there is a good chance that some accounts will not be included in the custom reports, or that they will be repeated. You can find these issues by comparing the original default financial statements to the modified versions.
Cash	*Complete the bank reconciliation.* The main company checking account usually processes a large number of transactions, and so is almost certain to contain a transaction that the company either did not record, or recorded incorrectly. Consequently, it is very useful to either complete a full bank reconciliation before closing the books, or to complete a preliminary one a few days prior to closing the books.
Accounts receivable	*Reconcile trade receivables account.* There should be no journal entries impacting the trade accounts receivable account, so review the account for such entries.
Accounts receivable	*Reconcile other receivables account.* The other accounts receivable account is the home for many stray receivables, such as for employees and company officers, and is commonly subject to adjustment. If the balance in this account is large, review it every month.
Inventory	*Verify cutoff.* Verify that the recordation of received goods and shipped goods switched to the following accounting period as of midnight on the last day of the reporting period.
Inventory	*Verify inventory quantities.* Ensure that someone audits the inventory quantities in the warehouse on a regular basis, and follows up on errors found. This improves the likelihood that the ending inventory balance and the cost of goods sold are correct.
Inventory	*Audit bills of material.* In a standard costing system, the bills of material are used to compile the cost of ending inventory. Adopt an ongoing review system to verify that these bills are correct; otherwise, the ending inventory balance will be incorrect.

Area	Description
Inventory	*Verify inventory layers.* If an inventory layering system is in place, verify that the costs assigned to the cost of goods sold were properly taken from the correct inventory layers, and that the costs in those layers are correct.
Prepaid assets	*Monitor account.* Verify that all items listed as prepaid assets were not consumed during the month; if they were, charge them to expense.
Fixed assets	*Match detail to account balances.* Fixed assets are frequently recorded in the wrong accounts. Therefore, make sure that the asset classification totals in the fixed asset register match the fixed asset account balances in the general ledger.
Fixed assets	*Review sale transactions.* If fixed assets were sold during a period, verify that the transactions were correctly recorded. In particular, verify that the associated amounts of accumulated depreciation were removed from the inventory records, and that gains or losses were properly recorded.
Fixed assets	*Recalculate depreciation.* Verify that the correct useful lives have been assigned to all fixed assets, and that depreciation terminates at the end of the useful lives of fixed assets.
Accrued liabilities	*Review accrual calculations.* Review all accrual calculations for such items as wages, vacation pay, sick pay, commissions, and royalties, and verify that the general ledger accrual accounts have been properly adjusted for these calculations.
Revenue	*Match invoices to funding.* If a business has contracts with its customers, verify that there are sufficient funds available before issuing invoices. Otherwise, the invoices will be rejected by customers, and the company must subsequently reduce the amount of recorded revenue.
Revenue	*Review shipping log.* Compare the sales register to the shipping log to verify that all items shipped to customers have been billed.
Revenue	*Approve accrued revenue.* Have the controller review the proposed accrual of any revenue transactions.
Income taxes	*Verify percentage.* Verify that the income tax rate used to calculate the income tax liability is the estimated average amount that the company expects to incur during the calendar year.

Sample Analytical Review

Account	December	November	% Change	$ Change	Issue
Prepaid assets	$80,000	$60,000	33%	$20,000	Deposit on new machinery
Accounts receivable	720,000	480,000	50%	240,000	Christmas sales surge
Inventory	120,000	350,000	66%	-230,000	Draw down for Christmas sales
Debt	400,000	200,000	100%	200,000	Funding for receivables
Revenue	600,000	250,000	1405	350,000	Christmas sales surge
Cost of goods sold	390,000	175,000	123%	215,000	Christmas sales surge
Employee benefits	50,000	25,000	100%	25,000	Christmas bonuses

Additional Controls for Public Companies

Any publicly-held organization is required to bolster its existing suite of financial statement controls with the participation of the following three groups:

- Outside auditors
- Audit committee
- Chief executive officer (CEO)

If a company is publicly held, its auditors are required to review its financial statements for the first, second, and third quarters of its fiscal year. The auditors must complete many audit steps before they will allow the financial statements to be issued, and those audit steps are essentially a massive cluster of detective controls.

Since the Form 10-Q cannot be issued without the permission of the auditors, there is no rush to release the financial statements. Thus, there is no tradeoff between the speed of release and the quality of the financial statements; instead, the auditors will work through their review procedures as fast as possible, but are primarily concerned with the quality of the final product.

Despite the presence of the auditors, do not consider them to be a backstop for any failed or missing internal controls. Instead, have a sufficient system of controls already in place for the auditors not to find any problems with the financial statements. A better way to use these reviews is to carefully examine any reports by the auditors of exceptions found, and to then institute new controls to mitigate the issues found.

A requirement of being publicly-held is to have an audit committee, which is a sub-group of the board of directors. This group must formally vote in favor of all quarterly and annual financial statements before they are released in the Forms 10-K and 10-Q. A diligent audit committee may occasionally spot an error or inconsistency in one of these Forms, or they may request clarification of certain statements made within the Forms. Nonetheless, only a few members of an audit committee usually have a strong financial background, so it is unlikely that the committee will spot significant issues. Consequently, the audit committee represents a relatively weak control over the financial statements.

The CEO is required to formally approve any financial statements filed with the Securities and Exchange Commission. It is possible that the CEO may spot problems in the financial statements, but only if he or she has significant financial knowledge of the company (which is not always the case). Thus, this should be considered a weak control.

In short, the participation of additional parties in the production of financial statements provides little additional control in the case of the audit committee and CEO; however the outside auditors may spot a number of issues that the controller can use as the basis for constructing additional controls.

Balancing Controls against Speed

There is a trade-off between installing a formidable array of closing controls and issuing financial statements on a timely basis. In brief, the more controls you install, the longer it takes to issue financial statements. However, the more controls you install, the more accurate the financial statements are likely to be. Thus, the controller needs to evaluate the tradeoff between speed of delivery and the accuracy of the delivered financial statements.

This balance between controls and speed tends to fluctuate over time. A common series of events is for a business to have an established set of procedures in place for issuing financial statements; management decides that it wants to receive them sooner, so the controller peels away the more time-consuming controls and delivers the financial statements within the time frame requested by management. Then an outlier event arises that would have been found if the eliminated controls were still in place, which leads to some embarrassment within the accounting department, followed by the re-imposition of those controls needed to guard against the outlier event.

In short, it is common to initially abandon some controls in favor of the faster release of financial statements, followed by a modest retrenchment that adds back some controls. The result is an adequate set of controls and the somewhat faster issuance of financial statements.

Summary

The discussion in this chapter makes it clear that a large number of controls could potentially be installed over the production of financial statements. It is quite likely that you do not need all of them, especially if the underlying accounting systems for recording transactions are well-constructed. Consequently, you should continually consider the controls being used, and judge whether adjustments can be made to achieve a system that strips away non-essential controls while still producing reasonably accurate financial statements in a timely manner.

You might consider using a more rigorous set of controls at the end of the fiscal year, so that the annual financial statements are subjected to a considerably more detailed review. This approach might be worthwhile if the year-end financial statements are to be released outside the company. The same logic holds for the quarterly financial statements of publicly-held companies; adopt an enhanced set of controls when quarterly reports are to be issued, and scale back the control effort for other months.

Chapter 22
Record Keeping for Closing the Books

Introduction

Closing the books can involve the production of a large number of transactions within a short period of time, after which there can be quite a debris field in the accounting department. Once the financial statements have been issued, you should collect, organize, and store this information in a month-end binder. Similarly, prepare a year-end book that documents the financial transactions for the entire year, as well as a few additional documents if you are filing reports with the Securities and Exchange Commission (SEC). This chapter discusses all three types of documentation.

Month-End Record Keeping

A considerable amount of information should be assembled into a month-end binder as part of the monthly closing process. The intent of having this binder is to document the decisions made and the journal entries used to create the financial statements. Key components of this binder are:

- *Master activity list.* Put the master list of closing activities in the front of the binder, and initial each step as it is completed. This provides proof to both internal and external auditors that the closing process is being consistently applied.
- *Journal entries.* Include every journal entry, with the backup calculations supporting each one.
- *Schedules.* Include the fixed asset register, as well as the accounts receivable aging and accounts payable aging reports. These provide proof of the balances in key accounts. Depending on the inventory system in use, you may also want to include an ending inventory report.
- *Account reconciliations.* Include the reconciliation of all accounts having material ending balances.
- *Bank reconciliation.* Include not only the bank reconciliation, but also the list of all checks and deposits in transit at the end of the month.

> **Tip:** It is better to start assembling the month-end binder *during* the closing process than *after* it. This reduces the chance that documents will be lost, since they are immediately being stored in the correct location.

The month-end binders should be well-organized, because it is very likely that the auditors will want to review them to obtain supporting information for various transactions that occurred in the past year. Also, if the company is sold at some point in the future, the due diligence team of the acquirer may want to review the documentation supporting the financial statements.

Year-End Record Keeping

The record keeping requirements at the end of the year are, at a minimum, the same as those for the end of each month. In addition, if the company's depreciation expense has been so small that you have waited until year-end to record it for the entire year, then calculate the amount of the expense and include it in the documentation for the last month of the year.

In addition to the usual month-end binder that is prepared for the last month of the year, you should also prepare a year-end book. This book should only contain paper reports, rather than electronic ones, so that it can survive archiving for a number of years. The year-end book contains the following items:

- *Financial statements.* This is the complete audited financial statements with disclosures.
- *Trial balance.* This shows the ending account balances for all accounts. If you have a trial balance in the year-end book, there is no need to also include a chart of accounts.
- *General ledger.* This is the detailed general ledger for the entire year. It is likely to be by far the largest document in the year-end book, and may be the one most referenced, since it contains a great deal of information about what happened during the year.
- *Subsidiary ledgers.* If there are subsidiary ledgers, print them out for the full year and include them in the book.
- *Ending inventory report.* Print a list of the year-end inventory, which includes the units, costs, and extended costs for all items in stock.
- *Fixed asset register.* This is a summary of all fixed assets owned by the company at year-end. You may also want to retain a listing of all assets that were disposed of during the year.
- *Fixed asset roll forward.* This is a report summarizing the changes in the fixed asset accounts from the beginning to the end of the year.
- *Invoice register.* This is a summary of all invoices created during the year.
- *Ending accounts receivable aging report.* This report should match the balance in the trade accounts receivable account in the general ledger. If the totals do not match, provide a reconciliation of the difference.
- *Ending accounts payable aging report.* This report should match the balance in the trade accounts payable account in the general ledger. If the totals do not match, provide a reconciliation of the difference.

The preceding list contains the key items that absolutely should be included in the year-end book. In addition, consider including the budget for the year.

Do not include *any* source documents in the year-end book, such as invoices, because they are extremely voluminous. The intent of the year-end book is to provide a summary of what happened during the year without going into a massive level of detail. Ideally, these materials should fit into just a few binders that can be easily stored.

The information listed for the year-end book is sufficiently detailed to be an excellent source document in case someone later conducts due diligence on the company, or if an audit is conducted several years later. At a minimum, it is an excellent archive of information, in case the electronic information for the same period is eventually removed from the accounting software.

Related Podcast Episode: Episode 199 of the Accounting Best Practices Podcast discusses the year-end book. It is available at: **accountingtools.com/podcasts** or **iTunes**

Public Company Record Keeping

If a company is publicly held, retain some additional documentation related to the quarterly Form 10-Q and annual Form 10-K filings. This documentation is:

- *Audit committee approval.* The audit committee must review and vote in favor of releasing the quarterly and annual financial statements. Retain a copy of the committee minutes documenting these votes.
- *Officer approval.* The chief executive officer and chief financial officer must formally certify that the financial statements present fairly, in all material respects, the financial condition and results of operations of the company. Retain signed copies of these certifications.
- *Auditor approved copy.* If the auditors approve a specific version of either form for filing with the SEC, retain a copy of it, as well as documentation of the approval by the auditor for the filing. This is helpful in case the auditors later claim that they did not give permission for their opinion to be included with the financial statements.

The documentation recommended here is primarily to provide proof that the company has adequate internal controls over the production of its SEC filings.

Summary

Record keeping for the closing process is extremely important, for several reasons. Internal auditors use it to verify that the closing process is being consistently followed. External auditors refer to it for evidence regarding the reasons for general ledger entries. The controller uses it to refer back to why entries were made in the past. Potential acquirers may read through it to gain insights into the company's financial processes. For all these reasons, you should carefully assemble the documentation related to the production of financial statements, and archive it for a number of years.

Chapter 23
The Soft Close and Virtual Close

Introduction

Closing the books is one of the more detailed and complicated procedures that a company must deal with, and must be so in order to generate sufficiently accurate financial statements for general consumption. Some controllers and CFOs have found a way to mitigate the work of closing the books by using a soft close or virtual close. In this chapter, we will describe both concepts and the situations in which they can be used.

Related Podcast Episode: Episode 160 of the Accounting Best Practices Podcast discusses the soft close. It is available at: **accountingtools.com/podcasts** or **iTunes**

The Soft Close

A soft close refers to closing the books at the end of a reporting period without many of the more rigorous steps used in a normal closing process. By doing so, the accounting department can issue financial statements with minimal effort and then return to its normal day-to-day activities. The soft close approach has the added advantage of allowing the accounting staff to issue financial statements very quickly – usually the day after the end of a reporting period.

This enhanced closing speed comes at a cost, for the accuracy of the financial statements is reduced by the various revenue and expense accruals that are no longer being applied to the financial statements. This means that the results reported through a soft close may be materially inaccurate. Or, they may have more variable results from month to month because accruals are not being used to smooth out results over multiple periods.

The reduced accuracy level makes the soft close impractical for reviewed or audited financial statements that are read by outsiders. Auditors would likely refuse to render a favorable opinion on such financial statements. Also, outsiders would be receiving information for which there would be a heightened risk of material errors, which places the company at risk of knowingly issuing inaccurate financial statements.

However, it may be perfectly acceptable to use the soft close for internal management reporting, where total accuracy is not entirely necessary. Internal recipients would be more familiar with the areas in which the soft close provides less accurate information, and could build this knowledge into how they interpret the reports. For example, if the accounting department is only bothering to record depreciation at the end of the year, recipients of the report can be made aware of this fact, and adjust their estimates of the company's results accordingly for all interim periods.

A reasonable compromise is to use a more thorough closing process whenever a complete set of financial statements is needed for the use of outsiders, and the soft close for all other months. This means that, for example, a publicly-held company could adopt a detailed closing process for its quarterly financial statements (which are issued to the public), and a soft close for all other months. A privately-held company could get away with eleven months of soft closes, and a more detailed close at the end of its fiscal year. This means that, depending on the circumstances, the majority of the monthly closes could potentially be reported under a soft close procedure.

The majority of closing steps are typically avoided during a soft close. For example, the following actions might be skipped:

- Account reconciliations
- Expense accruals
- Intercompany eliminations
- Overhead allocations
- Physical inventory counts
- Reserve account updates
- Revenue accruals

Many of these steps involve reversing entries that are created specifically for the financial statements, and then reversed at the beginning of the next reporting period. Other steps, such as physical inventory counts and account reconciliations, are designed to detect errors. If a company elects to conduct a long series of soft closes, this means the error detection steps are being turned off for a long time, which increases the risk of significant errors finding their way into the financial statements.

> **Tip:** If there are to be a number of consecutive soft closes, consider conducting some of the error-checking routines at intervals, to see if any errors have occurred that should be corrected.

If the results of a business are particularly susceptible to an item that has been removed from the soft close checklist, add the item back onto the list of closing tasks. For example, if the wage accrual is a large one, consider calculating and accruing it in every reporting period, irrespective of the type of close that the company uses.

The nature of a business may mandate that certain closing steps cannot be avoided, or else there will be material errors in the financial statements. For example:

- *Asset-intensive business.* If there is a large investment in fixed assets, and these assets are routinely being acquired or disposed of, it may be necessary to update the depreciation journal entries on a regular basis.

- *Inventory inaccuracies.* If there is a large investment in inventory and the inventory tracking system is primitive, a relatively frequent physical count may be necessary.
- *Irregular profits.* If profit levels are difficult to predict, it may be necessary to engage in extra closing steps in order to gain some assurance that the quarterly income tax liability is accurate.

If these issues can be surmounted, then the closing process for a soft close essentially involves completing all periodic billings to customers, recording billings from suppliers, and paying employees through the payroll system. The most problematic remaining activity is the accrual of supplier invoices that have not yet been received. If a company has a system in place for comparing received goods to authorizing purchase orders, it can readily calculate the amount of this accrual as soon as a reporting period is over, yielding accurate payable and expense figures for amounts due to its suppliers.

In short, a company can use the soft close concept to produce somewhat less accurate financial statements for selected reporting periods, thereby reducing the time required to close the books. This can be a useful concept if employed with caution, and when the recipients of the resulting reports have been warned about the potential shortcomings of the information they are receiving.

The Virtual Close

A virtual close involves the use of fully integrated company-wide accounting systems to produce financial statements at any time, on demand. This approach requires not only enterprise resources planning (ERP) systems, but also a great deal of effort to ensure that the underlying information is correct. The required investment is so large that you rarely see a virtual close in smaller companies.

The virtual close requires particular attention to the following areas:
- *Centralized accounting.* It is nearly impossible to achieve a virtual close without a great deal of accounting centralization, combined with ERP software. Conversely, that means an organization cannot have accounting operations scattered throughout its various locations. The reason is that far-flung accounting operations are much more likely to be using disparate accounting systems, from which it is more difficult to assemble information on an automated basis.
- *Standardized accounting.* Business transactions must be defined and treated the same way everywhere. Otherwise, the accounting staff must spend time investigating transaction irregularities throughout the organization, which introduces a manual component to the closing process.
- *Error tracking.* Any errors found must be tracked down and their underlying causes permanently eliminated. Otherwise, there are too many problems with virtual close financial statements to place much reliance on them.

The results of a virtual close may not be completely accurate, since some expense accruals, cost allocations, and reserves are difficult to automate. For example, if financial statements are to be produced every day, is it really possible to create an automated wage accrual for every day? Also, can the exact amount of supplier invoices really be correctly anticipated for every day? It is possible to avoid these issues by substituting standard costs for selected expense line items. For example, the cost of goods sold can be filled in by multiplying the standard cost of each product sold by the number of units sold. Similarly, a historically-correct labor expense can be charged based on production volumes and other factors. The result is a fully automated financial statement, though the accuracy of the result may not be great if the underlying standards diverge from actual results. Consequently, this approach only works well if a company is willing to spend a considerable amount of time revising its cost standards on an ongoing basis.

An alternative approach is to create a stripped-down version of the financial statements that only contains those elements that can be reliably recorded on a day-to-day basis. For example, management may realize that the core success of a business lies in revenues and the cost of goods sold, and so authorizes the creation of a daily income statement that stops at the gross margin percentage – all other operating expenses are skipped, and instead are only reported in the month-end reporting package. By taking this approach, management can focus on the most critical line items and take remediation steps as soon as possible. Similarly, a consulting business could focus on daily changes in revenues, billed hours, and payroll expense, since these are the key elements of its success.

A virtual close differs from a soft close in that the soft close requires a limited number of closing steps; and because of those closing steps, the soft close is usually only used at the end of a reporting period. Since a virtual close is essentially automated, there are no closing steps, which allows a company to run financial statements for any time period at all; thus, daily financial statements are possible.

The expense and long-term effort required to create a virtual close are not a good investment in slower-growth industries where there is little new competition and product cycles are lengthy. However, this cost can be worthwhile in the reverse situation, where the business environment is changing with great rapidity, and management needs rapid feedback to make decisions to pivot a company's direction. However, even in the latter case, a virtual close is only worth the effort if management is actually going to use the information to make decisions in a timely manner; if that is not the case, then a more traditional closing process may be a better and less expensive alternative.

The Reporting Package

When the soft close or virtual close is used, it is of considerable importance to strip the amount of reported information down to the absolute minimum. This means that only the basic set of system-generated reports should be issued – the income statement, balance sheet, and statement of cash flows. Any other report is likely to require additional work to generate, or will be inaccurate because a manual processing step is not being performed. For example, if the controller is not creating a wage accrual, this may be immaterial in relation to the entire company's income statement, but could be a material factor for the expenses report for the production department (where there tend to be a number of wage-earning employees).

If management insists upon receiving additional information, then the beneficial effects of the soft close or virtual close are being reduced. Though it may be possible to implement just a few manual closing procedures to accommodate report recipients, this can be a slippery slope, where adding "just a few" additional closing steps eventually results in a fairly lengthy and time-consuming close. Thus, it is best to hold firm on the information to be released, if the benefits of these closing methods are to be fully realized.

Summary

If a company does not have to share its financial statements with outsiders on a monthly basis, employing the soft close could be an excellent alternative for the majority of reporting periods. It allows the accounting staff to issue financial statements with great speed, leaving the staff with more time for other accounting functions. If you elect to use this approach, prepare the way by discussing with recipients of the financial statements any line items that are likely to be less accurate; this could even become a standard disclaimer that accompanies every set of financial statements issued using a soft close.

The virtual close has been and is likely to remain a viable alternative for larger organizations with sufficient funds to invest in sufficiently robust accounting systems. Other organizations could consider a "poor man's" version of a virtual close, where report recipients only receive a daily flash report that contains a few line items addressing the most actionable information.

Glossary

A

Accelerated filer. A company having an aggregate market value owned by investors who are not affiliated with the company of less than $700 million, but more than $75 million. This measurement is as of the last business day of the most recent second fiscal quarter.

Accounts receivable ledger. A subsidiary ledger in which you record all credit sales made by a business.

Accrued revenue. Sales that have not yet been recorded through the normal customer invoicing process, even though they have met all accounting guidelines for revenue recognition.

Adjusted trial balance. An unadjusted trial balance to which adjusting journal entries have been added, both to correct errors in the initial version of the trial balance and to bring the financial statements of the business into compliance with the relevant accounting framework.

Adjusting entry. A journal entry that is used at the end of an accounting period to adjust the balances in various general ledger accounts to meet the requirements of accounting standards.

Allowance for doubtful accounts. A reserve for bad debts that offsets the accounts receivable balance on the balance sheet.

Audit. The review and verification of an entity's accounting records, as well as the physical inspection of its assets. The auditor then attests to the fairness of presentation of the financial statements and related disclosures. An audit is more time-consuming and expensive than a review.

B

Balance sheet. A report that summarizes all of an entity's assets, liabilities, and equity accounts as of a given point in time. It is also known as the statement of financial position.

Bank reconciliation. A comparison of the cash position recorded on an entity's books and the position noted on the records of its bank, usually resulting in some changes to the entity's book balance to account for transactions that are recorded on the bank's records but not the entity's.

C

Carrying amount. The recorded amount of an asset, net of any accumulated depreciation or accumulated impairment losses.

Cash equivalent. A short-term, very liquid investment that is easily convertible into a known amount of cash, and which is so near its maturity that it presents an insignificant risk of a change in value because of changes in interest rates.

Chart of accounts. A listing of all the accounts used in the general ledger, usually listed in order by account number.

Chief operation decision maker. A person who is responsible for making decisions about resource allocations to the segments of a business, and for evaluating those segments.

Closing entries. Journal entries that are used to flush out all temporary accounts at the end of an accounting period and transfer their balances into permanent accounts. Doing so resets the temporary accounts to begin accumulating new transactions in the next accounting period.

Condensed income statement. An income statement with many of the usual line items condensed down into a few lines.

Contra account. An account that offsets a related account. If the related account is an asset account, then the contra asset account is used to offset (reduce) it with a credit balance. If the related account is a liability account, then the contra account is used to offset (increase) it with a debit balance. There can also be contra equity and contra revenue accounts.

Contra revenue. A deduction from gross revenue, such as sales returns, sales allowances, and sales discounts.

Contribution margin income statement. An income statement in which all variable expenses are deducted from sales to arrive at a contribution margin, from which all fixed expenses are then subtracted to arrive at the net profit or loss for the period.

Control account. An account in the general ledger in which information is summarized from a subsidiary ledger.

Cost pool. A grouping of individual costs, typically by department or service center. Cost allocations are then made from the cost pool. For example, the cost of a maintenance department is accumulated in a cost pool and then allocated to those departments using its services.

Credit. An accounting entry that either increases a liability or equity account, or decreases an asset or expense account. It is positioned to the right in an accounting entry.

Cycle counting. The process of counting a small proportion of the total inventory on a daily basis, adjusting the inventory records for errors found, and investigating the causes of those errors.

D

Debit. An accounting entry that either increases an asset or expense account, or decreases a liability or equity account. It is positioned to the left in an accounting entry.

Deferred revenue. A payment from a customer for either services that have not yet been performed or goods that have not yet been shipped by the recipient of the payment.

Deposit in transit. Cash and/or checks that have been received and recorded by an entity, but which have not yet been recorded in the records of the bank where the entity deposits the funds.

Depreciation. The gradual and systematic charging to expense of a fixed asset's cost over its expected useful life.

Direct costs. Costs that can be clearly associated with specific activities or products.

Direct method. A method of presentation for the statement of cash flows that presents specific cash flows associated with items that affect cash flow.

Discrete view. The assumption that the results reported for a specific interim period are not associated with the revenues and expenses arising during other reporting periods within a fiscal year.

Double-entry accounting. A record keeping system under which every transaction is recorded in at least two accounts; there is no limit on the number of accounts used to document a transaction, but the minimum is two accounts. There are two columns in each account, with debit entries on the left and credit entries on the right. The total of all debit entries must match the total of all credit entries.

E

Earnings per share. A company's net income divided by the weighted-average number of shares outstanding. This calculation is subject to a number of additional factors involving preferred shares, convertible instruments, and dividends.

Extended trial balance. A standard trial balance to which are added categories extending to the right, and in which are listed the account totals for the balance sheet and the income statement.

F

Fair value hedge. A hedge of the exposure to changes in the fair value of an asset or liability that are attributable to a specific risk.

Financial statement disclosures. Explanatory and supplemental notes that accompany the financial statements issued by a business.

First in, first out method. A method of inventory valuation that operates under the assumption that the first goods purchased are also the first goods sold.

Form 10-K. A document that a publicly-held company must file with the Securities and Exchange Commission once a year, detailing its financial results for the preceding year.

Form 10-Q. A document that a publicly-held company must file with the Securities and Exchange Commission every quarter, detailing its financial results for the preceding quarter and the year-to-date.

G

General ledger. The master set of accounts that summarize all transactions occurring within an entity.

Generally Accepted Accounting Principles. A set of authoritative accounting standards issued by several standard-setting bodies, which entities should follow in preparing their financial statements.

Gross margin. Revenues less the cost of goods sold.

Gross profit method. A method for calculating the approximate amount of ending inventory, based on the estimated cost of goods sold.

I

Indirect method. A method of presentation for the statement of cash flows that begins with net income or loss, and then adds or subtracts non-cash revenue and expense items to derive cash flows.

Income statement. A financial report that summarizes an entity's revenue, cost of goods sold, gross margin, other expenses, taxes, and net income or loss. The income statement shows an entity's financial results over a specific time period, usually a month, quarter, or year.

Intangible asset. A non-physical asset having a useful life greater than one year. Examples of intangible assets are trademarks, patents, and non-competition agreements.

Integral view. The concept that results reported in interim financial statements are an integral part of the full-year financial results.

Interest capitalization. The inclusion of any interest expense directly related to the construction of a fixed asset in the cost of that fixed asset.

International Financial Reporting Standards. A set of authoritative standards set by the International Accounting Standards Board, which an entity must comply with if it wishes to create financial statements that are accepted in those countries mandating the use of IFRS.

Item master. A record that lists the name, description, unit of measure, weight, dimensions, ordering quantity, and other key information for a component part.

L

Large accelerated filer. A company having an aggregate market value owned by investors who are not affiliated with the company of a minimum of $700 million. This measurement is as of the last business day of the most recent second fiscal quarter.

Last in, first out method. A method of inventory valuation that operates under the assumption that the last goods purchased are the first goods sold.

Ledger. A book or database in which double-entry accounting transactions are stored or summarized.

Lifting fee. The transaction fee charged to the recipient of a wire transfer, which the recipient's bank imposes for handling the transaction. The term also applies to foreign bank processing fees, which may be applied to a variety of other financial transactions besides a wire transfer.

Lower of cost or market. A rule requiring a business to record the cost of inventory at the lower of its cost or the current market price.

M

Matching principle. Under this principle, record the cause and effect of a business transaction at the same time. Thus, when you record revenue, also record within the same accounting period any expenses directly related to that revenue.

Multi-step income statement. An income statement that uses multiple subtotals to aggregate such information as the gross margin, operating expenses, and other income.

N

Net operating loss carryforward. A loss experienced in an earlier period that could not be completely offset against prior-period profits. This residual loss can be carried forward for up to 20 years, during which time it can be offset against any reported taxable income.

Non-trade receivables. Amounts due for payment that are not related to the normal customer invoices for merchandise shipped or services performed.

Not sufficient funds. Refers to a check that was not honored by the bank of the entity issuing the check, on the grounds that the entity's bank account does not contain sufficient funds.

O

Other comprehensive income. A statement that contains all changes not permitted in the main part of the income statement. These items include unrealized gains and losses on available-for-sale securities, cash flow hedge gains and losses, and foreign currency translation adjustments.

Outstanding check. A check payment that has been recorded by the issuing entity, but which has not yet cleared its bank account as a deduction from cash.

Overhead absorbed. The manufacturing overhead that has been applied to products or other cost objects.

P

Payroll cycle. The length of time between payrolls. Thus, if a business pays its employees every Friday, that is a one-week payroll cycle.

Periodic inventory system. An inventory calculation method under which the ending inventory balance is only updated when you conduct a physical inventory count.

Perpetual inventory system. The continual updating of inventory records to account for additions to and subtractions from inventory.

Petty cash. A small amount of cash kept on hand in a business to pay for incidental expenses.

Post-closing trial balance. A listing of all balance sheet accounts containing balances at the end of a reporting period.

Posting. The process of copying either summary-level or detailed entries in an accounting journal into the general ledger. Posting is needed in order to have a complete record of all accounting transactions in the general ledger.

Purchase ledger. A subsidiary ledger in which is recorded all purchases made by a business.

R

Recurring entry. A journal entry that is configured in the accounting software to repeat itself for a predetermined number of periods.

Reporting unit. An operating segment or one level below an operating segment. An operating segment is a component of a public entity that engages in business activities and whose results are reviewed by the chief operating decision maker, and for which discrete financial information is available.

Retail inventory method. An inventory valuation method used by retailers to estimate their ending inventory balances. It is based on the relationship between the cost of merchandise and its retail price.

Reversing entry. A journal entry made at the beginning of an accounting period, which reverses selected entries made in the immediately preceding accounting period. A reversing entry is typically used in situations when either revenue or expenses were accrued in the preceding period, and you do not want the accruals to remain in the accounting system for another period.

Review. A service under which an auditor obtains limited assurance that there are no material modifications that need to be made to an entity's financial statements for them to be in conformity with the applicable financial reporting framework (such as GAAP or IFRS).

S

Sales allowance. A reduction in the price charged by a seller, due to a problem with the sold product or service, such as a quality problem or a short shipment.

Sales discount. A reduction in the price of a product or service that is offered by the seller in exchange for early payment by the buyer.

Sales return. Merchandise sent back by a customer to the seller, presumably due to defects.

Segment. A distinct component of a business that produces revenue, and for which the business produces separate financial information that is regularly reviewed internally by a chief operation decision maker.

Single-step income statement. An income statement format that contains a single subtotal for all revenue line items and a single subtotal for all expense line items.

Social security wage cap. The annual compensation level above which no additional social security tax is paid for an individual.

Soft close. Refers to closing the books at the end of a reporting period without many of the more rigorous steps used in a normal closing process.

Standard costing. An inventory valuation method that assigns a standard cost to each item in stock, and then tracks any variances between standard and actual costs.

Statement of cash flows. An element of the financial statements that contains information about the flows of cash into and out of a company.

Statement of retained earnings. An element of the financial statements that reconciles changes in the equity accounts of a business.

Subsidiary ledger. A ledger designed for the storage of specific types of accounting transactions. The information in a subsidiary ledger is then summarized and posted to an account in the general ledger.

T

Temporary account. An account used to hold balances during an accounting period for revenue, expense, gain, and loss transactions. These accounts are flushed into the retained earnings account at the end of an accounting period.

Trade receivables. Amounts billed by a business to its customers when it delivers goods or services to them in the ordinary course of business. These billings are typically documented on formal invoices.

Trial balance. A report listing the ending debit and credit balances in all accounts as of the date of the report.

U

Unadjusted trial balance. The listing of general ledger account balances at the end of a reporting period, before any adjusting entries are made to the balances.

V

Virtual close. A closing process that involves the use of fully integrated company-wide accounting systems to produce financial statements at any time, on demand.

W

Weighted average method. A method of valuing ending inventory and the cost of goods sold, based on the average cost of materials in inventory.

Index

CPSIA information can be obtained
at www.ICGtesting.com
Printed in the USA
FFHW011243280219
50772881-56180FF